Lecture Notes in Computer Science 4871

Commenced Publication in 1973
Founding and Former Series Editors:
Gerhard Goos, Juris Hartmanis, and Jan van Leeuwen

Editorial Board

T0223140

Marc Cavazza   Stéphane Donikian (Eds.)

Virtual Storytelling

Using Virtual Reality Technologies for Storytelling

4th International Conference, ICVS 2007
Saint-Malo, France, December 5-7, 2007
Proceedings

 Springer

Volume Editors

Marc Cavazza
University of Teesside
School of Computing
Middlesbrough, TS1 3BA, UK
E-mail: m.o.cavazza@tees.ac.uk

Stéphane Donikian
IRISA/INRIA
Campus de Beaulieu
35042 Rennes Cedex, France
E-mail: donikian@irisa.fr

Library of Congress Control Number: 2007939972

CR Subject Classification (1998): H.4, I.3, I.2, C.3, H.5, I.4, I.7.2

LNCS Sublibrary: SL 3 – Information Systems and Application, incl. Internet/Web and HCI

ISSN   0302-9743
ISBN-10   3-540-77037-2 Springer Berlin Heidelberg New York
ISBN-13   978-3-540-77037-4 Springer Berlin Heidelberg New York

Springer is a part of Springer Science+Business Media

springer.com

© Springer-Verlag Berlin Heidelberg 2007

Typesetting: Camera-ready by author, data conversion by Scientific Publishing Services, Chennai, India
Printed on acid-free paper   SPIN: 12197507   06/3180   5 4 3 2 1 0

Preface

In September 2001 the First International Conference on Virtual Storytelling was organized in Avignon, France. This was the first international scientific event entirely devoted to the new discipline that links the ancient human arts of storytelling to the latest technologies of the virtual reality era. Then, Virtual Storytelling 2003 was held during November 20–21, 2003, in Toulouse, France, and Virtual Storytelling 2005 was held during November 30–December 2, 2005, in Strasbourg, France.

Since autumn 2003, there has been a strong collaboration between the two major virtual/digital storytelling conference series in Europe: Virtual Storytelling and TIDSE (Technologies for Interactive Digital Storytelling and Entertainment). Thus the conference chairs of TIDSE and Virtual Storytelling decided to establish a 2-year turnover for both conferences.

Narratives have evolved from their early role in human knowledge transmission into the main content of cultural production. With the advent of mass media, they are now at the heart of one of the world's largest industries.

The advent of the digital era has enhanced and accelerated this evolution: image synthesis, digital special effects, new human–computer interfaces and the Internet allow one to not only realize more sophisticated narrative forms but also to create new concepts as video gaming and virtual environments. The art of storytelling is becoming evermore complex. Virtual reality offers new tools to capture and to interactively modify the imaginary environment in ever more intuitive ways, coupled with a maximum sensory feedback. In fact, virtual reality technologies offer enhanced and exciting production possibilities for the creation and non-linear manipulation in real time of almost any story form. This has led to the new concept of virtual storytelling.

Virtual Storytelling 2007 aimed to gather researchers from the scientific, artistic and industrial communities to demonstrate new methods and techniques, show the latest results, and to exchange concepts and ideas for the use of virtual reality technologies for creating, populating, rendering and interacting with stories, whatever their form, be it theater, movie, cartoon, advertisement, puppet show, multimedia work, video games, artistic installation, . . .

During the conference program, invited guests gave us interesting views about disciplines related to virtual storytelling but not already directly involved in this multidisciplinary topic. We hope that more connections will exist in the near future. An invited session provided an overview of the ongoing EU projects NM2, IPERG and INSCAPE. Moreover, a panel discussion provided a better understanding of the potential future uses of interactive storytelling techniques in the media industry. In addition, practical demonstrations of systems, tools and concepts were presented in the demo area.

We hope that participants in Virtual Storytelling 2007 found exciting guidelines for future scientific and artistic research as well as ideas for new applications and developments.

The members of the Program Committee deserve special acknowledgment for their amazing reviews done during the summer time.

Last, but not least, our thanks also go to the organization team, Edith Blin-Guyot and Angélique Jarnoux, and to Yann Jehanneuf for the design of the poster.

December 2007

Marc Cavazza
Stéphane Donikian

Acknowledgment

Virtual Storytelling 2007 was organized by the Bunraku team of the INRIA Research Centre Rennes - Bretagne Atlantique. However, the conference only came about thanks to the financial support of various institutions: GDR Informatique Graphique, Fondation Michel Métivier, The Media and Networks Competitiveness Cluster, and the Regional Council of Brittany. We would also like to thank IFIP for its sponsorship.

Organization

Chairs

Marc Cavazza	University of Teesside, UK
Stéphane Donikian	IRISA/INRIA, France

Program Committee

Elisabeth Andre	University of Augsburg, Germany
Ruth Aylett	Heriot-Watt University, UK
Olivier Balet	C-S, France
Antonio Camurri	DIST, University of Genoa, Italy
Ronan Champagnat	L3i, IUT de La Rochelle, France
Jaanis Garancs	rix(L) interactive media laboratory, Riga, Latvia
Stefan Göbel	ZGDV, Germany
Stefan M. Grünvogel	University of Applied Sciences Cologne, Germany
Jean-Pierre Jessel	IRIT, France
Craig Lindley	Gotland University and Blekinge Technical College, Sweden
Michael Mateas	University of California, Santa Cruz, USA
Ana Païva	INESC-ID, Portugal
Catherine Pelachaud	University Paris 8, France
Mark Riedl	Institute for Creative Technologies, USA
Ulrike Spierling	University of Applied Sciences, Erfurt, Germany
Gérard Subsol	LIRMM, France
Nicolas Szilas	TECFA, University of Geneva, Switzerland
Richard Wages	NOMADS Lab / UASC-IMP, Cologne, Germany
Eku Wand	HBK, Braunschweig University of Art, Germany
Michaël Young	Liquid Narrative, USA

Table of Contents

Invited Session: Related EU Projects

Poster and Demo Session

Authoring Tools and Story Models

Visual Scenario Representation in the Context of a Tool for Interactive Storytelling

Martyn Dade-Robertson

Culture Lab, Newcastle University, Grand Assembly Rooms, Kings Walk, NE1 7RU, UK
martyn.dade-robertson@ncl.ac.uk

Abstract. Tools, such as Macromedia Director and Flash which are commonly used in the development of interactive stories, are based upon linear means of representation i.e. timelines, reflecting their evolution from animation packages. In the development of INSCAPE, however, which is a tool dedicated to the creation of interactive stories, we have been able to readdress the notion of visual scenario representation for interactive stories through the development of a 'Story Editor' component which acts as a means of organising story assets and presenting story structures as coherent patterns of information. This paper describes the process which has resulted in the development of a Story Editor component which will be released in INSCAPE's Beta application at the end of 2007. It outlines the theoretical grounding of this work as well as providing a description of the design approach and its implications for the further development of interactive storytelling authoring tools.

Keywords: INSCAPE, Interactive Story Telling, GUI, Information Visualisation, Topological Space, Topographical Space.

1 Introduction

This paper outlines ongoing research on the development of INSCAPE, which is a software tool to allow non-specialist users to develop interactive stories. In particular, the paper will focus on the visual representation of stories through the use of topological graphs. We note that applications such as Macromedia Director and Flash, which are commonly used in the development of interactive stories, are based upon linear representation systems i.e. timelines, reflecting their evolution from animation packages. In the development of INSCAPE, however, which is a tool dedicated to the creation of interactive stories, we have been able to readdress the notion of visual scenario representation for interactive stories through the development of a 'Story Editor' which acts as a means of organising story assets and presenting story structures as coherent patterns of information. The process of developing this component has involved a combination of theoretical investigation, practical design and implementation. The evaluation and the initial findings of this process are presented here.

M. Cavazza and S. Donikian (Eds.): ICVS 2007, LNCS 4871, pp. 3–12, 2007.

2 Background to INSCAPE

INSCAPE is a four year European 6th Framework project, integrating partners from both academic and commercial organisations from nine European countries. INSCAPE was commissioned in 2004 with the stated aim of developing '...*a software suite for authoring, publishing and experiencing interactive multimedia stories and contents.*' [1]. Furthermore, it has been proposed that the INSCAPE software should be capable of being used by inexperienced computer users across a wide subject domain and a variety of creative end users: '*just as PowerPoint has enabled anyone to prepare professional-looking presentations, just as MIDI has democratised and revolutionised music by empowering home users to create ambitious music, INSCAPE's vision is to offer creative people a means to readily transform their ideas into appealing interactive stories using a scalable and intuitive authoring environment.*' [1]

INSCAPE is to achieve its ambitious aims by integrating a number of different software modules from different providers into one piece of software, bringing together aspects of interactive programming and authoring which, before now, have needed multiple applications. This suite of software tools included tools to:

- Write and organise story scenarios
- Acquire story sets from images or videos with automated wizards
- Import, manage and customise 2D and 3D story props and actors
- Include dialogues, sounds, music and visual effects
- Create and direct all scene, camera and actor's actions without programming
- Control user experience through a wide range of Human Interface Devices
- Preview stories in real-time whilst authoring
- Publish and experience interactive stories on the Internet [1]

Furthermore, the project structure has allowed for a group of potential end users to become involved in the development of the software. These end users each represented a particular market sector including:

- Science and Industry
- Education and Entertainment
- Animation and Cartoons
- Communication and Marketing
- Cinema and Television
- Live Performances

Each of these market sectors provides a different view on authoring interactive stories and these differences emerged during the summer of 2006 when an Alpha version of the software was released and the software was tested and validated by a number of project partners.

The end users took part in two validation activities. The first, the functional validation, involved a systematic testing and scoring of all the software components and functions. In the second activity, the users undertook a scenario based validation, consisting of a set of assets and instructions on how to complete typical interactive projects. The first type of validation was completed by consortium members and the second was undertaken by a wider user group.

At the end of July 2006, the initial results of the user trials were released and it was found that there were considerable weaknesses in a number of key areas, most importantly in the design and implementation of the software's Graphical User Interface, (hereafter GUI) which, it was suggested, far from providing a user friendly and intuitive interface was an opaque barrier to the software's use. This finding led to a reconsideration of what interactivity and story telling meant in each market sector and of how the processes of developing interactive stories differed across the different domains.

3 Visual Representations of Interactive Stories

As part of the analysis of the outcomes of the evaluation, the process of authoring interactive stories in each domain was revisited. The Alpha implementation of INSCAPE was based on two key assumptions about the use of the tool:

1. That authoring interactive stories reflects traditional methods of production and workflow consisting of Design, Pre-Production, Production and Post-Production. These stages were integrated into the software as 'Rooms' accessed through a tabulated menu and containing tools which were relevant to each stage.

2. That a visual means of representation could be found that allowed the author to unite both the story structure and the programming structure. In the case of INSCAPE this representation was described as the StoryScape and consisted of a node and link graph where nodes were objects within the story and links represented interactive 'transitions' or conditional relationships (Fig. 1.).

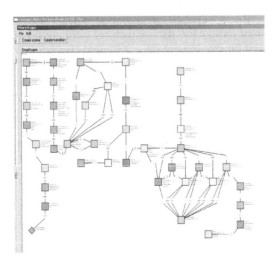

Fig. 1. Screen grab of the StoryScape component of INSCAPE

These assumptions were challenged by the evaluation of the Alpha release. It was discovered that neither the interface conventions nor the concepts behind them were flexible enough to cope with the range of definitions for interactive stories across the different sectors and, as a result, substantially differing views emerged from the various end user groups on both the strategies and the products of their approaches. The role of the GUI was, therefore refocused, following the Alpha review, on the following tasks:

1. To represent and support varying process structures, beyond the traditional production model.
2. To represent and support the authoring of non-linear story structures through a visual interface which allows the user to organise their assets logically and does not restrict them to predefined models of interactivity or story telling.
3. To represent and provide a means of authoring complex interactive systems without the need to program in a syntactically complex programming language.

The second task posed the most significant challenge. Through the reappraisal and redesign of the INSCAPE GUI, it was proposed that the similarities and differences in ways of authoring interactive stories would emerge and that a more coherent authoring system could, through such investigation, be designed. The evaluation of the Alpha release also revealed the importance of separating the processes of collecting and organising assets; creating the story structures for an interactive application and creating the programming structures.

3.1 Distinguishing Interactive/Programming Structure from Story Structure

A key problem we faced in the design of the GUI was disentangling the notions of story structure (i.e. the main events in the story divided into logical units or chunks and assembled as a topological pattern) and interactive/programming structure (i.e. the interactive relationships between programmed objects and behaviors). In the Alpha implementation of INSCAPE, these structures were considered to be the same. The StoryScape worked on the principle that an interactive story can be divided into minimal units, described as scenes, which are connected together through 'transitions', representing the associations between scenes.

A scene consists of an object, such as an image, 3D model or sound; a property, for example 'display image' or 'play sound' and a transition property, usually triggered by an interactive action such as moving a joystick or clicking on a hotspot. For example, a very simple interactive application might consist of two scenes, 'Scene 1' and 'Scene 2' each containing an image, a hotspot and the property 'display image'. 'Scene 1' and 'Scene 2' are then linked via a conditional transition which is triggered when the hotspot object in 'Scene 1' is clicked using the mouse, causing the new scene with its new image to load.

Even for comparatively simple scenarios, a large number of 'scenes' were necessary to articulate both the story and interactive potential of the scenario. In a notable scenario used to demonstrate INSCAPE, the user is faced with a comparatively simple interactive story (in this case based on a simulation) where they are asked to perform three tasks within a simulated space station:

Task 1. To navigate through a Space Station to the airlock.

Task 2. To navigate outside the Space Station to a predefined location to perform a repair.

Task 3. To perform the repair on the space station.

This is essentially a linear narrative composed of three events where the user either succeeds or fails to move on to the next task. However, in the StoryScape, the complexity of the interactive structure, which involved the use of global (relevant to all scenes) sounds, objects and actions, as well as separate representations of the hardware interaction devices, meant that the StoryScape was composed of 42 different and incoherent 'scenes' to cope with every possible interactive permutation (illustrated in Fig.1.). This clearly provided a scalability problem and rendered the usefulness of the StoryScape, as a means of story visualization, limited. It became clear, therefore, that it was necessary to separate programming/interactive structure from a global view of the story structure.

3.2 Topological Models of Story Structures

Despite the weaknesses of the StoryScape model, the end users taking part in the Alpha validation responded positively to the notion of a graphical representation of the story structure by highlighting this component as being one of the most novel aspect of the INSCAPE package. There was a recognition that some form of graphical representation to aid the author whilst developing interactive stories is a necessary feature.

There are numerous concepts describing different organisational strategies for digital productions. For example, in Hypertytext storytelling models of story structure, formal patterns consisting of lexias (text chunks) are used as part of the grammar of interactive storytelling. Bernstein points out, in his history of hypertext patterns in hypertext storytelling, that once hypertext systems began to be used outside technology development laboratories, the early hope for systems which would allow for the free association of documents and information objects, gave way to a realisation that structural patterns were necessary if such systems were to be used effectively [2]: '*Before 1987, hypertext writing tools were laboratory curiosities; after 1987, systems like Guide, HyperCard, and Storyspace became readily available and were widely employed. Early systems often reflected the prevalent concern with navigation. For example, Peter Brown, Guide's developer, argued that emphasizing a hierarchical structural backbone would render hypertexts more comprehensible to users. To the widespread emphasis on tree-structured hypertexts was added speculation on the utility of hypercubes, toruses, and lattices (and Petri nets), while Polle Zellweger argued in an immensely influential paper that guided tours along clearly-marked paths help keep readers oriented* [3].'*

Other authors have also noted the importance of structural patterns in early models of interactive storytelling, describing various graph structures as representing the organization of '*narrative events*' [4].

In all these commentaries there appears to be a tendency to consider narrative organization as being akin to some method or diagrammatic visualization and this conclusion was supported by the our end user feedback.

3.3 Stages and Situations

In defining the minimal coherent units of representation, we looked toward generic storytelling scenarios provided by INSCAPE's end users. The structures defined above refer to a logic of spatially organised storytelling. This does not mean to say that the stories authored using such structures necessarily took place in topographically coherent locations (although this was sometimes the case) but rather that they represent topologically coherent systems where the patterns of relationships represent an important structuring principle.

Although some, for example Crawford [5], have theorised about and demonstrated models of interactive storytelling which do unite programming and narrative structure through the development of agent based stories, in practice, it was found that, during our evaluation of the INSCAPE alpha release, even in the process of conceptualising relatively sophisticated emergent forms of interactivity, the early to middle stages of interactive story development required the use of broad structural diagrams as a means of articulating story ideas. Such structures act to break down the stories into manageable chunks or minimal coherent units. The rationale for this method of conceptualising interactive stories emerges because stories are usually organised with relation to contained chunks (chapters, scenes, acts etc). Furthermore, these chunks are very often associated with particular locations or journeys from place to place or the triggering of groups of events. If we add on the 'layer of interactivity', we no longer have the constraints of linearity but, in its place, these experiences can be organized through a spatial/diagrammatic articulation. The constant of spatial organisation gives us the most flexibility whilst providing a logical structure on which to build our representations.

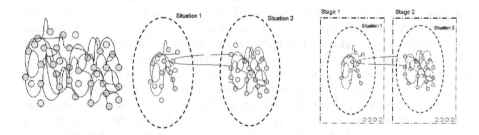

Fig. 2. Diagrams to show the concept of 'Stages' and 'Situations' in the context of INSCAPE

These story structures should, however, be separated from a story's interactive/programmed structure. A useful model might be to consider an interactive story as a complex web of interactive and inter-reactive objects (whether physical, virtual or code). Such structures are topologically complex. However, in the context of a particular model of interactive story, it is possible to group objects together based on a common property. Using Aristotle's model of drama [6], this common property can be defined as either Time, Space or Action. Simply put, all drama takes place in some time, some place and is motivated for a reason. The starting point for our visualisation was 'some place'. We hypothesised that, since all actions take place within a particular location, this would provide a basic organisational principle leading to two of the founding concepts for INSCAPE's visualisation of story structures - 'stages' and 'situations'. A Stage is represented as a container, in this case a 2D box which contains all the non-active elements which usually make up the background of a story. A Situation, on the other hand, can only exist within a Stage (events must take place some where) and contains active objects e.g. characters, behaviors and interactive objects. The user defines the scope of those actions, and thereby what constitutes a situation in INSCAPE terms (see Fig.2.). This approach can incoreprate a great many interactive story production types and still serve the purpose of providing a division into relevant and manageable chunks, as well as giving a reasonable and comprehensive overview.

In terms of implementation, the stage and situation model offers significant flexibility since the programmatic aspects of the story have been separated from the story structure.

3.4 Example of Stage and Situation Implementations

To develop the Stage and Situation concept we isolated a number of examples of use which emerged from the INSCAPE end user discussions as follows:

Example 1: Structuring a story based in a Real or Real-Time Virtual Environment.

In this case the story may need to be spatially consistent and spatial relationships are constant and defined. The environment itself may not be interactive but it defines the location of the action through a sequence or pattern of spaces which are represented as separate stages.

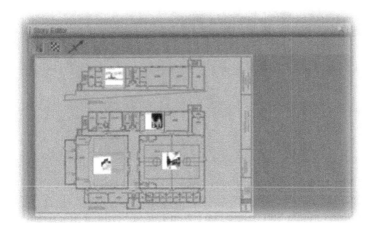

Fig. 3. Mock up showing stages associated with physical locations on a room plan

Situations may also be directly associated with Stages i.e. the active elements in a story are Stage specific so, in the Story Editor, a stage will always and only contain one situation. The configuration of such Stage/Situation chunks may be organised as follows:

Linear where the user is forced to go from one location to another and cannot return.

Free Stages where the user is able to navigate freely from Situation to another Situation in any order but where a single Stage contains a single Situation.

Free Stages but Dependent Situations where the user is able to navigate freely but where interacting in the situation on one stage will leads to the experience of a different situation on another.

Similarly, the same models can be conceptualized for a real space, for example a museum, gallery or interactive installation. In this instance, however, instead of a virtual space we refer to a real spatial organisation this can consist of locations in a single room, a number of rooms or even a number of different buildings.

Example 2: Structuring a Story based on a Linear Script or Story Board.

Despite the possibilities of nonlineality, a dominant model of interactive storytelling is never-the-less linear with user controlled pacing of the action with obstacles which must be overcome or minor detours taken but with a strong focus on a core linear story. In sectors such as TV production, the starting point for an interactive application may be a linear structure defined by a story board and a script which are the traditional tools used in this type of media production. Like the examples defined above, the units of the story are defined by spatial location. However, unlike these scenarios there does not need to be a spatial constant and a Stage becomes a container for what might be described as a Scene defined by a sequence of shots and a cut between one Scene (and hence location) and another Scene.

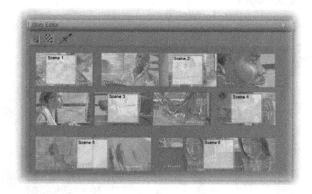

Fig. 4. Mock up showing stages associated with a linear storyboard

Example 3: Structuring a Story Based on a Non-Linear Script or Storyboard

As with Example 2, Non-Linear Scripts or Story Boards are divided into spatial units defined as Scenes. However, rather than being linearly arranged they can be associated to each other through a range of structures – e.g. branching cyclical and recursive.

Often such structures are authored by defining the individual scene elements and then relating them to one another through conditional transitions. For example,

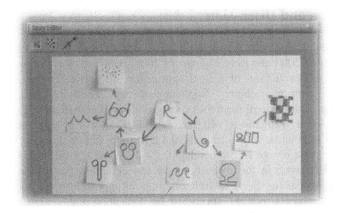

Fig. 5. Mock-up of a non-linear story based on a network node link model

hypertext stories are often authored in this way – using hyperlinks to cause a transition from one scene to another.

The images below show such a structure which has initially been developed using post-it notes and arrows. Each post-it has been translated into a stage with conditional transitions defining where the user is able to travel in the structure.

Example 4: Structuring a Story Based on Chapters and Sections

In the authoring of interactive material, for example for an online text book or educational resource, it may make sense to use strong categories to distinguish between different subjects. It may be necessary for the user, in this case, to complete tasks before moving on to the next section or to navigate in a particular order.

Here Stages can each represent a section or chapter of the interactive scenario. Each Stage may contain multiple situations each one reflecting a puzzle, for example, which is self contained.

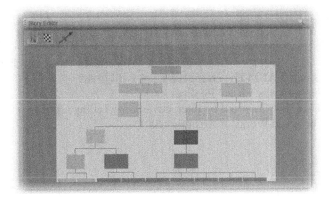

Fig. 6. Mock-up of a schematic and hierarchical chapter based model

4 Conclusion and Discussion

This research and design work represents the early stages of INSCAPE's development and, for the rest of 2007 and the early part of 2008, continued development will lead to the release and evaluation of a Beta application. In particular, the Story Editor component is currently being implemented by Zentrum für Graphische Datenverarbeitun and this will form the core part of the INSCAPE tool. Following the release of the Beta, validations will be undertaken to assess this model for the visualisation of interactive story scenarios and it is only after this process that we will be able to make firm design recommendation for the development of this sort of tool in the future. However, in the mean time we can conclude that topological visual representations appear to offer a flexible and natural approach to the organisation of stories and that story structures appear to be critical to the conceptualisation of interactive stories and applications, particularly in their early development. Such visualisations of Story Structure, however, despite their usefulness, should not be confused with programming/interactive structures which are topologically separate and may be substantially more complex.

Acknowledgements

This research is performed in the frame of the INSCAPE Integrated project (EU RTD contract IST-2004-004150) which is funded by the European Commission under the sixth Framework Programme. More information is available at www.inscapers.com. The design work shown here was produced as a result of a collaboration with Björn Thuresson at the Kungliga Tekniska Hoegskolan and the implementation of the Story Editor will be initiated by Zentrum für Graphische Datenverarbeitung. I am also grateful to the reviewers for their constructive comments.

References

[1] http://www.inscapers.com
[2] Bernstein, M.: Structural Patterns and Hypertext Rhetoric. ACM Computing Surveys, pp. 31–34 (1999)
[3] Zellweger, P.: Scripted Documents: A Hypertext Path Mechanism. In: Proceedings of the ACM Hypertext 1989, pp. 1–14 (1989)
[4] Ryan, M.: Narrative as Virtual Reality (2001)
[5] Crawford, C.: Chris Crawford on Interactive Story Telling (2005)
[6] Aristotle: The Basic Works of Aristotle (2001)

Adding Aspects of "Implicit Creation" to the Authoring Process in Interactive Storytelling

Ulrike Spierling

FH Erfurt, University of Applied Sciences,
Altonaerstr. 25, 99085 Erfurt, Germany
spierling@fh-erfurt.de

Abstract. In Interactive Digital Storytelling (IDS), new design processes are needed for authors to fully embrace the emergent properties of this dynamic novel medium. As a counterpart to traditional explicit authoring in storytelling, "implicit creation" is introduced as a conceptual framework. By describing the development steps of a specific IDS application – the Killer Phrase game – and starting out with explicit methods, the conditions for adding implicit creation are discussed, which lead to suggestions for future research.

Keywords: interactive digital storytelling, implicit creation, authoring, emergence, emergent narrative, storyworld.

1 Introduction

Interactive Digital Storytelling (IDS) provides opportunities and challenges for the future creation of entertainment and education applications by combining aspects of story, simulation and games [18]. A difficulty frequently emphasized in IDS is that of maintaining coherence in a story with an interesting plot while also allowing the audience to interact with it. This challenges traditional ways of conceiving stories, because either the participant's interaction can destroy a well-crafted plot line, or the author's plot may be so tightly woven that interaction is reduced to only frustratingly meaningless choices.

This challenge is currently addressed by the research field of Interactive Digital Storytelling in the development of sophisticated story engines, which ensure the coherence of a story on behalf on an author at interactive runtime sessions. The task is particularly ambitious in realtime multi-agent environments, in which users can interact with a storyworld with only few restrictions. Prior to this user interaction, the authors of this experience have the important task of configuring the behaviour of individual agents and a story engine, a major component of the overall goal of content creation. This is the reason for the current interdisciplinary divide between engineers and people who have the ideas for content: designers, authors and writers. The divide is caused by difficulties with the process of creation. Aspects that have been recently discussed are:

M. Cavazza and S. Donikian (Eds.): ICVS 2007, LNCS 4871, pp. 13–25, 2007.

- **Programming:** There has been much discussion about the requirement of the author's ability to program in order to achieve creative goals in IDS [11].
- **Anticipation of Emergence:** There has been less discussion on the general difficulty of anticipating the emergent course of actions generated automatically or semi-automatically by the interaction of agents (software agents and users). When the constraints for interaction are loosened, the "story" can take unexpected directions. The flow of the resulting "emergent narrative" can better be explained by the metaphor of role playing than by storytelling [10].

This contribution discusses both aspects, but with an emphasis on trying to get to the bottom of the aspect "emergence", and what it means for the creative process. "Emergent narrative" is a recently discussed concept, often identified as a paradox. The merit of employing a potential emergent system for IDS is here seen not as a goal in itself, but as a possible way to avoid the clash between pre-scripted narrative and the freedom offered and afforded by a virtual environment. An emergent property is one that exhibits perpetual novelty [7] each time the system runs, under the influence of a sequence of input combinations. Hence, it supports user agency by generating a variety of constellations at runtime, which are, on the other hand, hard to foresee, and can only be addressed "implicitly" by a designer.

After presenting related work, "implicit creation" is introduced as a concept opposite to "explicit" authoring. Issues of IDS creation are discussed with the help of an example application: the "Killer Phrase" game designed with the platform *Scenejo*. Based on conclusions drawn from this process, the next steps towards a conceptual model of implicit creation are extrapolated. These go beyond the vision that the main benefit of developing authoring tools is that they can prevent writers from programming by providing a GUI for the task of behaviour description. The concluding insight is that the coding itself is not the main problem, but that a whole new design process of Interactive Storytelling needs to be embraced by new authors, letting them define and configure the parameters of the story that "implicitly" lead to an interactive narrative experience.

2 Related Work

Current IDS implementations can have multiple forms, in which varying kinds of roles for participants, (virtual) actors and authors occur. The work presented in this paper focuses on a form that lets users and agents interact in real time with frequent turn-taking, leading to an emerging course of actions instead of following a pre-authored path. The term "emergent narrative" was introduced by R. Aylett [2]. The concept has been implemented in the demonstrator "FearNot" of the VICTEC project [3], which lets the user participate in a role play with virtual characters that are only defined by parameters. Each agent chooses actions based on a complex model of emotions and cognition. Currently, there is no authoring tool for the system; the virtual actors are directly programmed in XML-like structures. The architecture doesn't differentiate between a storyworld and models of the agents. A similar case has story engines based on HTN planning methods [4]. While authors can define a storyworld as a hierarchical ontological structure of goals and sub-goals for agents, it is hard to anticipate concrete actions that result from it. The project "Façade" [11] solves the anticipation problem by letting a drama manager take partial control over the flow of actions, while dialogue pieces are pre-authored within so-called "beats". Content creators had to program the drama manager. The underlying creative concept has been called "Expressive AI" [12]. All aforementioned approaches make partial use of automatically generated dialogue by using dialogue templates with partially scripted components. Storytron is another story engine project, which has been under development for several years [5] and which differentiates between engine and storyworld. It contains the authoring tool "SWAT" based on "verbs" directly defining possible actions, events and states in a storyworld.

This paper is based on previous work with the conversational storytelling platform "Scenejo" [21], using the simplest agents based on AIML chatbots and uncomplicated dialogue management with finite state machines. In contrast to the examples cited above, Scenejo still leaves much of the explicit decision making to authors, who are supported by a graphical authoring tool. Only a few IDS systems exist with first authoring tools, some of which were presented in a TIDSE 2006 workshop [20]: Scenejo [21], Cyranus [9], Scribe [13], U-Create [16]. Other storytelling tools built in EU-funded research [8] [14] don't address real-time multi-agent systems while they deal with cross-media and the constrained choice options in the TV-sector. With all these tools, the flow of the narrative plot can be directly defined by visual graph structures with explicit transitions between actions.

Some issues of creating IDS, such as artistic models and workflow, "Expressive AI" and storyworld creation problems, are debated in online forums[1]. In section 5, storyworld creation will be reconsidered. It can be concluded that there are story engines enabling forms of "emergent narrative" without accessible means of authoring and there are systems with authoring tools that allow for explicit definition of actions, following traditional metaphors of controlled content creation. As of yet, there is no real synthesis of the two. This is not only perceivable in the lack of respective tools, but, moreover, in the lack of relevant concepts that, in the following paragraphs, will be called "implicit creation". Systems supporting "explicit" authoring are in fact meaningful for the development of the field, because they allow non-programming creators to access IDS and create useful examples for further research. Hence, they are a valid starting point to be further developed towards "implicit" creation.

3 Explicit Authoring vs. Implicit Creation

First of all, it is argued that the way story "writers" craft their work changes significantly with the introduction of interaction. This is especially true in the creation of a piece to be run on a multi-agent platform allowing "emergent narrative", where it is impossible to define every little detail explicitly, in advance of the user interaction. The traditional method of creation, shaping every detail of the plot, is referred to herein as "explicit authoring". In contrast, "implicit creation" becomes necessary, where configurations of states "imply" certain behaviours of agents. As for a conceptual model of creation, new metaphors are needed to explain the main difference constituted by this indirect form of design.

---

[1] e.g., http://grandtextauto.gatech.edu/, http://storytron.com/smf/, http://tale-of-tales.com/

Figure 1 illustrates this difference by using the metaphor of gardening (this metaphor was used previously by W. Wright for simulation games, such as SimCity [15]). The left side of the illustration shows that with explicit creation, a creator generates content that serves as the predefined template for the runtime narrative to follow the given form, such as is the case in branching interactive storytelling. In this metaphor, it is a paper flower, crafted explicitly by the author in full detail and beauty. By contrast, the right side – with implicit creation – shows that a runtime narrative actually has to be "planted" beforehand by a creator. All details emerge while the plant is growing, and untypical variations can also occur in the runtime narrative. The difficulty of crafting finally lies in the design of the "seeds", independent of any ability to code. As such, this sketched creative process is the same as found in the design of simulation games. Moreover, the vision to "get a grip" on the emergent process is likely to shape up as an illusion, as the definition of emergence implies. As J. Holland [7] says: *"Much comes from little"* – meaning that emergence is defined by its unpredictable attributes, letting few rules give rise to extraordinarily complex situations.

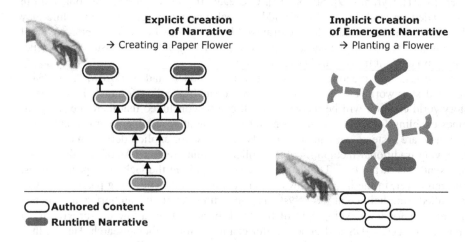

Fig. 1. The gardening metaphor explaining the difference between explicit and implicit creation for generating a narrative structure during runtime

As mentioned before, IDS is considered to be a combination of story, simulation and games – therefore, the art form requires more than traditional story creation as a telling of events. For a simulation game, a critical design step is the design of a dynamic model. Figure 2 shows the general concept of transition functions building the core of a dynamic model [7]. According to Holland, a "perfect model" would result in a complete detailed mapping of real world configurations to model states and of laws of change in the real world to transition functions in the model. However, as he points out, the art of model building lies in selecting the "right level of detail" that is useful for the purpose, distinguishing salient features from the non-essential and capturing the laws of change at the chosen level. It is very unlikely that we manage to observe the world successfully in every detail, and doing so would result in a model that is way too complex.

In the following sections, it will be argued that, for IDS, it is this "right level" of detail that has to be identified in order to apply emergent features. In other words, the claim is made that the design of a model as an abstraction, leading to emergent behaviour of a "desired" sort, must be a part of the creational process and, as such, part of the content. The modelled behaviour is not (only) the responsibility of the underlying runtime engine, which more or less provides underlying environmental conditions (for example, psychological and physical models resembling "reality"). It will further be assumed that for each "interactive story" (aka "storyworld") created, there is a need to identify the usefulness of "emergence" for its narrative elements and make this a part of the design workflow – considering that narrative properties exist that don't necessarily have to show "perpetual novelty" (see section 1), and therefore don't need to be modelled as emergent features, and can be scripted in a more traditional manner.

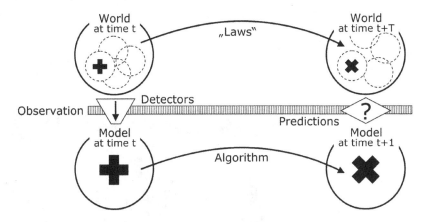

Fig. 2. The observed world configurations and their identified "laws of change" have to be transferred to a dynamic model of states and calculable transition functions ("algorithm"). (Illustration adapted from [7]).

The next section describes a case study, illustrating the experiences made with the model building and authoring process. Starting from an "explicit" view on authoring, first steps towards implicit creation are made. Finally, further needs are outlined with their consequences for implicit creation.

4   The Creation Process of the Killer Phrase Game

The "Killer Phrase Game" is a digital conversational game where the player is the moderator of a discussion between two debating characters. The application is running with the platform *Scenejo* [21]. *Scenejo* connects several A.L.I.C.E. chatbots [1] in a conversational loop of turn-taking, which is controlled by a drama manager component. On top of the creation possibilities of AIML[2], the mark-up language for "explicitly"

---

[2] AIML: Artificial Intelligence Markup Language. The knowledge base for the chatbot A.L.I.C.E. [1] is implemented in AIML.

defining dialogue, the authoring tool provides condition definitions for utterances, processing and affecting each bot's inner states separately. The virtual characters attained in this manner are animated heads talking with TTS, while their textual conversation is also displayed on screen. The user is able to interrupt the conversation by typing text. As such, the interaction concept of *Scenejo* strongly resembles that of Façade [11]. In fact, any new content created would result in a similar interaction style – a user takes turns in a conversation with several digital characters.

The killer phrase game has been designed as an experiment for a University seminar on "moderation and mediation".[3] The game tackles the topic of how to identify and react to so-called "killer phrases" within a discussion. Killer phrases are "creativity killers", often used in a knee-jerk manner, that destroy new ideas before they are discussed with solid arguments. The game assumes a scenario with two parties, the planners and the residents, arguing about novel plans for an airport expansion. The partly predefined conversation between the two parties, carried out across the table, contains killer phrases. The learner plays the role of the moderator and has to manage the meeting (see game screen in Figure 3).

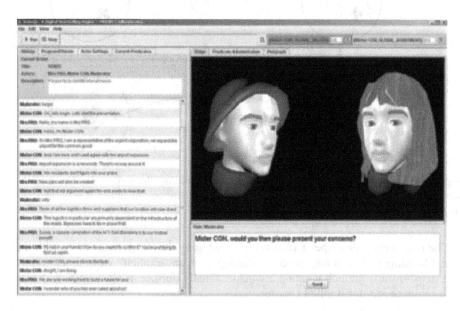

Fig. 3. The Killer Phrase Game prototype running in the *Scenejo* Platform

Although the application is called a "game", there are also elements of narrative expression and of simulation. The design tasks included: 1.) generation of narratives containing characters, actions (performed as utterances), changing states and turning points for possible endings, 2.) a simulation model made up of states and transitions, and finally 3.) the game design defining local objectives for the player, and tuning / testing the gameplay.

---

[3] More detailed insights on the educational achievements of the concept have been published in [18] and [19].

4.1 Building a Story and a Model: Experiences

The design conditions for the game were affected by its educational purpose. Rather than by artistic motivation, the work was done in iterative brainstorming sessions by an interdisciplinary team, consisting of the instructors of the course "moderation and mediation", and of the designers and programmers of the platform *Scenejo*. While the *Scenejo* designers provided the logical frame for a computable conversation, which was a concept of actions (utterances), states and rules, the domain experts were supposed to provide its content – decisions on concrete conversational states and defined rules calculating the story's transitions and turning points. At the beginning of this process, it turned out that it was much easier for the domain experts to imagine concrete conversations than to explain them as an abstract model. So, the easier start was to provide concrete cases of potential conversations in the form of a linear script of explicit dialogue lines – particularly at first, stories with a "best case" and a "worst case" progression and ending.

In order to achieve interactivity in the sense of a gaming simulation, the necessary next step was the modelling of dependencies between utterances, according to the principle sketched in Figure 2 (states and transitions defining a "behaviour" of the world). This transfer is not a straightforward task. The easier part was to analyse the scripts and categorise the single utterances, for example, into killer phrases and groups of arguments. Building a simulation model, however, required the connection of these groups of utterances to world states that can change over time. Identifying world states at "the right level of detail" required the knowledge of the domain experts, given that the model was supposed to be simple for the first implementation.

The first achieved model (see Figure 4) made use of the character-centered approach of *Scenejo*. Each virtual actor is modelled with its/his own mind states. During play, these individual states will be affected by events (for example, by actions of

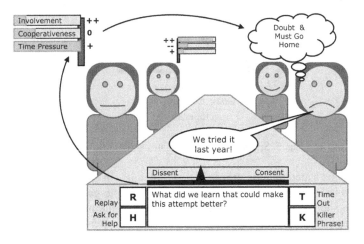

Fig. 4. Design sketch of the conceived structural elements of the "killer phrase" game, such as the parameter states of each virtual actor

users or other virtual actors). For example, offending one character would count down the value of his cooperativeness. The moderator may have to act to raise this value again, since only with a high level of cooperativeness, will this character finally agree on a compromise.

This is an abstract model, tailored to a certain game goal, yet without personality traits for each actor. Modelled traits would affect the transition rules in a way that lets different characters react differently to the same actions and events. This would be useful to enable apparent novelty and idiosyncrasies in the conversational turns each time the game would be played, and will be considered as future work. As a drawback in terms of the educational purpose, we expected that – next to an immense increase in complexity – the correlations that can be made between actions and outcome would be disguised. Instead, for the first prototype, we were looking for reduced intricacy, also in terms of getting a grip on the authoring process, which was conceived at the same time. Finally, the next hitch was the proper assignment of the model's states with concrete bot utterances and potential user utterances.

As a result, the initial model had been reduced again to an even more abstract and simple game-like model. Figure 5 shows the simplified model, which was then implemented. Instead of modelling each character's mind, a generalized view is taken by only modeling overall levels of stress – here: the "Killer Phrase Level". This model places a scale on the overall "mood", with the effect that valid arguments of each party can only be played out by the system if the killer phrase level is low.

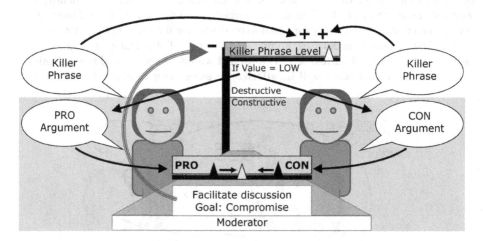

Fig. 5. Simplified model of states and transitions

Thus, it can be stated that the "chosen level of detail" (in Holland's terms, compare section 3) has led to a result that makes a point as a simple gaming simulation and as an interactive short story, at least creating awareness of the phenomenon of a "killer phrase". Compared to "reality", the implemented model appears as an oversimplification, far from Holland's "perfect model". Phrasing it in narrative terms, a model of a simple "storyworld" has been created by people who wanted to make a point. This model is part of the content and, at first, independent of potentially underlying engine models resembling physical realities (such as psychological models).

These preparations, outside of the authoring tool, showed the indirect work of turning an explicitly scripted dialogue into a model that "implies" how the conversation can go if not scripted in detail. This major step has to be done by story artists or by simulation designers, who are completely involved in the content matter, and not by the engineers of the runtime platform. For example, as a common practice in modelling gaming simulations for organisational change, the "Critical Incident" technique is used to turn oral stories into a model, by segregating essential dependencies.

4.2 Affordances for the Authoring of Actions, Events and States

Transforming the conceived model into a runtime application requires methods to define procedures generating actions and events to influence states. The way this can be accomplished depends on the platform available. In the case of the Killer Phrase game, the *Scenejo* authoring tool provided an interface for non-programmers. It works in accordance with its unique platform peculiarities, which construe actions as utterances of individual characters (bots), finally to be coded in AIML.[4]

The actions (utterances) of each bot have to be constructed with pre-conditions and post-conditions. A pre-condition consists of 1.) a text pattern of another agent's utterance (bot or user) and optional 2.) state conditions required for the action to be triggered. A post-condition is 1.) an optional state change, and 2.) the spoken utterance. A so-called "Stimulus-Response" element manages this procedure in *Scenejo*. The killer phrase game contains threads of dialogue between two bots, which can be interrupted by the user. To code these dialogues in the above way, it is necessary to match the post-conditions of one bot with the pre-conditions of the other, and vice versa. The "Stimulus-Response" interface also allows the author to define utterances not only in direct speech, but also in an abstract form, to denote a dialogue act. For example, a dialogue act can be named "Reproach Ignorance Killerphrase", connecting to a selection of possible concrete utterances, such as "We residents don't figure into your plans" or "We're only asked our opinion after everything is already set in stone".

On a higher level of abstraction, dialogue graphs can be structured into scenes. Scenes are always connected by an explicit connection; at this level, no emergence is at work, but only branching paths as the result of certain choice events.

4.3 Conclusions for Explicit Authoring and Implicit Creation

The creation process of the Killer Phrase game on the *Scenejo* platform showed limitations and possibilities of explicit writing methods, as well as of implicit techniques.

In terms of accessibility for newcomers to the modelling process, it was easiest to start with explicitly phrased text in a linear order on several task levels. For turning the dialogue script into something more procedural – letting a similar dialogue "emerge" from interaction, each time with variations – it was necessary to define rule-based models. Such "implicit creation" has been achieved for the following aspects:

- The game state varies based on user interaction and on some randomisation in the bot's action selection, depending mostly on the development dynamics of the "Killer Phrase" state and "Agreement" level state in the designed model.

---

[4] The main *Scenejo* authoring tool components have been described in [21].

- Interruptions within the dialogue threads are possible at any given moment, since the utterances are modelled as conditional actions.
- Abstract dialogue acts can result in variations of concrete utterance templates.

The following aspects have still been authored explicitly:

- The utterances are hand-crafted. Therefore, it can't be excluded that exact repetitions in the spoken text occur. This can be diminished by creating a huge body of variations explicitly. Turning to complete "implicit creation", i.e., generating the language, requires modelling outreaching current possibilities – ontologies of the theme (airport expansion), of discussion styles, and more.
- The order of actions within a dialogue thread is predefined, unless a user interrupts. However, the order of all available dialogue threads varies according to the game state model. "Implicit creation" would have to result in a conversational model of the argument.
- The game contains a small higher-level plot structure, providing a predefined branching point to win or lose the game (compromise or escalation). More sophisticated models would contain planning structures and goals for the actors to be tuned on a higher level.

Although only few aspects of this application were model-based instead of explicitly scripted, it showed emergent performance, in the sense that it turned out to be difficult to anticipate the runtime behaviour completely during the authoring phase. Possible utterances were explicitly formed, but not their order, and only some of their connections. From a perceptual point of view, there might be no difference between the appearance of a successfully emergent aspect and a failure in authoring. The consequences are that the phase of tuning and testing gets intricate, and that "debugging" tools for dynamic content are needed, in the sense of inversely tracking down responsible rules for an occurring effect, in order to fine-tune them. Thus, the process of creation becomes similar to programming complex software, even if no programming language, but rather visual editors are used. The *Scenejo* tools have proven to be accessible and effective. However, the authoring process on the action level, including the definitions of pre- and post-conditions, is nonetheless a tedious task close to programming.

5 Steps Towards Implicit Creation for Authors

In this section, the concept of emergence is contrasted with the notions of storytelling and creation. The phenomenon of patterns created by an ongoing emergent process is usually seen as the opposite of anything based on intentions, such as creation. However, there is a creative, inductive process of finding rules that attempt to model patterns of interest – a selection. J. Holland, 1998: *"Emergence must somehow be bound up in the selection of the rules (mechanics) that specify the model, be it game or physical science. [...] Knowing what details to ignore is not a matter of derivation or deduction; it is a matter of experience and discipline, as in any artistic or creative endeavor."* [7, p. 113]

There is a correlation between the above concept and writing a novel or other forms of "traditional" storytelling. D. Herman, who provided an integrating view on narrative theories including other disciplines [6], defined the notion of a "storyworld" as an "ecology of narrative interpretation", from the perspective of recipients. Actions, events and states are parts of the inventory of "local principles of storyworld design" [6, p. 27]. Presented actions in a story are mostly incomplete and "underspecifying" the storyworld – much of it is only implied, without being explicitly articulated during narration. For example, one pithy dialogue line in a film can have three functions [17]: 1.) provide information, 2.) display emotions, and 3.) reveal traits by its diction. The art of storytelling and the art of model building both rely on omitting details. Nevertheless, they are not the same and have to be distinguished. Figure 6 illustrates the dual meaning of a storyworld.

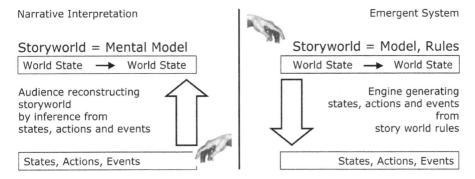

Fig. 6. Two meanings of "storyworld": Left, the recipient's mental model, built from interpreting created states, actions and events (according to [6]). Right, the designer's created dynamic model, leading to generated states, actions and events (after [7]).

"Implicit creation" in IDS is the content creator's task of letting actions, events and states result from automatic generation during narration, by specifying a dynamic model (a storyworld). Various engines with underlying dynamic models for the generation of perpetual variations of actions already exist: scientific models from physics and psychology, such as for gravity, vision, kinematics, emotions, cognition and linguistics. However, actions based on models of "reality" alone do not tell a story or provide a storyworld. The concern with developing unique storyworlds as a basis for coherent actions is part of the content creation, not of engineering. Faced with the complexity of emergent systems, content creators need to approach implicit creation in steps, starting with explicit creation methods for its greater accessibility. There is a need for future research in identifying appropriate steps and developing supporting tools.

6   Conclusion

In this contribution, the notion of "implicit creation" has been introduced. It paraphrases concepts and metaphors (such as the gardening metaphor) for authors who attend to the building of emergent narrative, even when it is not necessary for all possible narrative structural aspects to be rendered as emergent properties. The difference with explicit creation is that the created content does not fully describe the resulting actions, states and events in every detail, but it "implies" them. The current discussion on authoring systems mainly focuses on GUI tools that free people from programming, in the sense of replacing the code generation form of typing by clicking. While this is commendable, it is not the only problem for authors. Instead, conceptual models for implicit creation still have to be created and communicated.

References

1. ALICE: Homepage of the A.L.I.C.E. Artificial Intelligence Foundation (last accessed August 31, 2007), online: http://www.alicebot.org
2. Aylett, R.: Narrative in Virtual Environments - Towards Emergent Narrative. In: Proceedings, AAAI Fall Symposium on Narrative Intelligence, TR FS-99-01, AAAI Press (1999)
3. Aylett, R., Louchart, S., Dias, J., Paiva, A., Vala, M.: Fearnot! - an experiment in emergent narrative. In: Panayiotopoulos, T., Gratch, J., Aylett, R., Ballin, D., Olivier, P., Rist, T. (eds.) IVA 2005. LNCS (LNAI), vol. 3661, pp. 305–316. Springer, Heidelberg (2005)
4. Charles, F., Lozano, M., Mead, S.J., Bisquerra, A.F., Cavazza, M.: Planning Formalisms and Authoring in Interactive Storytelling. In: Proceedings of TIDSE 2003, Darmstadt (2003)
5. Crawford, C.: Storytron Interactive Storytelling (last accessed August 31, 2007), Project Website: http://www.storytron.com/
6. Herman, D.: Story Logic: Problems and Possibilities of Narrative. University of Nebraska Press, Lincoln (2002)
7. Holland, J.H.: Emergence: From Chaos to Order. Oxford University Press, Oxford (1998)
8. Inscape Consortium: Inscape Storytelling EU Project Website, Research Papers (last accessed: August 31, 2007), http://www.inscapers.com/downloads_research_papers.html
9. Iurgel, I.: Cyranus – An Authoring Tool for Interactive Edutainment Applications. In: Pan, Z., Aylett, R., Diener, H., Jin, X., Göbel, S., Li, L. (eds.) Technologies for E-Learning and Digital Entertainment. LNCS, vol. 3942, Springer, Heidelberg (2006)
10. Louchart, S., Aylett, R.: Solving the narrative paradox in VEs - lessons from RPGs. In: Rist, T., Aylett, R., Ballin, D., Rickel, J. (eds.) IVA 2003. LNCS (LNAI), vol. 2792, pp. 244–248. Springer, Heidelberg (2003)
11. Mateas, M., Stern, A.: Procedural Authorship: A Case-Study Of the Interactive Drama Façade. In: DAC. Proceedings of Digital Arts and Culture, Copenhagen (2005)
12. Mateas, M.: Expressive AI – A hybrid art and science practice. Leonardo: Journal of the International Society for Arts, Sciences, and Technology 34(2), 147–153 (2001)
13. Medler, B., Magerko, B.: Scribe: A Tool for Authoring Event Driven Interactive Drama. In: Göbel, S., Malkewitz, R., Iurgel, I. (eds.) TIDSE 2006. LNCS, vol. 4326, Springer, Heidelberg (2006)
14. nm2 Consortium: nm2 – New Millenium, New Media. EU Project Website (last accessed: August 31, 2007), http://www.ist-nm2.org/publications/deliverables/deliverables.html
15. Pearce, C.: Sims, BattleBots, Cellular Automata God and Go. A Conversation with Will Wright. Game Studies Journal 2(1) (2002), http://www.gamestudies.org/0102/
16. Sauer, S., Osswald, K., Wielemans, X., Stifter, M.: U-Create: Creative Authoring Tools for Edutainment Applications. In: Göbel, S., Malkewitz, R., Iurgel, I. (eds.) TIDSE 2006. LNCS, vol. 4326, Springer, Heidelberg (2006)
17. Schütte, O.: Schau mir in die Augen Kleines. Die Kunst, gute Dialoge zu schreiben (in German), Verlag Lübbe (2002)

18. Spierling, U.: Learning with Digital Agents – Integration of Simulations, Games, and Storytelling. In: Burmester, Gerhard, Thissen (eds.) Proceedings of Digital Game Based Learning – Symposium Information Design 2005, Universitätsverlag Karlsruhe, pp. 115–147 (2006)

19. Spierling, U.: "Killer Phrases": Design steps for a game with digital role playing agents. In: Proceedings of ISAGA 2007. 38th ISAGA Conference, Nijmegen, The Netherlands (2007)

20. Spierling, U., Iurgel, I.: Pre-Conference Demo Workshop "Little Red Cap": The Authoring Process in Interactive Storytelling. In: Göbel, S., Malkewitz, R., Iurgel, I. (eds.) TIDSE 2006. LNCS, vol. 4326, Springer, Heidelberg (2006)

21. Spierling, U., Weiß, S., Müller, W.: Towards Accessible Authoring Tools for Interactive Storytelling. In: Göbel, S., Malkewitz, R., Iurgel, I. (eds.) TIDSE 2006. LNCS, vol. 4326, Springer, Heidelberg (2006)

Wide Ruled: A Friendly Interface to Author-Goal Based Story Generation

James Skorupski[1], Lakshmi Jayapalan[2], Sheena Marquez[1], and Michael Mateas[1]

[1] University of California, Santa Cruz
Computer Science Department
1156 High Street, Santa Cruz, California, 95064
`jskorups@cs.ucsc.edu, smarquez@ucsc.edu, michaelm@cs.ucsc.edu`
[2] Electronic Arts

Abstract. We present Wide Ruled, an authoring tool for the creation of generative stories. It is based on the Universe author-goal-based model of story generation, and extends this model by providing support for reader interactivity, episodic memory elements, and an extensive graphical interface that is aimed at authors with little or no experience with computer programming and artificial intelligence planning techniques. The design of the interface is based around common interface conventions, narrative terminology, and step-by-step guidance through the creation of complex plan preconditions and actions. We also present initial user evaluation of this work-in-progress, which shows how our tool can be used by those with varying technical backgrounds to author dynamic stories with our tool. This feedback also suggests potential improvements of the interface to the underlying story representation and generation model.

Keywords: Story generation, author modeling, interactive narrative.

1 Introduction

The creation of interactive story experiences, in which interaction deeply affects the story, requires both expertise in authoring (compelling plot arcs, dialog, character conflicts, etc.) and technical expertise in computational and generative story representations. Either developers must be experienced artists and technologists (which, while ideal for certain types of innovation [11], is unfortunately rare), or they must work in multi-disciplinary teams that are segmented into distinct technical and non-technical pursuits. The multi-disciplinary team approach, while appropriate for large commercial projects, is inappropriate for small-scale development, impedes rapid experimentation, and is pedagogically inappropriate for small course projects. Wide Ruled is a story modeling tool that attempts to fit in this area of cross-over between algorithms and art, by providing a non-technical interface to a generative story engine based on the decidedly technical Universe story model [6, 7].

The experience of one of the authors (Mateas) in teaching Interactive Narrative over the last few years formed the genesis of the Wide Ruled project. Many of the students in the first few years of the course, while having some programming

M. Cavazza and S. Donikian (Eds.): ICVS 2007, LNCS 4871, pp. 26–37, 2007.

experience, generally had arts and humanities backgrounds rather than formal CS backgrounds. A portion of the course is devoted to surveying AI approaches to story generation and management, including classic generators such as Universe [6, 7], Tale-Spin [12] and Minstrel [17], as well as more contemporary work in interactive drama. For those students who chose to incorporate an AI approach to story generation into their course projects or masters theses, they almost always chose Universe, writing partial, simplified implementations of the Universe model and building their interactive stories on top of that [e.g. 4, 8]. For students from both technical and non-technical backgrounds, the Universe story model, with its hierarchical pursuit of multi-character story plans (plot fragments) in response to author goals, appears to offer an effective compromise between generative complexity and authorial simplicity. However, since each student project created a custom, partial (and often buggy) implementation of Universe, this strongly limited the amount of time students were actually able to spend working on the content of their experiences. This observation led to the creation of Wide Ruled, a general purpose Universe-based authoring tool accessible to non-programmers, which will ultimately support a variety of front ends for story interaction. While the version of Wide Ruled presented in this paper outputs textual stories, its execution model is generic enough to be applied to any story medium, including interactive video games.

By designing a simple visual interface to author-based story planning that makes use of non-technical language wherever possible, our authoring environment is designed to provoke a feeling of familiarity and relevance to the task of story-telling, and at the same time maintain the flexibility and power of the underlying planning engine.

2   Related Work

The difficulty of authoring is a common concern in interactive storytelling, for AI-based approaches in particular. Many authors have described authoring issues involved in creating autonomous characters and drama managers [e.g. 9, 15, 10]; such work, however, tends to describe authoring methodologies, rather than specific tools aimed at non-programmers. In this related work section, we limit ourselves to discussions of such tools.

A number of tools facilitate the construction of story graphs, in which the author explicitly represents possible paths through the story. Some examples include: InAuthor [1], which supports authoring geographically-aware spatial stories, AESOP [14], which provides a story-graph tool for pedagogical interactive dramas, U-Create [13], which provides graph authoring capabilities as part of a larger mixed reality authoring suite, INSCAPE, which provides graph authoring as part of a modular interactive story authoring environment [18], and SceneMaker [3], which supports more complex hierarchical story graphs with probabilistic transitions. The strength of story graphs is that they provide a readily understandable visualization of the potential story space, while their weakness is that they are a non-generative formalism, forcing the author to manually express the combinatorial possibilities in the story space, thus effectively limiting plot-level variation. The goal of Wide Ruled is to therefore make a more generative plan-based approach accessible to authors from a wide variety of backgrounds.

Other authoring tools have provided support for more plan-like story representations. DraMachina [2] defines dramatic units in which relationships between units are implicitly specified via propositional formulas over dramatic units. The Bowman plan authoring interface provides support for mixed-initiative narrative plan authoring within a plan-space planning framework [16]; it has not yet been tested with story authors.

Jayapalan created the first version of Wide Ruled [5]. Besides the evaluation, the work reported in this paper included extending the subgoaling mechanism in the underlying generation model and substantially revising the user interface.

3 Design

Wide Ruled implements the Universe author-based model of planning, which formulates a dynamic story as a plan that acts within the context of a story world. The world contains *objects*, including *characters*, *environments*, and *plot points* (see below). The space of potential stories is modeled as a set of *author goals*, each of which has one or more *plot fragments* which can fulfill these goals. Plot fragments (plans), the core of the story generation process, are activated based on the satisfaction of required *preconditions*; the *actions* of a plot fragment can display dynamic story text, pursue any number of author goals, and create or modify story world objects. With this representation, the underlying story generation engine selects

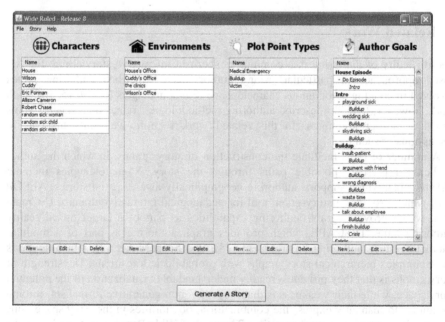

Fig. 1. The main window in Wide Ruled

an initial author goal and executes valid plot fragments and their pursued subgoals to generate a single instance of story. This approach is strongly related to HTN planning where the task decompositions (plot fragments) coordinate the activities of multiple characters rather than individual characters. This is in fact the Universe model's contribution to the story generation literature, being the first system to model the pursuit of authorial plans, which coordinate multiple characters, in pursuit of authorial goals. Subgoals within plot fragments can pass parameters into the plot fragment that is selected to satisfy the subgoal, providing a mechanism for maintaining consistency in the characters and story-world objects involved in the action. By being able to represent complex hierarchies of plot fragments that satisfy author goals, Wide Ruled, like the Universe model that it is based on, can generate complex and varied stories automatically.

Interactivity can be incorporated in the Universe model in a number of ways, including: the third-person interaction of manipulating initial conditions of the story world, the third-person interaction of manipulating the story-world during the planning process (thwarting or aiding the currently executing author plan), and the first person interaction of making choices for one of the characters within the story world. Wide Ruled currently supports this latter interaction model, allowing a user, acting as a character within the story world, to select amongst a set of plot fragments that are related to that chosen character. The user is effectively incorporated into the planning process, making decisions among plot fragments during subgoal pursuit when those plot fragments are relevant to the player character.

Figure 1 shows the initial and main window of Wide Ruled. Here, the user is presented with three lists of named story world objects, including characters, environments, and plot point types, and a list of author goals and the plot fragments that can satisfy them. An author can perform a consistent set of operations on each list, including renaming by double clicking on each element, and creating, editing, or deleting by selecting an element and using the respective buttons below. The menu bar at the top of the window provides options for creating a new blank story world, saving an existing one to a file, or loading a previous story world from a saved file. Finally, the prominent story generation button at the bottom of the window initiates the (interactive) story generation process.

3.1 Objects

Objects are uniquely named entities possessing a set of user-defined attribute/value pairs. Character and event objects exist before the generation of a story, thus defining the story world. Plot points, on the other hand, are episodic memory elements that represent significant story events. They are created by plot fragment actions.

Characters. Characters in Wide Ruled are modified using the editor interface displayed in Figure 2. Each character has three classes of attributes – traits, relationships, and aspirations/fears. Traits are a set of named attributes that are shared amongst all characters in the story world. Each trait can be one of three types of information: text, yes/no, and numeric. Relationships are named attributes that have a target, which is a reference to another character, and a number value representing the strength of that relationship. Aspirations/fears are named attributes that, unlike shared

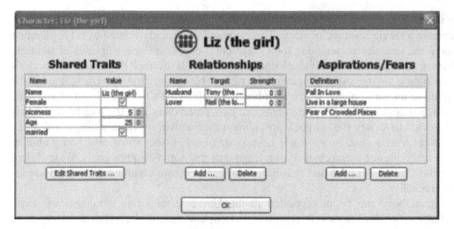

Fig. 2. The character editor window lists the traits, relationships, and aspirations/fears of a specific character. The add and edit buttons support the creation of new attributes.

traits and relationships, don't possess any associated value, but can simply exist or not exist for each character. In order to aid in the authoring process, Wide Ruled provides many sample shared traits, relationships, and aspirations/fears that can be selected when creating new attributes.

Environments. Environments in Wide Ruled are analogous to characters, but conceptually refer to locations in the story world. The editing of each environment is identical to the character editing process described earlier, however only shared traits and relationships are valid attribute types, and relationships refer instead to other environments, instead of characters. Environments are intended to serve as stages for story events; attributes provide the means for selecting appropriate stages as the story progresses.

Plot Point Types. Plot points are episodic memory elements that are designed to represent significant events that occur during the progress of a story, and are dependent on the order of events. As such, are created and edited only during the story generation process, and the main Wide Ruled window only allows for the creation of specific types of plot points. Each named plot point type refers to a potential plot point with a user-defined set of attribute-value pairs. The values, like the values for the attributes of characters and environments, can be textual, yes/no, or numeric. In Figure 3, the simple editing interface for a single plot point type is shown. Here, the user can select only attribute names and types, and no values, since this type of object is only instantiated and manipulated during story generation.

Fig. 3. The plot point typ editor window

3.2 Author Goals

Author goals are the primary organizational component of story generation in Wide Ruled. Like the

Universe model, Wide Ruled generates stories by picking an initial author goal then executing plot fragment with a valid precondition, which may in turn pursue another author goal. As seen in Figure 1, the main window displays author goals as the top level entity of a hierarchical list. In this list, author goals are bolded elements, and each plot fragment that fulfills a specific author goal is indented underneath that goal in the list. In addition, if a plot fragment pursues another author goal, then the name of that goal is displayed in italics, indented underneath that plot fragment's name.

Goal Parameters. During story generation, author goals can be passed data values, either text, yes/no, or numeric, from plot fragments that choose to pursue them. These values are then in turn passed onto the plot fragment that is selected by the story generation engine for that author goal. In order to select the names and types of parameters for each author goal, the user can, from the main window in Figure 1, select any bolded author goal from the list and click the "Edit" button below. This will display a window, similar to the plot point type editor in Figure 3, which allows the user to add new parameters and their respective types.

3.3 Plot Fragments

Plot fragments are the unit of story world manipulation within Wide Ruled. When the story generation engine is creating a story, upon reaching an author goal, every plot fragment that fulfills that goal is analyzed to determine if all of its preconditions are satisfied. If these conditions are all satisfied, then the story generator puts that plot fragment into a list until all plot fragments are analyzed. When finished, the story generator then selects a random fragment from this list, and then performs the actions of that plot fragment.

The plot fragment editor window is activated by selecting a plot fragment name in the author goal hierarchical list in the main window of Wide Ruled. Shown in Figure 4, the plot fragment editor consists of four sections describing interactivity features, author goal settings, preconditions, and actions. The settings pane allows the user to change the parent author goal for the current plot fragment, and also displays the names and types of the author goal parameters that are passed onto this plot fragment during story generation. In addition, this pane allows the user to select whether this plot fragment can be repeated more than once throughout the course of story generation, which can occur if author goals are recursively pursued. The interactivity, precondition, and action panes are described in later sections of this paper.

Preconditions. Preconditions are sets of constraints that must be satisfied before a plot fragment can be chosen to fulfill a goal. Within these precondition tests, during story generation, object attributes are matched against values, and any attribute of a matched object can be saved to variables within a plot fragment. These attributes may be matched against literals, incoming author goal parameters, or variables bound in previous precondition tests. A wizard is used to construct each test in a precondition, allowing the selection of the type of object to match against, attribute constraints, and options to bind attribute values to variables. This precondition creation wizard is show in Figure 5.

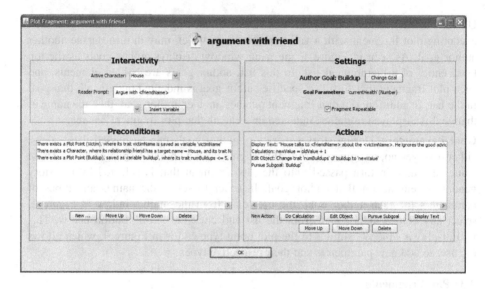

Fig. 4. The plot fragment editor window

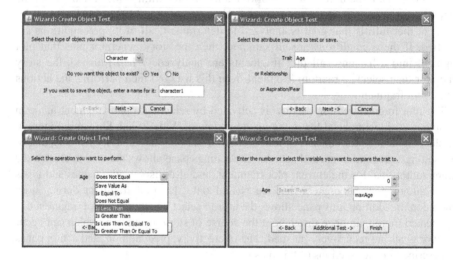

Fig. 5. The precondition creation wizard. The interface proceeds from left to right, and top to bottom. Any additional test or variable save for this precondition is appended by clicking the "Additional Test" button in the final window, which returns the user to the upper right window for further tasks within the current precondition test.

Within the plot fragment editor shown in Figure 4, precondition tests are displayed as a list of simple sentences that explain, in a straightforward way, the condition that must be true for each one to be satisfied. We designed these sentences to resemble English language statements, so that non-technical users would not be intimidated by any confusing notation. The story generation engine analyzes precondition tests in the order they are listed; by selecting one and using the "Move Up" and "Move Down" buttons below this list, the user may modify this order. This order is important if one precondition test compares an object attribute against a variable that is stored in another precondition test. If analysis occurs in the incorrect order, a variable may not be bound before it is tested against, resulting in the failure of that precondition test, invalidating the entire plot fragment during story generation.

Actions. Actions are the core of the story generation process. They are tasks that can output story text, create new plot fragment variables, manipulate the story world, or activate other author goals to pursue. Any of the plot fragment action can make use of variables within the plot fragment. These include author goal parameters or variables saved within any of the precondition tests. Like precondition tests, each action is executed in the order they are displayed in the plot fragment editor in Figure 4. Similar to the precondition list, plot fragments are displayed as a list of textual sentences that are designed to be as non-technical and understandable as possible.

Display Text. The text display action is the function that allows the author of a Wide Ruled story to output the actual text of the generated story. A parameterized text template language allows outputted text to depend on variable values.

Calculation. The calculation action allows the user to create a new plot fragment variable that is a summation, subtraction, division, or multiplication of two literal numbers, two plot fragment number variables, or one of each of these kinds of data. The ability to perform simple mathematical operations within a plot fragment allows for the flexibility of having object attributes with continuous variability.

Edit Object. The object editing action allows an author to create a new instance of a character, environment, or plot point, or edit any existing object. If the author wishes to edit an object, it must be bound to a variable within one of the precondition tests or created within a previous plot fragment action. The name of this bound variable is selected in the first window of the precondition creation wizard in Figure 5. The process of editing or creating objects is presented in a wizard interface similar to that of the precondition creation wizard. The wizard walks the player through assigning initial attribute values to a newly created object, or changing attributes of an existing object.

Pursue Subgoal. The subgoal pursuit action allows the user to select an author goal to pursue when executing the ordered actions of this plot fragment. If the selected goal requires author goal parameters, then the user must choose values to pass on from amongst the similarly-typed variables within the current plot fragment or the incoming author goal parameters.

3.4 Generation

The process of story generation within Wide Ruled is a recursive depth-first descent through a hierarchy of pursued author goals. The process begins with a randomly chosen initial author goal with no parameters and at least one valid plot fragment (one with fully satisfied precondition tests), and proceeds until all the ordered actions of every plot fragment in this descent have been completed. During this traversal, if a plot fragment fails, then the story generator reverts any story world and story text changes made by the fragment's actions, and returns to the parent author goal to search for another valid plot fragment. If no valid plot fragments remain, the entire author goal fails. Failure of an entire plot fragment occurs when any author goal pursuit action within that plot fragment fails. If the initially chosen author goal fails, then another one with at least one valid precondition is pursued. While reverting on failure is possible for textually generated stories (essentially be "crossing out" text that has already been output), reversion is inappropriate for real-time visual story worlds. Future versions of Wide Ruled will explore backing-up on plan failure without reversion, using special plan "clean up" actions to maintain coherence when abandoning a story trajectory.

3.5 Interactivity

The Wide Ruled model of interactivity involves allowing the reader to override the random choice of the story generator and select which of the valid plot fragments to activate for the current author goal, if more than one exists. In order to mimic the decisions of a specific character instead of the decisions made by the story generation algorithm, each plot fragment can have a designated *active character*, chosen in the interactivity pane of the plot fragment editor in Figure 4. This active character can be one of the predefined characters created in the character editor, or it can be set to a dynamically bound character variable saved within any of the precondition tests. In order to provide a more understandable selection menu to the player, instead of simply listing static plot fragment names, the author may enter a player prompt in the plot fragment editor. The player, before generating the story, can select the character he or she wishes to play from the "Story" menu in the main window of Wide Ruled. During story generation, if the current author goal has valid plot fragments with an active character identical to the player character, then the player is presented with a set of prompts to choose from. We consider this mechanism to be a debug mechanism for exploring how abstract player choices affect story generation. In future integration of Wide Ruled with a more visual representation (e.g. game engine), rather than presenting explicit, dynamically generated menus, as is done for textual generation, story-plan interaction would be enabled by having player choices in the concrete world *implicitly* select among potentially applicable plot fragments in the more abstract story structure.

4 Results

The Wide Ruled tool was presented in an assignment for an Interactive Narrative class offered by the Computer Science Department at the University of California, Santa Cruz. The assignment instructed the students to take a generative story world each had previously formulated in a story grammar, and then implement and extend the story using Wide Ruled. Ten students participated in a survey after completing their respective Wide Ruled story worlds. The students consisted of nine persons with backgrounds in computer science or engineering, and one with a background in the liberal arts. Prior to authoring, students were given a 30 minute lecture on the main features and story representation concepts within the system, four pages of electronic documentation, and two example Wide Ruled story worlds. One of them was a Wide Ruled version of the story in the popular American medical mystery drama "House".

It contained extensive manipulation of all story world objects, including multiple plot points, and varied use of preconditions, but its plot fragment structure was more linear, with each plot fragment pursuing typically only a single author goal. To demonstrate a more complex hierarchical story structure, we also provided them with an implementation of the "churn" plot fragment and its related actions, as described by Lebowitz in his work on Universe. This example demonstrated a large plot fragment with five precondition tests and seven actions that pursued other author goals, but did not make use of environments or plot points. After participants had completed authoring (they had 2 weeks), they filled out an anonymous survey in which they provided by qualitative and quantitative feedback on their experience.

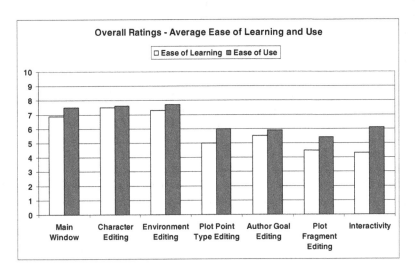

Fig. 6. The overall usability ratings for each component of Wide Ruled - 1 is hard, 10 is easy

The average overall ratings of the various components of Wide Ruled are depicted in Figure 6. While it appears that the character and environment editor portions of Wide Ruled received positive feedback, the responses indicate that most participants had trouble learning and regularly using the plot point type, plot fragment, and author goal editors. Not surprisingly, the editing of plot fragments, the most complex aspect of our tool, was considered to be one of the hardest tasks to learn and the hardest to use. The survey indicated that the primary difficulty was due to a lack of an ability to edit existing precondition tests or actions, or duplicate them to create similar entities with slight differences. The negative feedback to the author goal and plot fragment story structure components in general appears to demand a more intuitive explanation of the story generation process to users of the program. In terms of interactivity, the overall level of relative dissatisfaction with our model of interaction and qualitative survey feedback suggests that placing interactivity as a component of the story planning process is not a highly intuitive or conceptually simple way of integrating user input into the story generation process. In other, more positive results, two users that had low self-ratings of their background in programming and software design both reported that they used two to three precondition tests per plot fragment, the average across participants. This result suggests that the potentially complex notion of matching multiple constraints against the story world state was presented in an intuitive manner. Unfortunately, throughout the entire set of evaluated students, many of the generated stories displayed a primarily linear plot fragment structure (low author goal count), similar to the structure of the "House" sample story world described earlier. The power of the Universe model, and thus the Wide Ruled system, is its ability to represent complex hierarchical author goal relationships. This tendency for students to write less hierarchical plot fragments did not fully exploit this flexibility, and may have been a result of bias from the earlier story grammar assignment, in which students wrote relatively abstract, fairly shallow grammars. Finally, the aspiration/fear attributes of characters also rarely used, and their task was primarily subsumed by shared traits with yes/no values.

5 Conclusions and Future Work

We have shown that it is possible to build a visual story authoring environment based on Universe, a classical AI model of story generation. Such authoring tools have great potential to put more powerful, generative interactive story models in the hands of story artists. Despite the mixed results of our evaluation, the results were strong enough to warrant further development of Wide Ruled, especially given our experience with non-technical students being attracted to the Universe model. Based on feedback from the evaluation, our next steps will include adding the ability to edit and duplicate existing precondition tests and actions, implementing a visual depiction of plot point manipulation by plot fragments, allowing authors to explicitly see the creation and testing of plot points, further investigation into the authorial usefulness of separating aspirations and fears from shared traits, and adding explicit support for character group affiliations. For player interaction, in addition to the active character interaction model currently implemented, we will integrate a third-person interaction model in which the player modifies world state during story generation. In the longer term, we will explore the use of a comic strip style interface for both story generation and drag and drop authoring. Finally, with this improved version of Wide Ruled, we'll perform a broader authoring study utilizing a larger set of participants with non-technical backgrounds.

References

1. Barrenho, F., Romao, T., Martins, T., Correia, N.: InAuthoring environment: Interfaces for creating spatial stories and gaming activities. In: Proceedings of the 2006 ACM SIGCHI international conference on advances in computer entertainment technology (2006)
2. Donikian, S., Portugal, J.: Writing Interactive Fiction Scenarii with DraMachina. In: Göbel, S., Spierling, U., Hoffmann, A., Iurgel, I., Schneider, O., Dechau, J., Feix, A. (eds.) TIDSE 2004. LNCS, vol. 3105, Springer, Heidelberg (2004)
3. Gebhard, P., Kipp, M., Klesen, M., Rist, T.: Authoring Scenes for Adaptive, Interactive Performances. In: AAMAS-2003. Proceedings of the Second International Joint Conference on Autonomous Agents and Multiagent Systems, pp. 725–732 (2003)

4. Hochhalter, B.: Triad. Digital Media masters thesis, Georgia Institute of Technology (2004), http://steel.lcc.gatech.edu/ms_projects/hlogas/
5. Jayapalan, L.: Wide Ruled: A Generative, Interactive Story Authoring Environment. Digital Media masters thesis, Georgia Institute of Technology (2005), http://egl. gatech. edu/?cat=4
6. Lebowitz, M.: Story-Telling as Planning and Learning. Poetics 14, 483–502 (1985)
7. Lebowitz, M.: Creating Characters in Story-Telling Universe. Poetics 13, 171–194 (1984)
8. Logas, H.: Agency: A Character-Centric Approach to Single Player Digital Space Role Playing Games. Digital Media masters thesis, Georgia Institute of Technology (2004), http://steel.lcc.gatech.edu/ms_projects/hlogas/
9. Loyall, A.B., Neal Reilly, W.S., Bates, J., Weyhrauch, P.: System for authoring highly interactive, personality-rich interactive characters. In: Proceedings of the 2004 ACM SIGGRAPH/Eurographics Symposium on Computer Animation, pp. 59–68 (2004)
10. Mateas, M., Stern, A.: Structuring Content in the Façade Interactive Drama Architecture. In: AIIDE. Proceedings of Artificial Intelligence in Interactive Digital Entertainment (2005)
11. Mateas, M., Stern, A.: Build It to Understand It: Ludology Meets Narratology in Game Design Space. In: DiGRA. Proceedings of the Digital Interactive Games Research Association (2005)
12. Meehan, J.: Tale Spin. In: Shank, R.C., Riesbeck, C.K. (eds.) Inside Computer Understanding: Five Programs Plus Miniatures, Lawrence Erlbaum Associates, Mahwah (1981)
13. Sauer, S., Osswald, K., Wielemans, X., Stifter, M.: U-Create: Creative Authoring Tools for Edutainment Applications. In: Proceedings of TIDSE 2005, pp. 163–168 (2005)
14. Silverman, B., Johns, M., Weaver, R., Mosley, J.: Authoring Edutainment Stories for Online Players (AESOP): A Generator for Pedagogically Oriented Interactive Dramas. In: Balet, O., Subsol, G., Torguet, P. (eds.) ICVS 2003. LNCS, vol. 2897, Springer, Heidelberg (2003)
15. Sobral, D., Machado, I., Paiva, A.: Managing Authorship in Plot Conduction. In: Balet, O., Subsol, G., Torguet, P. (eds.) ICVS 2003. LNCS, vol. 2897, Springer, Heidelberg (2003)
16. Thomas, J., Young, M.R.: Author in the Loop: Using Mixed-Initiative Planning to Improve Interactive Narrative. In: The ICAPS 2006 Workshop on AI Planning for Computer Games and Synthetic Characters (2006)
17. Turner, S.T.: The Creative Process: A Computer Model of Storytelling and Creativity. Lawrence Erlbaum Associates, Mahwah (1994)
18. Zagalo, N., Göbel, S., Torres, A., Malkewitz, R.: INSCAPE: Emotion Expression and Experience in an Authoring Environment. In: Göbel, S., Malkewitz, R., Iurgel, I. (eds.) TIDSE 2006. LNCS, vol. 4326, Springer, Heidelberg (2006)

Story Manager in 'Europe 2045' Uses Petri Nets

Cyril Brom[1], Vít Šisler[2], and Tomáš Holan[1]

[1] Charles University, Faculty of Mathematics and Physics, Prague, Czech Republic
{brom,holan}@ksvi.mff.cuni.cz
[2] Charles University, Faculty of Philosophy, Prague, Czech Republic
vsisler@gmail.com

Abstract. *Europe 2045* is an on-line multi-player strategy game aimed at education of high-school students in economics, politics, and media studies. The essential feature of the game is that players face various simulated scenarios and crises addressing contemporary key issues of the unified Europe. These scenarios are branching and can evolve in a parallel manner. In this paper, we present a technique for specifying plots of these scenarios, which underpins the story manager of *Europe 2045*. The technique is based on a modification of Petri Nets. We also detail one particular scenario concerning the current crisis in Darfur. On a general level this paper discusses the strengths and weaknesses of implementation of Petri Nets in virtual storytelling.

1 Introduction

The idea of using computer games to support training and learning objectives is more than 30 years old [4]. Recent works have explored the potentialities of commercial strategy games and simulations in formal education and their alleged advantages over classical e-learning and edutainment tools, e.g. [6]. Indeed, many of such games have been experimentally integrated to formal curricula in the last four years. Perhaps the most prominent case studies have been conducted with *The Sims 2*, *Civilization III*, and *Europe Universalis II* [6, 12, 15], but other attempts exists as well. The results from these pilots are promising, but also ambiguous in some aspects, e.g. [15]. Hence, so called "serious" or "educational" games are starting to achieve increasing amount of attention. These games are, contrary to commercial games, *intentionally developed as educational tools*, which makes their integration into formal education easier. For example, a role-playing game prototype *Global Conflicts: Palestine* has been recently evaluated in a Denmark high-school with positive outcome [7]. Another studies are being conducted, including *FearNot!*, an anti-bullying educational game [1], and *Revolution*, a multi-player educational role-playing game concerning American War of Independence [5, 8].

As a part of European funded project "Integration of IT Tools into Education of Humanities" we develop an educational game *Europe 2045*, which is likely the first on-line multi-player strategy game worldwide aimed at education of high-school students in economics, politics, and media studies. The implementation part is finished and the game is presently being tested. Five preliminary studies have been already carried out, each with about 10 high-school or undergraduate university

M. Cavazza and S. Donikian (Eds.): ICVS 2007, LNCS 4871, pp. 38–50, 2007.

students. A large-scale pilot evaluation is planed for November 2007 in a high-school in Prague, Czech Republic. The game is intended to be fully applied in spring 2008.

Europe 2045 features three layers of game-play. Each student (1) represents one EU member state in the game and is responsible for its governmental policies, economical development, and social issues. Additionally, in cooperation with the other players, (2) he or she is engaged in setting politics of the whole EU. Nevertheless, the essential feature of the game is that (3) each player faces various simulated scenarios and crises addressing contemporary key issues of the unified Europe, including migration, population aging, international relations, and energy independence. Not only have these scenarios a strong educational potential, but also they introduce storytelling into the game. Storytelling has played an important role in humanities education since the advent of formal schooling ([4]). Stories help to build a learning context, through them the students can better understand the problematic, they increase their involvement, and consequently their motivation.

Specifying plots of stories and controlling the course of a game in accordance with these plots is a well known problem. It was indeed one of the most challenging goals we faced during the development. Essentially, the game had to be designed in order to meet the following requirements:

a) the story plots to be branching,
b) the story episodes to be both global, i.e. concerning the whole Europe, and local, i.e. concerning a particular state or a set of states,
c) the episodes to can happen in parallel, because we have more than 20 countries, which could be played simultaneously, each having defined different episodes,
d) the episodes to be triggered by various initial conditions depending on the time, EU economy etc.,
e) the technique for specification of the plots to be intuitive enough for a high school teacher or another user (typically an undergraduate university student of humanities) to be able to design new scenarios for the game.

Finally, we have chosen a modification of Petri Nets [2] as the plot specification technique. Although this modification is used for *Europe 2045*, the technique is quite universal and can be use in other applications as well. The goal of this paper is to present this technique and discuss its strengths and weaknesses. We first detail the game *Europe 2045* in Section 2, focusing on how the stories are narrated in the game. In Section 3, we review previous research on methods of controlling a story in games and storytelling applications in general. Section 4 details the Petri Nets modification and its implementation. Section 5 demonstrates a part of a scenario concerning the Darfur crisis. Section 6 concludes.

2   'Europe 2045'

This section details the game *Europe 2045*. We first describe the game from the perspective of a player, focusing on its storytelling aspects, and then overview the technical background.

Europe 2045 is an on-line multiplayer game in which each student (i.e. a player) governs one state by setting its policies, taxes, and subsidies while discussing

European and global issues with other players. The game contains economical and social model which simulates population aging, migration, evolution of the market, transfers of industry and services, changes in environment, moods of citizens, and a substantial number of other variables describing particular states and European Union as a whole (e.g. culture, infrastructure, education, etc.).

On the European level, all the players are encouraged by the game to take active part in decision making. The narrative structure of *Europe 2045* serves for three purposes. First, it introduces new topics and agenda for students' discussions. Second, unfolding new events in accordance with players' previous decisions, it serves as a global feedback for the students and as a method for sharpening the discussion. Both these kinds of events are global, i.e. they are common for all the players and concern EU as well as international issues (e.g. conflict in Darfur has intensified). The third class of events provides individual players with a feedback about the results of their previous actions concerning their own states; hence, these events are local (e.g. citizens in France protest against university fees, or unemployment in Czech Republic has reached 15%).

The game proceeds in rounds, one round is one game year. An atomic "beat" of a scenario is called an *affair*. It is an event that takes place in one round and can be triggered by players' actions or results from the economical and social model or affairs from previous rounds. An affair is communicated to the player via a textual description in the game newspaper (*NP news item*) or via a short animation in TV, which is being displayed at the beginning of every round (*TV news item*). In some cases, an affair also has an *impact* on the economical and social model, i.e. it influences state of a country or the whole EU. Typically, an affair can result in increasing the EU budget, increasing the level of pollution in particular states, crippling agriculture production, etc.

Some affairs introduce issues that require decision to be taken by the players (e.g. accepting another state's proposal, sending humanitarian mission to the area of a conflict, etc.). These decisions are intended to be taken during a discussion, typically in the class under the teacher's supervision, and voted through a *ballot*. One affair often triggers more ballots, each constituting precisely formulated question ("Do you vote for sending European humanitarian mission to Darfur area?") with three possible answers (yes/no/abstain). The ballots chosen by the game designers aim to cover all the main possible solutions usually proposed by real politics in similar cases. When the answers can not be schematized to the yes or no option, the ballot contains number (3-4) of more detailed solutions. The decision chosen by the players influences the economical and social model and the affairs to be triggered in the next round.

The game offers more different campaigns to be played, each of them focusing on different problematic (e.g. energy independence, international relations, environment). For each campaign, specific affairs and a scenario describing relations between them have to be designed. New campaign also comprises distinctive animations for the TV, articles for the newspaper, items for the in-game encyclopaedia, teachers manual, and handouts for students.

Technically, the game is a client-server application; the students play the game via the Internet (Fig. 1). The server part comprises PHP scripts generating the game interface, the story manager written in PHP as well, and the social-economical simulation, which is written in Java. Almost all parts of the interface are programmed in Flash (see Fig. 2). The social-economical simulation features a simplified model of EU economy. Technically, the model is a multi-agent simulation [16], where each agent is either a country, or an abstract representation of an EU industry, like travel industry, mining industry, agriculture etc. In a simplified fashion, at the end of each round, an agent–country computes next state of the country, while an agent–industry carries out decisions in which country to build new factories, mines etc. based on particular variables of the countries (e.g. mining industry agent would prefer countries with low environmental tax, travel industry agent would prefer countries with nice environment, high culture and developed infrastructure). We remark that this simulation is coarse grained in the sense that it does not feature human-like agents.

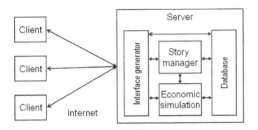

Fig. 1. Architecture of *Europe 2045*

2a

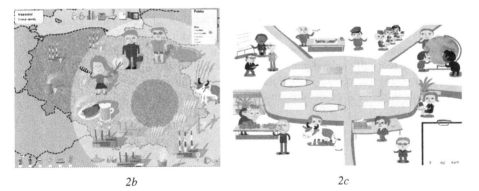

2b   2c

Fig. 2. a) The TV news. b) The interface, through which the player governs its country. c) The balloting interface.

3 Related Work

The issue of generating/controlling stories in games and storytelling applications is notoriously known. Most techniques come from games and experimental simulations featuring human-like actors. As said above, *Europe 2045* does not employ such actors. Rather, the story events are more abstract; they deal with whole populations, with a country economy etc. However, formally, the problem is very similar. We remind that we had several requirements on the storytelling technique in *Europe 2045* ranging from parallelism of the stories to the technique to be of use to undergraduate university non-IT students (see Sec. 1).

A well known branch of techniques for specifying plots are deterministic finite-state machines (dFSMs) [e.g. 13, 14]. Each state represents a story episode, and a transition is a trigger that detects the end of the episode and starts a next one. Natural advantage of dFSMs is that they are formal, and yet graphical (Fig. 3), which makes them easily intelligible. However, a classical dFSMs was not suitable for us, since they cannot cope with the issues of parallelism (req. b), c)). On the other hand, non-deterministic FSMs can cope with it, but they are not easily comprehensible (e)). Similarly to dFSMs, we encountered these parallelism difficulties when considering adopting the "beat approach" by Mateas [9].

In the field of emergent narrative, planning formalism is often used [1, 3, 11]. This technique can cope well with the requirements a), b), c), d), but it is not too friendly for a non-AI expert (req. e)). Since we are interested in pre-specified plots but not in automatic story construction (because the story must fit into the formal curricula), to use the HTN ("hierarchical-task network") formalism would be like using a sledgehammer to crack a walnut, with having the unintelligibility disadvantage. To tackle e), one could introduce a "presentation layer" for an HTN system to disguise the underlying representation and develop an authoring interface; however, this is time-consuming activity.

We needed something that would have *natural* comprehensibility advantage like the dFSMs, but could cope with the parallelism at the same time. The best candidate technique we found was Petri Nets, which is a specification technique frequently used in software engineering. Petri Nets have been already employed in storytelling. Natkin & Vega [10] used them to a retrospective analysis of a computer game story. In our previous work [2], we used it to prototype a story plot of a large simulation featuring human-like agents. However, none of these work implemented a story manager for a real full-fledged game, which is the case of *Europe 2045*.

Actually, many variants of Petri Nets exist. For our purposes, we specified our own modification, which will be detailed in the next section.

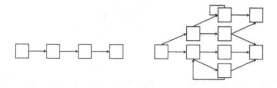

Fig. 3. Story plots as dFSMs. The linear plot is on the left, the branching on the right.

4   Petri Nets in 'Europe 2045'

This section gives description of our modification of Petri Nets. Generally, Petri Nets consist of containers (or places, represented by a circle: $\bigcirc$), tokens ("the pellets": ●), actions (or transitions, ▭), and transition function (→). The containers contain the tokens. If a sufficient number of tokens is contained in specific containers, an action is triggered. After firing an action, the tokens that helped to fire this action are removed, and some new tokens are generated (see Fig. 4a). Which tokens fire which action and which action generates tokens to which containers is specified by the transition function (and depicted by arrows). At one instant, several containers can contain tokens, which allows for concurrent triggering of actions (as opposed to dFSMs). The types of containers, tokens, and transition functions vary a modification from modification. For more thorough introduction to Petri Nets, we recommend the reader to consult [10].

The important feature of Petri Nets is that they are formal, and yet allow for graphical depiction, which mirrors all of their (or most of their, depending on the complexity of a particular Petri Nets variant) formal features. In other words, Petri Nets are a formal system, which has its own presentation layer. Hence, they fit well as a specification interface between a designer and a programmer. Indeed, in *Europe 2045*, we use our Petri Nets modification in two ways. First, they are employed in an informal manner as a specification tool for a game designer (and for university students who develop new game episodes as a part of their course). Second, a rigorous counterpart of this informal specification tool presents the architectural underpinnings of the story manager developed by our programmer. Thanks to the advantages of Petri Nets, the conversion of specifications into code is straightforward.

Our modification of Petri Nets was demanded to mirror the features of stories of *Europe 2045* described in Sec. 2. Particularly, the model must have seized the round-based nature of the game, the affairs, the ballots, and the presentation of news items. Hence, the model works with two types of actions, one of which is further coupled with the so-called ballot, and triggering of actions happens only between two rounds. These two features are also the most significant distinction of our model from a typical Petri Nets. We now describe individual components of our model. Then, we describe how they are integrated together and introduce the story manager algorithm.

Actions. We have two types of actions: *affairs* (⬜), and *news items* (⬚). Both of them can be started between two rounds by a trigger, as described later. When an affair is triggered, it can influence the game by its game *impact*. An impact can be for example: "migration to EU decreases in this round by x", or "the EU budget increases in this round by y & agriculture production in the states X, Y, Z is crippled by the factor of z". This impact is immediate, i.e. its result is computed by the economic simulator before the next round starts (see Fig. 1). Contrary to affairs, news items never have a game impact. In a plot specification, impacts are not described graphically, only textually.

Both kinds of actions can communicate to the player several news items in the next round, using either the game newspaper, or the game TV. Only an affair can invoke (in the next round) one or more *ballots* about a proposal related to the affair.

When the next round finishes, both affairs and news items can generate a new token to a specific container. Fig. 4a depicts an action, which generates one token. In Fig. 4b, there is depicted an affair "Darfur conflict" invoking a ballot about "sending an EU mission to Darfur" proposal in the next round (which in case of agreement generates two tokens, each to a particular container – see next).

Ballots. In a typical ballot (⬭), each student has three possibilities: he or she can agree, disagree or abstain, but more complicated cases are also allowed. The result of a ballot can influence the game, however, not necessarily straight-forwardly. To determine, how the game is influenced (i.e. which game impact to apply), a *what-next function* is defined for each ballot. This function returns its value based on the voting result. The simplest what-next function is trivial: it returns "+" if the proposal was agreed and "–" if it was not. This function is used in Fig. 4b. A more complicated what-next function can for example return A if the total size of armies of the states that agreed is more than 75% of the size of all EU states' armies, B if it is between 50% and 75%, and C if it is less than 50%.

A game *impact* is then defined for each return value of a what-next function. Additionally, every ballot can generate one or more tokens similarly to actions. How many tokens and to which containers are generated again depends on the result of the what-next function. In a portrayal, the return values of the what-next function are depicted next to the arrows originating from the ballot and pointing to the containers to which the tokens are to be generated. What-next functions are specified textually.

Tokens. We employ state-less aging tokens, in contrast to our previous work [1], where we used aging tokens with state (in so-called coloured Petri Nets modification). A token starts to age after it is generated to a container, but not removed in the next round. The *age* is given in number of rounds the token stays in the container.

Triggers and Containers. Triggers are evaluated at the beginning of each round. We use three types of them. First, we have *token-generating triggers*. These are associated with containers. Similarly to [1], containers with the triggers are depicted as a double circle (◎), as opposed to containers without a trigger (◯). Every time the condition of such a trigger holds, a new token is generated into the container. Presently, we use only the form of "when the round x starts → generate one token". These triggers essentially start the game or schedule the episodes to particular rounds. The number of a round, i.e. x, is depicted next to the container, as in Fig. 2b.

Second type of triggers is an *action-starting trigger*, whose meaning is obvious. Theoretically, an action-starting trigger cannot start its action directly for a conflict between two triggers can rise because they want to remove the same token (Fig. 4c). Hence, if the condition of a trigger holds, the trigger only marks its action to be started, and the respective tokens to be removed.

A typical action-starting trigger has the following form: "if there are n tokens in a particular container & f → mark the desired action", where f is a function of game state returning a boolean value (e.g. f can be "is EU budget in this round bigger then x EUR?"). The condition can also question the age of a token. In the portrayal, we write the ID of the trigger condition next to the arrow pointing to the action, as depicted in Fig. 4d. The condition itself is specified textually. Nothing next to the arrow, or only the age, means the condition: "if there is at least 1 token (of the specified age)".

To cope with conflicts, we define *conflict resolving triggers* that unmark one of the marked actions. This solution is based on our previous work [2]. The default conflict-resolving mechanism is to unmark one action randomly, but more elaborated solutions can be used, e.g. prioritising the actions. However, note that these triggers have been introduced to have the mechanism theoretically consistent; so far, we have not used them in our scenarios for they are not too intelligible for non-IT experts.

To sum up; in our Petri Nets modification, we use tokens without states but with aging, we use two types of actions (news items and affairs), and we can couple an affair with one or more ballots. Instead of transition function, we use three types of triggers, which can have relatively complicated conditions. Tokens can be generated by both ballots and actions.

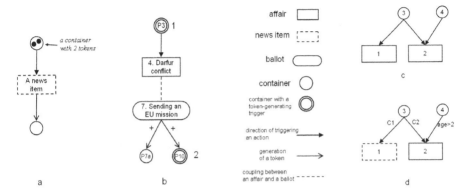

Fig. 4. a) A simple net. One token is needed in the upper container to start the news item, which then generates a token to the bottom container. b) A token-generating trigger generates a token to Container P3 in the first round. In fact, this starts the scenario. Affair 4 invokes Ballot 7 immediately. Between round 1 and 2 and if the what-next function of Ballot 7 returns "+" (which is in the simplest case when the ballot proposal has been agreed), two tokens are generated; one to P7a, one to P10. Additionally, a token-generating trigger generates one token into P10 in the second round regardless of the result of the ballot. c) If there is both one token in Container 3 and one token in 4, it is not clear whether to start Action 1 or 2. A conflict resolving trigger must be invoked. d) News item 1 is started when Condition C1 holds. Affair 2 is started when condition C2 holds *and* there is at least one token in Container 4 older than 2 rounds. Note, that in fact, the overall condition of trigger starting Affair 2 is "C2 & age_of_token_in_Cont4>2". If there is a conflict between this trigger and the trigger starting News Item 1, the conflict-resolving trigger is invoked as in the case (c).

1) Evaluate all token-generating triggers and generate tokens based on the results.
2) Evaluate all action-starting triggers and mark the respective actions to be started and the tokens to be removed.
3) For every token that is marked more than once: trigger the appropriate conflict-resolving trigger and consequently unmark one or more actions.
4a) If there is no marked action, then **end** this scenario.
4b) Otherwise, prepare all the marked actions to be run: generate newspaper & TV news based on the news items, consider the impact of the affairs, prepare the ballots of the affairs.
5) Remove all marked tokens, increase the age of remaining tokens.
6a) Run new round. Display the news, and ballots, ...
6b) End the round.
7) Calculate the results of the ballots & their what-next functions.
8) Generate new tokens based on the run actions and on the what-next functions of the ballots.
9) Compute the game impacts of the ballots based in their what-next function.
10) Go to 1

Fig. 5. The story manager algorithm. Note, that the steps 1-5 are concerned with a round k, while 7-10 with the round $k+1$.

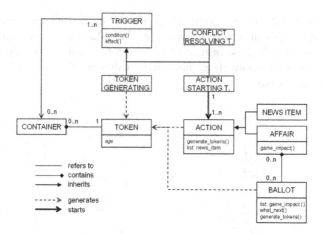

Fig. 6. Overall description of Petri Nets we uses given in a UML-like class diagram. Based on this schema, the story manager in Europe 2045 works. Relations of the "Conflict resolving trigger" are not depicted for clarity.

Game designer specifies the plots according to the above mentioned principles. Additionally, each entity of the model has a unique ID, which serves as a referencing mechanism to additional textual description (concerning e.g. the trigger conditions) as well as corresponding animations and news articles.

Petri Nets serves also as an architectural ground for our story manager. During a game, the plot specification is evaluated between each two consecutive rounds using the algorithm in Fig. 5. We remark that theoretically, some difficulties may be encountered in marking of tokens in Step 2 (for each trigger, we need to mark the tokens of appropriate age that has not been already marked, which may require searching for an appropriate ordering of triggers). Additionally, ordering of actions in Step 4b may matter (the total impact of "action A after action B" can differ from the total impact of "action B after action A"). Thought these issues are of theoretical interest, we did not tackled them rigorously for they could be addressed easily in an *ad hoc* manner even for our largest scenarios (Fig. 7).

Fig. 6 overviews how all the components of the model are integrated together. In the next section, we give an example of a large plot called "Darfur conflict".

5 Darfur Example

One of the largest and perhaps the most informative plots is *Darfur scenario* (Fig. 7). For brevity, we will not describe here the whole plot, rather we will illustrate how the building blocks of our Petri Nets work on the plot.

This scenario starts in the first round by an affair communicating via TV that the crisis in Darfur has escalated and invoking four ballot proposals. Based on the results of the ballots, the crises further develop. The important point is that it can evolve in several branches at the same time. For example, if students agree both on a form of development aid (Ballot 8) and a humanitarian aid (Ballot 5), both the affairs "Development aid begins" (8a) as well as "Humanitarian aid begins" (5a) are triggered in the second round. Additionally, either Affair 10a "Big migration increase", or Affair 10b "Small migration increase" is started. Which affair is started depends on conditions 7A and 7B.

The trigger conditions, ballot results and what-next-functions are not depicted graphically. They are rather specified textually and referred via IDs from the portrayal. Hence, the trigger starting Action 10a "Big migration increase" has the condition "if there are less than 3 tokens in P10" (Condition 7A), while the trigger starting 10b wants "at least 3 tokens" (Condition 7B). Notice also, that Container P10 has a token-generating trigger, which generates one token into P10 in the second round. This means that even if all the proposals are disagreed, large increase in migration to EU still occurs.

Similarly, it is specified textually that in the ballot "Lost reaction" (12), students have three possibilities: to reinforce the mission, to pull out the mission or to ask NATO for help. The what-next-function of this ballot is trivial (this is again specified textually) – to which container will be generated a token depends only on the result of the ballot (ids: 12A, 12B, 12C). It is also specified that Ballot 12 has no game impact, but the affair "Mission failed" (20) has game impact: "migration to EU is increased by x".

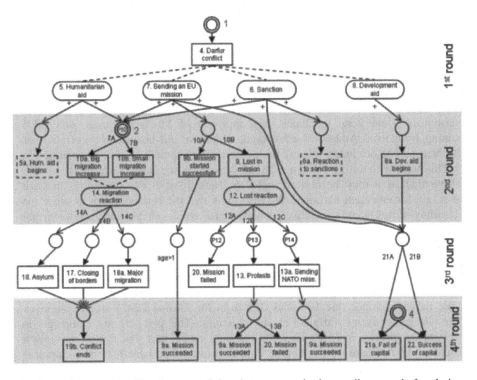

Fig. 7. Darfur scenario. The elements of the plot are organised according rounds for clarity. Container's ids that are not referred from text are not depicted. For clarity, several actions are depicted twice (9a, 20). Compare this figure with Fig. 3. We think that such scenario would be hard to describe by a deterministic FSM.

The scenario ends in the fourth round by a final series of affairs. However, notice, that other scenarios can be unfolded in parallel. In the basic campaign of *Europe 2045*, there are two additional scenarios of the size of "Darfur", and several dozens of small scenarios comprising from one to three actions. The campaign lasts 10 rounds (game years).

6 Discussion and Conclusion

In this paper, we have introduced serious game *Europe 2045*, which is a multi-player round-based strategy game aimed at education of high-school students in economics, politics, and media studies. The game is fully implemented and it is presently being evaluated. A large-scale pilot is planed for November 2007 in a high-school in Prague, Czech Republic. The game is intended to be applied in spring 2008.

A player in the game faces, among other things, various simulated scenarios addressing contemporary key issues of the unified Europe. This essentially introduces storytelling into the game. We have addressed the issues of specifying plots of the scenarios, and of unfolding stories by developing a Petri Nets modification that serves both for the purposes of a game designer and as an architectural ground for the story manager in the game.

The strength of Petri Nets is that they (at the same time) allow for graphical and yet formal description, they are easily comprehensible, and allow for describing branching stories evolving in parallel. The comprehensibility was demonstrated by the fact that the technique was explained to college students of humanities during a course (during about an hour and half) and they were subsequently able to use it to specify their own "toy" campaigns. For this strength, we favoured Petri Nets over deterministic finite state machines, beat-approach of Michael Mateas, and HTN planning formalism. Additional advantage, which we did not use however, is that Petri Nets can be run independently on the underlying simulation, as demonstrated in [2]. This helps with testing plots (e.g. are all the parts of the story reachable?).

Nevertheless, it must be noticed that Petri Nets fit well only for stories that are preset, not for emergent narrative. We also think that the beat approach is better for controlling stories featuring relatively small virtual worlds inhabited by (a few) virtual humans – this approach is more flexible. Additionally, if one needs a story with preset plot, which however do not evolve in parallel, deterministic FSM would be likely sufficient. Finally, it must be stressed that our technique is a branching one: after all, the author must specify all branches in advance. The potential risk of combinatorial explosion of branches must be avoided by manual "cutting" by the author.

We have developed one 10-round campaign for *Europe 2045*, which comprises about 70 game events (affairs, or news items). The plot of this campaign is programmed directly in PHP. This allowed us a quick start, but it also presents a limitation. To facilitate the development process, we would benefit from a graphical authoring tool, especially because we aimed at creating a second campaign and several undergraduate humanities students, who do not know PHP, develop other campaigns as a part of their university course. Developing this tool presents our future work. However, note that even in this tool, Petri Nets would be presented to the user *as such*, there would be no need for adding another presentation layer disguising the underlying representation (as may be the case of HTN planning – see Sec. 3). In fact, Petri Nets are a sort of rule based system, and it is this underlying rule based system that they innately present in a graphical form, further, Petri Nets can be even viewed as a methodology constraining the space of possible rules that can be written down.

Acknowledgments. The research on usage of Petri Nets in storytelling was partially supported by the Program "Information Society" under project 1ET100300517, and by the Ministry of Education of the Czech Republic (Res. Project MSM0021620838). The project "Integration of IT Tools into Education of Humanities" is financed by the European Social Fund, the state budget of the Czech Republic, and by the budget of Municipal House Prague. The authors would like to thank to all the partners of the project: Generation Europe, Ciant, gymnasium Sázavská, and Association for International Affairs, and to all the people who helped, most notably to Petr, Edita, Jakub, Lenka, Ondřej, Martin, and Michal.

References

1. Aylett, R.S., Louchart, S., Dias, J., Paiva, A., Vala, M.: FearNot! – An Experiment in Emergent Narrative. In: Panayiotopoulos, T., Gratch, J., Aylett, R., Ballin, D., Olivier, P., Rist, T. (eds.) IVA 2005. LNCS (LNAI), vol. 3661, pp. 305–316. Springer, Heidelberg (2005)
2. Brom, C., Abonyi, A.: Petri-Nets for Game Plot. In: Proceedings of AISB Artificial Intelligence and Simulation Behaviour Convention, Bristol, vol. 3, pp. 6–13 (2006)
3. Cavazza, M., Charles, F., Mead, S.J.: Planning Characters' Behaviour in Interactive Storytelling. The Journal of Visualization and Computer Animation 13, 121–131 (2002)
4. de Freitas S.: Learning in Immersive worlds: A review of game-based learning. JISC (Joint informational Systems Committee) report (2006) (June 6, 2007), http:// www.jisc. ac.uk/ eli_outcomes.html
5. The Education Arcade: Revolution, a role-playing game (June 6, 2007), http://www.educationarcade.org/revolution
6. Egenfeldt-Nielsen, S.: Beyond Edutainment: Exploring the Educational Potential of Computer Games. PhD Thesis, University of Copehagen (2005)
7. Egenfeldt-Nielsen, S., Buch, T.: The learning effect of 'Global Conflicts: Middle East'. In: Santorineos, M., Dimitriadi, N. (eds.) Gaming Realities: A Challenge for Digital Culture, pp. 93–97. Fournos, Athens (2006)
8. Francis, R.: Revolution: Student's experiences of virtual role play within a virtual reconstruction of 18th century colonial Williamsburg (an unpublished manuscript)
9. Mateas, M.: Interactive Drama, Art and Artificial Intelligence. Ph.D. Dissertation. Department of Computer Science, Carnegie Mellon University (2002)
10. Natkin, S., Vega, L.: Petri Net Modelling for the Analysis of the Ordering of Actions in Computer Games. In: Proceedings of Game-ON, pp. 82–92 (2003)
11. Reidl, M.O., Stern, A.: Believable agents and Intelligent Story Adaptation for Interactive Storytelling. In: Göbel, S., Malkewitz, R., Iurgel, I. (eds.) TIDSE 2006. LNCS, vol. 4326, pp. 1–12. Springer, Heidelberg (2006)
12. Sandford, R., Ulicsak, M., Facer, K., Rudd, T.: Teaching with Games. Using commercial off-the-shelf computer games in formal education, Futurelab, Bristol, UK (June 6, 2007), www.futurelab.org.uk/download/pdfs/research/TWG_report.pdf

13. Sheldon, L.: Character Development and Storytelling, ch. 7, 14. Thompson Course Technology (2004)
14. Silva, A., Raimundo, G., Paiva, A.: Tell Me That Bit Again.. Bringing Interactivity to a Virtual Storyteller. In: Balet, O., Subsol, G., Torguet, P. (eds.) ICVS 2003. LNCS, vol. 2897, pp. 146–155. Springer, Heidelberg (2003)
15. Squire, K.: Replaying history: Learning World History through playing Civilization III. PhD thesis, Indiana University (2004)
16. Wooldridge, M.: An Introduction to MultiAgent Systems. John Wiley & Sons, Chichester (2002)

Narrative Construction in a Mobile Tour Guide

Mei Yii Lim and Ruth Aylett

School of Mathematical and Computer Sciences,
Heriot Watt University,
Edinburgh, EH14 4AS, Scotland
{myl,ruth}@macs.hw.ac.uk

Abstract. Storytelling capabilities are vital aspect of a tour guide. In this paper, we present a mobile tour guide that emulates a real guide's behaviour by presenting stories based on the user's interests, its own interests, its belief and its current memory activation. This research moves away from the concept of a guide that recites facts about places or events towards a guide that utilises improvisational storytelling techniques. Contrasting views and personality are achieved with an inclusion of emotional memories containing the guide's ideology and its past experiences.

1 Introduction

A tour guide should provide interesting stories to encourage learning so as to create a meaningful tour experience. Based on a brief survey of tour guide experiences, factors like role, interest, experience, type of tour, length of tour, guide's belief, guide's personality and visitor group are found to influence the presentation of information. Most guides tend to incorporate beliefs and past experiences, whether his/her own or that of others whilst narrating a story. Different guides have different presentation styles and some guides are more talkative than others. Most of the time, they present general information about the tour, particularly about what can be immediately seen. They usually welcome interaction in order to gain an indication of the visitors' interests before they provide in-depth information on a particular subject. Visitors' age, origin, race and group size also contribute to the type of story told and the level of detail in which it is told. Indoor tours are usually more continuous, while outdoor tours involve more idling moments due to walking from one place to another.

In recent years, many tourist guidance applications have been developed, to list a few: C-MAP [1], HIPS [2], SAGRES museum [3] and PEACH [4]. Our work differs from these systems in that the guide does not only present facts but also its own ideological perspectives, expressing its viewpoint about a particular event, just as a real guide does. This is consistent with Tozzi's finding that one of the most striking features of historical investigations is the coexistence of multiple interpretations of the same event, depending on the storyteller's perspective [5]. By seeing things from a particular perspective coupled with his own knowledge and understanding, a user will be able to analyse, reflect, evaluate and use the source of information critically to reach a conclusion of why different historical interpretations exist, hence producing a deeper learning experience [6].

M. Cavazza and S. Donikian (Eds.): ICVS 2007, LNCS 4871, pp. 51–62, 2007.

2 Inspiring Our Work

Terminal Time [7] is a history engine that combines historical events, ideological rhetoric, familiar forms based on TV documentary and artificial intelligence algorithms to construct custom-made historical documentaries for mass audiences taking into account the audiences' polls. The system utilises questionaires as the user interface and an applause meter measures the audience reaction to the possible answers to each question. The computer program creates historical narrative that strongly emphasizes the audience's ideological preference, with the history unfolding based on the winning choice. The engine uses multimedia material covering the past 1000 years of world history as the source for narrative construction. This system addresses questions concerning the relationship of perspective to the construction of history. Instead of trying to reconstruct alternative long views of history based on ideological biases, we attempt to make the users aware of the availability of different ideological perspectives on a specific historical event. Whilst Terminal Time generated stories in response to audiences' generic ideological viewpoints, we take into account both the user's and the guide's interests. Our system adopts improvisational story generation based on a variety of factors (discussed in Section 4) rather than following a pre-defined storyline in support of a winning ideology.

Ibanez [8] proposed a story generation agent that can generate short stories using inference rules that combine historical facts and common-sense knowledge. At each step, the guide decides where to go and what to tell dynamically. This system constructs stories by improvising, taking into account factors such as the distance from the current location to a destination, the already told story at the current moment and the affinity between story element and the guide's profile. Three scores corresponding to these factors are calculated each time, which are then combined to calculate an overall score for each candidate pair of story element and location. Finally, the pair with the highest overall score value is chosen. If the granularity of the selected story element is not large enough to make a story of acceptable length, more story elements are selected. These elements are then translated from the virtual guide perspective, incorporating the guide attitudes that reflect the emotional impact on it of these story elements. Next, the story elements are enhanced by means of new information items generated by inferences from simple common-sense rules.

Generating narrative from a guide's viewpoint is also the problem we address. Hence, we utilise the approach just discussed. In general, Ibanez's work brings us a step nearer to the creation of an 'intelligent guide with personality'. It adopts a storytelling technique that links the memory and interests of the guide to their spatial location so that stories relevant to what can be immediately seen can be produced. However, what it lacks is the incorporation of the user's interaction. Whilst Ibanez's system omits user interests, we consider these together with feedback throughout the tour session as important factors that may affect the user's overall tour experience. Our guide makes use of interest attributes attached to story elements and locations that can be used to choose spots that interest the user and thus, allow personalised route planning and tours. While Ibanez' system generates stories by inferences based on facts and common-sense rules, we construct stories based on historical facts and the guide's past experiences. Instead of activating pre-defined attitudes and emotions, our guide behaviour is controlled by a biologically plausible model of emotion [9].

The problem of generating real-world tours has been explored in Geist [10], a project that developed an interactive storytelling system where stories are stored in the form of dramatic scenes, containing virtual characters, virtual buildings, storyboards, etc. By using pre-defined scenes to handle the virtual characters' behaviour, and by giving scene results back to the Story Engine, it selects the next scene to be played, in relation to the interaction of the user. Within the scenes, conversational interaction is used to permit a humanlike communication with the actors. Conversation is modelled taking into consideration social and emotional factors, story content sequences, immersion, user's perceptual focus, content information and navigational aspects. In a sense, our proposal deals with the same problem as Geist but we do not model the conversational aspects. Alternatively, a very simple interface for user's feedback is included. While Geist uses a database of explicitly pre-generated stories, our system constructs stories, step by step as in Ibanez's system.

3   The Mobile Tour Guide

The Mobile Tour Guide is an attempt to create guides with different personalities and beliefs, presenting users with different versions of stories about the same events or places. It is implemented on a PDA integrated with embedded text-to-speech system and a Global Positioning System. A server holds the guide's memories and performs processing. It sends the results of processing to the PDA on demand through wireless communication.

The guide commences the tour by introducing itself. There follows an ice-breaking session where the guide extracts information about the user's name and interests. After the user has entered and submitted the required data, the guide chooses attractions that match the user's interests, and plans the shortest possible route to the destinations. The guide navigates the user to the chosen locations via directional instructions as well as via an animated directional arrow. Upon arrival, it notifies the user and starts the storytelling process. The system links electronic data to actual physical locations so that stories are relevant to what is in sight. During the interaction, the user continuously expresses his/her interest in the guide's stories and agreement to the guide's argument through a rating bar on the graphical user interface. The user's inputs affect the guide's emotional state and determine the extensiveness of stories. The system's outputs are in the form of speech, text and an animated talking head.

4   The Narrative Constructor

4.1   Emotional Memory

Since a life story is always more interesting than simply bare facts, we argue that an emotional memory is important and necessary for the guide. The emotional recollection of past experiences will allow the guide to tell more believable and interesting stories. The user will be 'Walking Through Time' as the guide takes them through the site presenting its life experiences and reflecting the emotional impact of each experience. Holding to this view, the guide possesses a long-term memory that is made up of declarative memories, both semantic and emotional. Additionally, the guide's current memory holds information relating to recent processing.

Semantic memory is a memory for facts, including location-related informa-tion and the user's profile, while emotional memory is memory for experienced events and episodes. The guide's emotional memories are generated through simulation of past experiences. Consistent with Kensinger and Corkin's [11] pro-posal, the guide's emotional memory holds not only information about when, what and how an event happened, but also an 'arousal' tag and a 'valence' tag. The inclusion of the 'arousal' tag is analogous to the *Emotional Tagging* concept [12]. 'Valence' denotes how favorable or unfavorable an event was to the guide. When interacting with the user, the guide is engaged in meaningful reconstruc-tion of its own past [13], at the same time presenting facts about the site of attraction. This recollective experience is related to the evocation of previously experienced emotions through the activation of the emotion tags.

4.2   Ontologies and Entities

The guide defines two informal ontologies. First, a story element attributes ontol-ogy, which consists of the attributes used to annotate the story elements. These attributes and their corresponding interest areas - *General, Science, Military, Politics* and *Social* are hierarchically structured. Figure 1 shows the attributes ontology for the prototype version - the narrative domain being the 'Los Alamos' site of the Manhattan Project. Second, the guide profile ontology describes the guide's role and interests. In the prototype version, two guides are implemented, a scientist who is interested in topics related to *Science* and *Politics*, and a mem-ber of the military who is interested in topics related to *Military* and *Politics*. Both guides also have *General* knowledge about the attractions.

Besides these ontologies, the system contains definitions for basic entities, in-cluding *event, concepts, personnel* and *divisions*. These definitions are used to introduce related events, concepts, personnel and 'Los Alamos' divisions respec-tively, the first time they appear in the narrative process. These entities are tags in the story elements that serve as triggers to the remembering process during story activation and extension.

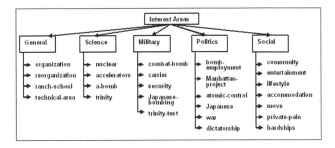

Fig. 1. Attributes ontology for the prototype version

4.3   Memory Organisation

As mentioned before, the guide possesses a long-term memory that is made up of declarative memories, both semantic and emotional. Semantic memory is memory for facts, including location-related information, ontologies and the definition of the entities. Facts form the basic *story elements (SEs)* used to construct stories and are basically free from any ideological perspective. Each element of the guide's semantic memory is composed of the properties presented in Table 1 with example, referring to the *SE* in Figure 2.

Table 1. The features of story element

Property	Description	Example
name	identification of the story element	*CU2*
type	the topic of story element	*Plutonium-bomb*
subjects	the subjects in the story element	*physics*
objects	the objects in the story element	*Oppenheimer, plutonium-bomb*
effects	the *SEs* that are caused by this *SE*, each effect has a weight associated	*CU3* with *weight 1*
event	a description of the event that took place, used to retrieve the guide's emotional response to the event (entity tag)	*plutonium-gun-problem*
concepts	basic entities of which the definition will be given on the first occurrence of these entities in the story (entity tag)	*plutonium*
personnel	the personnel involved in the story, not necessarily the subjects (entity tag)	*Robert-Oppenheimer*
division	the 'Los Alamos' division at which the story element happened (entity tag)	not applicable in this SE
attributes	each attribute has a weight associated and falls under one of the interest areas presented in the ontology	*a-bomb*
location	the physical location where the event occur, it can be of type "ANY" which means that the story element is general and applicable to any location, each location is also associated with a weight	*UCM*
text	the text encoding the event	refer Figure 2

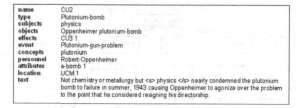

name	CU2
type	Plutonium-bomb
subjects	physics
objects	Oppenheimer plutonium-bomb
effects	CU3 1
event	Plutonium-gun-problem
concepts	plutonium
personnel	Robert-Oppenheimer
attributes	a-bomb 1
location	UCM 1
text	Not chemistry or metallurgy but <s> physics </s> nearly condemned the plutonium bomb to failure in summer, 1943 causing Oppenheimer to agonize over the problem to the point that he considered resigning his directorship.

Fig. 2. Sample story elements

While the semantic memory contains facts, emotional memory is a memory for those events that have an emotional impact on the guide. Each *emotional story element (EE)* has similar structure to the *SE* without *effects* and *subjects* attributes because the *EE* itself is the effect of a *SE* and the guide itself is the subject. In addition, the following tags are included:

arousal :   the arousal value when an event took place
valence :   the emotional valence value when the event occurred

4.4   Finding the Spot

The storytelling process, presented in Figure 3 starts upon arrival at a particular site of interest or upon user activation. Similar to Ibanez's system, the guide decides what to tell dynamically at any particular instant of time. The guide usually starts with a general description of the site before any interest-specific information is provided. This is achieved by assigning a higher weight to the *SEs* in the *General* interest group so that they receive higher priority. The guide's interests and the user's interests are persistent triggers of recollections and selections of stories. Additionally, the already told story elements aid recall by association of other related story elements.

Reminding is a crucial aspect of human memory and it can take place across situations. The story elements of the guide are retrieved based on processing-based reminding [14]. Processing-based reminding occurs during the normal course of understanding or processing new information. A *scene* or *location* is a kind of structure that provides a physical setting serving as the basis for re-construction. Therefore, the first step involves filtering out *SEs* that are not related to the current location. This is to ensure that the *location* of the story spot always corresponds to the user location. Furthermore, the changeability of dynamic memory makes people's memory act differently in apparently similar situations. We are usually reminded by similar events, those close to previously experienced phenomenon. Thus, *attributes* and *story type* are used to link and retrieve the guide's memories of similar events or circumstances. Additionally, an object or a person may also remind us of other similar or related object or person. Thus, *concepts* and *personnel* are also sources for remembering.

Three scores corresponding to: previously told stories; the guide's interests; and the user's interests are calculated. These scores are combined to obtain an

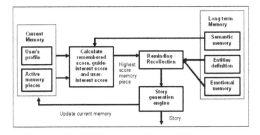

Fig. 3. The Storytelling Process

overall score for each *SE* in the current location. A *SE* with the highest overall score will become the starting spot for extension. Only stories that relate to the user's interests, the guide's interests and to previous stories should be presented, which means that the spot needs to have an overall greater than zero value to be passed to the next and final phase. The algorithm involved in finding the spot is presented in Figure 4.

```
For each pair (SE, loc) ∈ PAIRS
    For each concept c ∈ concepts(SE)
        If recentMemory contains c
            rememberedScore(pair) = rememberedScore(pair) + recentMemory(c)

    For each attribute a ∈ attributes(SE)
        If recentMemory contains a
            rememberedScore(pair) = rememberedScore(pair) + constantA

    For each personnel p ∈ personnel(SE)
        If recentMemory contains p
            rememberedScore(pair) = rememberedScore(pair) + constantP

        If recentMemory contains type(SE)
            rememberedScore(pair) = rememberedScore(pair) + constantT

    For each attribute a ∈ attributes(SE)
        guideInterestScore(pair) = guideInterestScore(pair) +
            attributeValue(SE, a) x guideInterestValue(a)
        userInterestScore(pair) = userInterestScore(pair) +
            attributeValue(SE, a) x userInterestValue(a)

For each pair (SE, loc) ∈ PAIRS
    rememberedScore =
        rememberedScore(pair) / maxRememberedScore
    guideInterestScore =
        guideInterestScore(pair) / maxGuideInterestScore
    userInterestScore =
        userInterestScore(pair) / maxUserInterestScore

    overallScore(pair) =
        rememberedScore(pair) x rememberedScoreWeight +
        guideInterestScore(pair) x guideInterestScoreWeight +
        userInterestScore(pair) x userInterestScoreWeight

    spot = pair ∈ PAIRS|overallScore(pair) ≥
        overallScore(pair') for all pair' ∈ PAIRS
```

Fig. 4. The algorithm for finding the spot of story

In the figure, *PAIRS* is the set of SE-loc pairs such that *loc* refers to the current location, there exists an entry in the database that relates *SE* to *loc*, and the *SE* has not been narrated yet. *concepts(SE)*, *attributes(SE)* and *personnel(SE)* give the sets of entities from the story element, *SE*. *type(SE)* denotes the type of the current *SE*. *recentMemory(c)* gives the value of the concept *c* in the current memory. *constantA, constantP* and *constantT* are fixed values between 0 and 1 that are added to the *rememberedScore* when entities in the current story element match the corresponding entities in the story elements of the previous step. *attributeValue(SE, a)* is the value associated with the attribute *a* in the *SE* while *guideInterestValue(a)* and *userInterestValue(a)* are values of the guide's interests and the user's interests relative to attribute *a* respectively. The user's profile, like the guide's profile contains a set of attributes that are related to his/her chosen interest area. Hence, a higher score will be obtained when the user's or the guide's interest attributes match the story attributes. *rememberedScoreWeight, guideInterestScoreWeight* and *userInterestScoreWeight* are the weights of the remembered score, guide's interest score and the user's interest score. Since we view the user's interest as the most important factor, followed by the guide's interest and finally the remembered score, these weight are in the ratio 20:15:12. It has to be noted that the choice of parameters' weight in the equations was for purely empirical reasons. Changing these values will change the pattern of *SEs* selection and the focus of stories.

4.5   Extending the Spot

After the spot has been selected, the guide proceeds to extend it. Given that one person can remind us of another person, one object can remind us of another object or one event can remind us of another event, story extension is activated based on *subject-object* links and *cause-effect* links as in Ibanez's system. Moreover, our guide uses *type, concepts, attributes* and *location* as activation factors. A story element with the *location* of type "ANY" can be activated during extension. Two story elements A and B are connected by subject-object link if one of the following conditions is satisfied: the subject of A and B is the same; the object of A and B is the same; the subject of A is the object of B; or the object of A is the subject of B. On the other hand, if A is the cause of B; or if A is the effect of B; or if A and B are causes of the third story element C; or A and B are effects of the third story element C, then a cause-effect link is established. These story elements can be organised using a network-like structure so that associative activation can be performed during extension.

The guide story extension process is the second step in Figure 5. All extensions are performed by JESS [15], a Java based rule engine to perform reasoning. Only *SE* that succeed the preceeding phases will continue to the subsequent phases of rule firing. At each extension cycle, the *SE* with the highest final evaluation value is selected. If the *SE* is extended through cause-effect link, then it will be ordered in such a way that the effect follows the cause. On the other hand, the order of selection is preserved if the *SE* is selected through the firing of subject-object link. When the desired granularity is reached and the combination of the story elements is large enough to generate a short story, the extension process is complete.

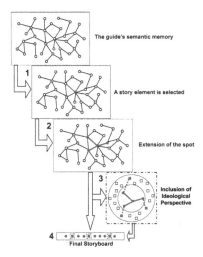

Fig. 5. The Story Extension Process (modified from [8])

4.6   Ideological Perspectives

Whilst it is true that the guide tells facts, at the same time it should not hide its feelings, beliefs and opinions. Hence, it includes its own experiences related to the facts during the storytelling, just as a real guide does. These experiences or events can be related to itself or others. We construct the guide's perspective from its emotional memory elements which lead to re-experience of emotions. The user rating on his/her degree of interest in the stories and the degree of which he/she agrees with the guide's argument after each story cycle, served as a determination factor for inclusion of ideological perspective. It is noteworthy that the guide includes its ideological perspectives only if it is currently competent and highly certain of the user's interests, that is, when user shows interest in the stories or agrees with its argument. Referring to Figure 5 again, this step is represented by the process in the dotted frame. The *EEs* are selected based on the activated *SEs* to ensure a smooth flow of storyline. To reduce complexity in the current version, a *SE* will lead to inclusion of only one *EE*. Hence, the number of *EEs* added is always less than or equal to the number of *SEs*.

Two examples stories without and with an inclusion of ideological perspectives are as below:

– *Estimates place the number of deaths caused by Little Boy in Hiroshima up to the end of 1945 at one hundred and forty thousands where the dying continued, five-year deaths related to the bombing reached two hundred thousands.*
– *Estimates place the number of deaths caused by Little Boy in Hiroshima up to the end of 1945 at one hundred and forty thousands where the dying continued, five-year deaths related to the bombing reached two hundred thousands. The experience of Hiroshima and Nagasaki bombing was the opening chapter to the possible annihilation of mankind. For men to choose to kill the*

innocent as a means to their ends, is always murder, and murder is one of the worst of human action. In the bombing of Japanese cities it was certainly decided to kill the innocent as a means to an end.

4.7   Generating the Story

The result of the above steps is a set of inter-related story elements and optional emotional story elements. These elements are stored in a structure with meta information about the extension process, including the relations among them, the reason for selection and the evaluation values. With this information, the system is ready to generate a complete story.

Since the set of *SEs* has been ordered during extension process, the next step is to order the *EEs*, where available. Each *EE* usually follows its associated *SE*. However, if two *SEs* have a cause-effect relationship, then the associated *EEs* will come after both *SEs*. Next, all the selected elements are combined taking into consideration the existence of *entities*. The guide retrieves the definition for each *entity*, (*event, concept, personnel* and *division*) that appears for the first time whether in *SEs* or *EEs*. This recall process - Schank [14] termed this dictionary-based reminding - occurs when the we search for the definition of an infrequent word or concept in our memory.

Each *subject* in the *SE* text is embraced in begin and end tags defined as <s> and </s>. These tags allow the system to recognise the *subject* of the *SE* and substitute it with an appropriate pronoun, retrieved from the database. With the completion of this step, the final storyboard is obtained. The resulting story is sent to the PDA and presented to the user.

After each story presentation, the guide updates its current memory so that it can be reminded of the current active memory elements in the next retrieval cycle. We have seen that the guide stores the current activation of *concept, personnel, attribute* and *type* in its recent memory. Analogous to human memory, a *concept* strength in the guide's memory increases when it is activated frequently and will be forgotten if not used after a few iterations. In contrast, the current activation of *personnel, attribute* and *type* remain in the current memory only for a single story cycle. The reinforcement and forgetting of *concept* strength are performed using the algorithm in Figure 6. *conceptsJustUsed* refers to the list

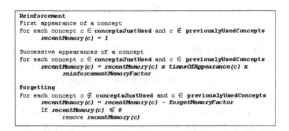

Fig. 6. Algorithm for reinforcement and forgetting of *concept* strength

of concepts that is active in the current story telling cycle while *previouslyUsed-Concepts* refers to the list of concepts that was active in preceeding cycles. *timesOfAppearance(c)* is the number of times c appears in the current cycle. *reinforcementMemoryFactor* specifies the degree of enhancement whilst *forget-MemoryFactor* defines the degree of forgetting of a concept c in the guide's memory.

5 Conclusion

This paper presents a mobile guide that adapts its story presentation based on the user's interests and opinions. We move away from a tour guide that recites facts to a guide that tells stories by improvising. Additionally, emotional memories is included so that the guide can tell its own autobiography, hence present a more believable and engaging narration. This point is confirmed by the evaluation with real users discussed in [16], which showed that with the inclusion of attitude, more interesting stories were generated and an enhanced tour experience was achieved.

For future work, we would like to explore on mood congruency effect in stories retrieval. People usually retrieve memory files that are directly consistent with their current mood [17], hence, it could be possible that a guide who tells stories based on its active emotions will be perceived as more realistic and believable. Moreover, to improve coherence for narrative construction, natural language approaches such as Rhetorical Structure Theory [18] ought to be considered.

Acknowledgements

Work supported by the European Union's Sixth Framework Programme, in the IST (Information Society Technologies) Thematic Priotity IST-2002-2.3.1.6 Multimodal Interfaces, HUMAINE (Human-Machine Interaction Network on Emotion) [19] (Contract no. 507422). The authors are solely responsible for the content of this publication. It does not represent the opinion of the European Community and the European Community is not responsible for any use that might be made of data appearing therein.

References

[1] Sumi, Y., Etani, T., Fels, S., Simone, N., Kobayashi, K., Mase, K.: C-map: Building a context-aware mobile assistant for exhibition tours. In: The First Kyoto Meeting on Social Interaction and Communityware (June 1998)

[2] O'Grady, M.J., O'Rafferty, R.P., O'Hare, G.M.P.: A tourist-centric mechanism for interacting with the environment. In: Proceedings of the First International Workshop on Managing Interactions in Smart Environments, Dublin, Ireland, pp. 56–67. Springer, Heidelberg (1999)

[3] Bertolleti, A.C., Moraes, M.C., da Rocha Costa, A.C.: Providing personal assistance in the sagres virtual museum. In: Proceeding of Museum and the Web 2001 (2001)

[4] Stock, O., Zancarano, M.: Intelligent interactive information presentation for cultural tourism. In: Invited talk at the International Workshop on Natural, Intelligent and Effective Interaction in Multimodal Dialogue Systems, Copenhagen, Denmark (June 2002)

[5] Tozzi, V.: Past reality and multiple interpretations in historical investigation. Stud Social Political Thought 2 (2000)

[6] NHC: History: The level descriptions (2006) (accessed October 15, 2006), http://www.ncaction.org.uk/subjects/history/levels.htm

[7] Domike, S., Mateas, M., Vanouse, P.: The recombinant history apparatus presents: Terminal time. In: Mateas, M., Sengers, P. (eds.) Narrative Intelligence, John Benjamins, Amsterdam (2002)

[8] Ibanez, J.: An Intelligent Guide for Virtual Environments with Fuzzy Queries and Flexible Management of Stories. PhD thesis, Departamento de Ingenieria de la Informacion y las Communicaciones, Universidad de Murcia, Murcia, Spain (2004)

[9] Lim, M.Y., Aylett, R., Jones, C.M.: Emergent affective and personality model. In: The 5th International Working Conference on Intelligent Virtual Agents, Kos, Greece (September 12–14, 2005)

[10] Braun, N.: Storytelling and conversation to improve the fun factor in software applications. In: Blythe, M.A., Monk, A.F., Overbeeke, K., Wright, P.C. (eds.) Funology, From Usability to Enjoyment, Kluwer Academic Publishers, Dordrecht (2003)

[11] Kensinger, E.A., Corkin, S.: Two routes to emotional memory: Distinct neural processes for valence and arousal. PNAS 101, 3310–3315 (2004)

[12] Richter-Levin, G., Akirav, I.: Emotional tagging of memory formation - in the search for neural mechanisms. Brain Research Reviews 43, 247–256 (2003)

[13] Dautenhahn, K.: The art of designing socially intelligent agents – science, fiction and the human in the loop (July 1998)

[14] Schank, R.C.: Dynamic memory: A theory of reminding and learning in computers and people. Cambridge University Press, United States (1982)

[15] Friedman-Hill, E.: JESS in Action: Rule-Based Systems in Java. Manning Publications Co., Greenwich (2003)

[16] Lim, M.Y., Aylett, R.: Feel the difference: A guide with attitude! In: The 7th International Conference on Intelligent Virtual Agents, September 17–19, 2007, Paris, France (to appear, 2007)

[17] Memory, A.: The role of emotion in memory. About Memory: Learning about Memory for Permanent Memory Improvement (2005), http://www.memory-key.com/NatureofMemory/emotion.htm

[18] Mann, W.C., Thompson, S.A.: Rhetorical structure theory: Toward a functional theory of text organization. Text 8(3), 243–281 (1988)

[19] HUMAINE: Human-machine interaction network on emotion (2004), http://emotion-research.net

Developing Virtual Storytellers for the Virtual Alhambra

José L. Fuertes [1], Ángel L. González [1], Gonzalo Mariscal [2], and Carlos Ruiz [2]

[1] Facultad de Informática. Universidad Politécnica de Madrid
Campus de Montegancedo. 28660 - Boadilla del Monte (Madrid). Spain
{jfuertes,agonzalez}@fi.upm.es
[2] SETIAM. CETTICO. FGUPM.
Campus de Montegancedo. 28660 - Boadilla del Monte (Madrid). Spain
{gmariscal,cruiz}@cettico.fi.upm.es

Abstract. Thanks to the technological advances in the last ten years, the recreation of 3D virtual worlds is becoming increasingly popular in several application fields. Desktop virtual reality is one of the best ways of reaching a good number of users through this technology. With the aim of improving the development of desktop virtual reality applications and increasing the relevance of the virtual experience, we defined the *Virtual Reality Framework* (VRF). This framework supports the creation of interactive systems for personalized and group guided tours in virtual worlds. The VRF can incorporate functionalities including context-sensitive information that a virtual guide will tell a user or group of users in a personalized manner. User interaction with the environment and with the intelligent virtual guides will lead to changes in the story told during the tour. In this paper we describe the Virtual Alhambra Project, which was the project that brought the VRF into being.

Keywords: Virtual Reality, Virtual Tourism, Virtual Storyteller, Interactive Storytelling.

1 Introduction

There are many monuments and sites of outstanding beauty on our planet. There is more than one way of experiencing and delighting in the charm of these sites. Visiting the monument in person is evidently the most impressive, but it is not always possible. When this is out of the question, videoed documentaries or photographic reports are a good option if you are looking for realism and an exact representation of the monument. The problem with this second option is that you have no control over what you can or cannot see, and even the order in which the images are viewed is programmed in videos. Additionally, if you have a question about the video you are watching, how do you find an answer? How can you gain access to the extra information? Thanks to technological progress, there has, for some time now, been an alternative way of visiting these beauty spots: virtual recreations of the sites [1].

Virtual recreation has a number of advantages over the use of videos and photos. For example, you can interact with the monument or decide what part of and in what order you would like to visit the site. Also visitor interaction with the environment is improved by giving users real-time access to information about the elements that

M. Cavazza and S. Donikian (Eds.): ICVS 2007, LNCS 4871, pp. 63–74, 2007.

prick their curiosity. There are some interesting initiatives, like the Louvre Museum's exhibition rooms [2] or SecondLife [3], a 3D virtual world built and owned entirely by its residents.

To achieve an interactive virtual experience [4], the interactive capability of the environment needs to be used to the full by providing guides, assistants and information points. All these are elements that exist in the real world and that are helpful for visitors for finding out more about the world around them. The primary aim of the virtual recreation system should be to resemble reality as closely as possible. The system should not be confined to simply making the most of the computer's graphical capabilities for representing images (static or dynamic) of reality, but should also be able to reproduce the experiences and impressions that visitors of the real environment take home. To make the experience more life-like, the virtual representations need to be enriched with intelligent virtual guides or virtual storytellers capable of explaining the most important aspects about the place the user is visiting. For example, [5] integrates a system of autonomous dialogue engines with narration to create a multi-modal storytelling environment and let multiple virtual and human participants act in a story.

Since the early descriptions [6], [7], most interactive storytelling systems have integrated artificial intelligence techniques [8], [9], [10], which generate narrative action sequences with 3D graphics and animations, staging these narrative actions to produce the actual interactive story, but some new theoretical approaches [11] focus on computational linguistics (as a form of "computational narratology").

This paper discusses the virtual recreation of the Alhambra in Granada [12] developed by CETTICO[1] and Sema Group, and funded by Legado Digital. The paper is organized as follows. First, we describe the problem leading to the need to build this system and the developed application's features. Then we remark on the technology used to develop the solution, focusing on the Virtual Guides System. This includes an outline of the process of building a storytelling system. We end with some final conclusions.

2   'Virtual Alhambra' Project

2.1 Motivation

Granada's Alhambra is an extremely interesting tourist, artistic and cultural site. It is Spain's most visited monument. There are strict restrictions on admission and on the duration of visits to certain parts of the grounds [13], and visitors are even barred from entering some of the monument's rooms. There are then plenty of reasons stopping people from visiting the monument in person.

Therefore, a number of fundamental aspects (beauty, cultural interest and visiting restrictions) come together to justify a virtual recreation. For this reason, Fundación Telefónica developed a virtual world for La Alhambra in arsVirtual [14]. Although the graphical quality of this recreation is good, it has some limitations: the user's

---

[1] Centro de Transferencia Tecnológica en Informática y Comunicaciones (Centre for Technology Transfer in Computing and Communications) is a division of the Fundación General de la Universidad Politécnica de Madrid.

range of movements is poor (all the user can do is turn around, and look up and down), there are no visits for groups, and it is more like a sequence of images than an interactive tour. To overcome these limitations, a virtual recreation should include interactive tours with guides and elements in the world from which the user can easily obtain additional information.

To solve the problems described above, we developed a virtual recreation, called the Virtual Alhambra (Fig. 1), with several key objectives:

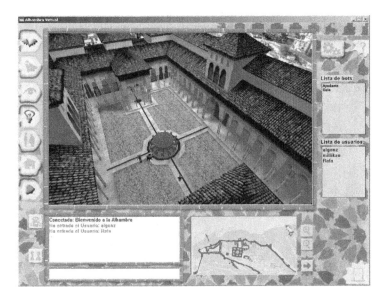

Fig. 1. *Virtual Alhambra* screenshot

- Give all those people who cannot or do not want to travel to visit the site in person access to the monument, exploiting what is known as virtual tourism.
- Try to reach as many people as possible by setting up a meeting point and an instructive and educational space. This is perfect for use by groups of people from primary and secondary schools and universities.
- Many parts of this age-old monument have suffered the ravages of time. One of the goals of this project is to do the historical groundwork to represent the Alhambra, removing all the damage it has suffered to date from the virtual recreation. This process of historical reconstruction is what is known as virtual archaeology [15].
- Assure the virtual visitor a comprehensive experience, not confined to a realistic visualization. To do this, the environment needs to react to actions that users constantly take in the virtual environment and provide feedback that at least mimics what would happen in the real environment. To improve the relevance of the virtual experience [16], it is necessary to deploy components to increase user interaction capabilities, provide expert assistants in the Alhambra and general- and special-purpose guides, and supply location-dependent information displayed to users according to their preferences and actions. These needs can be met by developing a system to manage virtual guides, also known as virtual storytellers.

2.2 System Features

In development terms, the Virtual Alhambra project is of considerable complexity and size, and has involved a sizeable group of researchers and developers [12]. Therefore, this paper will focus only on the key features of the Virtual Alhambra.

The Virtual Alhambra is a desktop virtual reality application, which can be placed in the virtual tourism slot. Its aim is to offer a virtual world experience within the environment of Granada's Alhambra. To achieve this goal, the system enables the user to relate not only to other users but also to intelligent systems that are in the same virtual space and time inside the monument. This communication will be visual (connected users will be able to see each other, see Fig. 2), through written language via chat (public or private) or speech conversation (public and private).

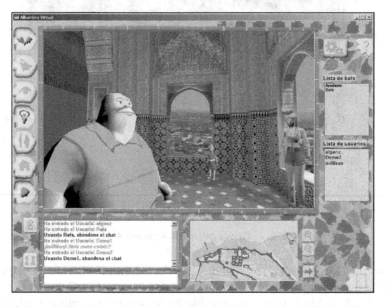

Fig. 2. Groups of users can visit the same virtual environment in the *Virtual Alhambra*

The user will be able to gather additional information during the virtual visit through the interaction elements there are within the virtual world: on the one hand there are softbots [17] that act as guides or assistants; on the other hand there are interactive information points as happens in reality. These components improve the user's experience of the visit by adding to and extending his or her interaction with the rest of the virtual world. A softbot can be associated with a representation in the virtual world as if it were a user. However, there is no human behind a softbot to manage it, and it behaves autonomously. When the user requests a guided tour (softbot), he/she can communicate with the softbot in different ways:

- Using a *questions menu*: the user is given a list of predefined questions based on his or her location. The visitor can choose the question he or she is interested in. This can help users to learn important information about the places they visit, without having in-depth historical or cultural knowledge.

- Using *natural language* to ask any question (see 'Virtual Guides System' section) through the chat.

In both cases, the user receives multimedia information and specific tours in response. The type of multimedia information is very wide ranging, from narrated explanations and explanatory videos to information displayed via web. The subsystems that provide these services are called assistants because they are able to help the user at definite times.

In addition, the user can request a personal or group guide. The guide gives the user a guided virtual tour, taking the user through the virtual world. The user can ask for extra information, as explained above, at any time. There are some differences between personal and group guides:

- *Personal guide*: thanks to the guides system's artificial intelligence, the features of the tours can be personalized depending on several parameters, like available time, areas of interest, preferred areas, or areas already visited. Each tour is associated with an interactive story where the guide narrates important aspects about each of the visited sections. The user can change the course of this narration either by asking the guide a question or interacting with the elements that there are in the world. When the user interacts with softbots or information points, the system can provide the virtual visitor with extra information about the place. The information is given as web pages, videos, texts, etc.
- *Group guide*: in this case, a group of users shares a virtual guide. If another user interacts with the guide (as described above), the story and the information received by all the group members will be modified as happens in real life.

The system can be run locally or across a network. Of course, guided tours and chat are only available when running the Virtual Alhambra online. Because of how intrinsically related the Internet is to the world of virtuality, the Virtual Alhambra can also take advantage of the potential of the world of the Internet and be used as a meeting place where users are free to act and interact according to their tastes and needs. This feature is applied in many Internet communities [18]. Additionally, each user can come away with a different picture of the Alhambra because different levels of detail are possible. They will depend on the each user's machine and network capacities. Also, to assure that performance is unaffected, the virtual world has been divided into separate rooms. The geometry and texture of these rooms is not downloaded until they are accessed.

To create the Virtual Alhambra, we defined the Virtual Reality Framework (VRF).

3 Virtual Reality Framework (VRF)

There are several tools for building or helping to build storytelling systems. One of these tools is DraMachina [19]. It is a powerful tool for interactive story editing and interactive story definition. This tool provides the user with an XML file containing all the information needed about the story. This file can be easily imported into a storytelling player system. MuViPlan [20] is an interactive guided tour framework. MuViPlan provides several tools and functionalities, such as editing tools, template definition and group guided tours. To develop the Virtual Alhambra not only did we need editing tools and group guided tours system capability, we also required a UIMS (User Interface Manager System) and intelligent virtual guides. Such features are helpful in building a better interactive system, including a 2D/3D user interface and personalized tours.

The *Virtual Reality Framework* (VRF) is based on earlier results obtained with a platform that was able to describe user interaction processes: COREUS (User Relations Builder) [21], [22], [23]. COREUS is a platform developed by CETTICO, to create and adapt user interfaces at runtime. COREUS needed to be extended to incorporate the virtual reality medium. This extension allows the construction of any virtual application: virtual tourism systems, demonstration systems, teaching applications, simulations...

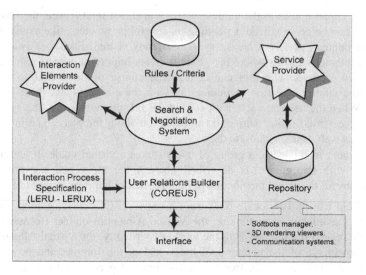

Fig. 3. Diagram of VRF architecture

VRF is a framework for building virtual reality-based systems that are furnished with other additional components, like a softbots manager for guides and tours (Virtual Guides System), multi-user and networking support [12], interface development system integration (COREUS), etc. Fig. 3 shows a high-level diagram of the framework's different parts. VRF's key features are:

- The framework components are independent. Each component is characterized by being able to provide a number of services.
- It uses an interpreted language, as suggested in [24], to represent the interaction process.
- VRF establishes the services and the protocol to integrate interaction elements like softbots into the framework (see 'Virtual Guides System' section). It now provides two types of interaction with virtual guides:
  - The first is based on the principle of closed questions and geographical location.
  - The second is based on the use of natural language and ontologies about the place where the visit is taking place.

- VRF establishes the requirements to be met by a component having 3D rendering capability for use in the framework. This allows the incorporation of different engines with different rendering capabilities depending on the situation at any time and technological advances.

The development of systems based on this framework is based on an interface modelling language and a user interface management system (UIMS) that is responsible for converting the described interface into a runtime. To make the most of the ideas that Puerta suggests in his works [24], we opted to define a flexible and extendible environment, without having to modify the system core. These interfaces are built using the following components:

- User Relations Specification Language (LERU) [22], [23] and its XML version (LERUX) [25]: this is an interface modelling language that can be used to describe the dialogue process, the visual appearance and the space/sound arrangement of the components that are going to participate in the interface. It also specifies the services that the components have to provide. We have defined an open language, whose full definition and interpretation depends on the elements participating in each interface. This requires a distributed and collaborative interpretation by all the components participating in the interface. LERU/LERUX defines the core of the language and the protocol to which both the interaction elements and the service providers should conform to be able to be incorporated into VRF by making the appropriate extensions to the language. This approach allows the incorporation of any new components into the framework.
- User Relations Builder (COREUS): this element implements the LERU/LERUX core interpreter, coordinates the different interface elements, performs the mapping at runtime between the description in the script and the rendering in a specific environment. Along general lines, the steps for generating an interface are:

1. Prepare the work area in which the interaction is to take place.
2. Determine the existence of constraints (window size, equipment capacity, existence of Internet connection...).
3. Perform the search and select the interaction elements. To do this, take into account the results of steps 1 and 2, the objective or purpose of the interaction element and the services to be provided.
4. Search required services providers (download contents, access databases, p2p communication system, etc.) to make the system operational.
5. Assemble the interface. This involves locating and assigning the materials that an interaction element should use to generate its *physical representation* within the interface. The materials to be used are determined depending on the purpose of the element and the context in which the interaction takes place. For example, it could be decided that a lower quality version of the model should be used to display a particular room.

As a result, this new platform was later applied to different projects (see conclusion). To do this, it had to be added to and extended with new functionalities. Its use in these projects validated the platform and demonstrated its utility, showing it to be reusable, modular and independent of the application domain.

4 Virtual Guides System

This system is a VRF module that is responsible for managing the tours that the user is given within a world. The tour is accompanied by an interactive story based, in this case, on historical facts related to Granada's Alhambra. The system will select what to show and tell of this story, creating a personalized interactive story for each user. The story varies depending on the actions the user takes within the world and the natural language question the user puts to the Virtual Guides System.

The Virtual Guides System is characterized by providing all the information required to define the guide's behaviour by means of a script language. These scripts are interpreted when a guide is activated, establishing the knowledge about the current location, the possible itineraries around the world and the possible decisions to be taken depending on user questions and actions [12]. The scripts that govern the behaviour of the guides (softbots) can be ready built or generated when needed from templates depending on user preferences and information available in the databases.

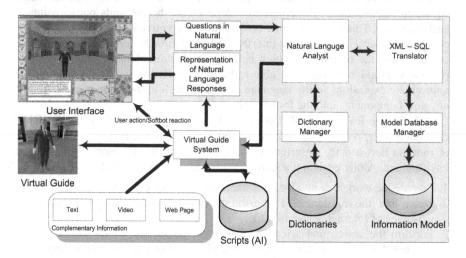

Fig. 4. Virtual Guides System with natural language processor

As already mentioned, the application allows the user to communicate with the virtual guide in natural language through the use of chat (see Fig. 4) driven by the Natural Language Dialogue Module. This component can be described as an improved information retrieval system (IRS) in the sense that it allows the user to ask in natural language about a particular topic (specific domain), in this case Granada's Alhambra. The technique used for natural language recognition is *shallow parsing* [26]. Our system is also capable of interpreting the actions that the user takes within the world and acting proactively by providing information related to the elements about which the user has shown interest. In both cases, the system responds correctly to the user based on the information that it contains. The user will be given the response directly through the chat system, which may be accompanied by additional information like videos or web pages related to the system response.

5   Building Process

As mentioned previously, VRF provides a set of script languages for story definition. The syntax of these languages is quite simple and they can be used by people with no programming skills. The development team can also use a set of tools (see Fig. 5) to import worlds (3DS Max or Blender 3D formats), specify predefined paths, specify predefined softbot responses (Story Builder) and, when a domain ontology is defined, automatically define new paths. This information will be used to personalize the visitors' tours.

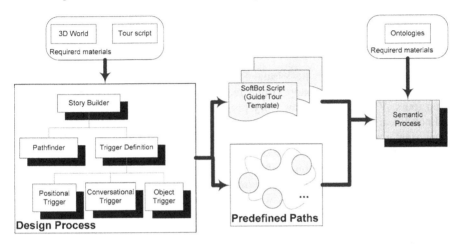

Fig. 5. Building process

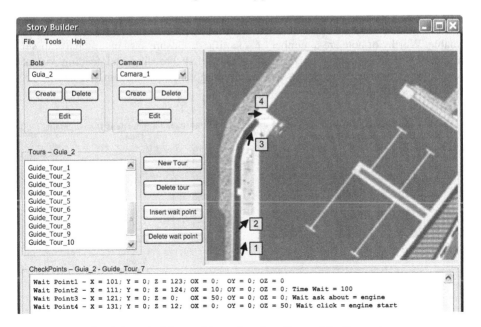

Fig. 6. Story builder used in sea bass breeding and feeding system

Scripts of the available tours and a version of the 3D world with all the rooms and interactive objects are needed before embarking on the building process. Using the Story Builder tool (Fig. 6), the story designer selects the specific points of the world included in the tour, defines camera positions and specifies visitor actions (position, conversation, interaction with objects…) to define each tour. The result will be the predefined paths and the templates for the intelligent bots.

Finally, the semantic process is useful for grouping rooms, defining new tours, new paths or path fragments based on the main subject of the virtual world. Domain ontologies are recommended as they achieve better results in this process.

6 Conclusions

In this paper we introduce the Virtual Reality Framework (VRF). This framework supports the creation of desktop virtual reality systems for personalized and group guided tours. VRF features allow story programmers and components developers to build non-linear stories with a high degree of interactivity between users and elements in the virtual environment. This gives users an intensely interactive, amusing, striking, and informative experience. The system allows the user to meet other visitors and autonomous intelligent systems (*softbots*) that are in the same place of the virtual world at the same time. They can interact by visual communication (movements, gestures and facial expressions), by written language (private and public chat), and by voice dialogue (private and public conversations). Thanks to the modularity of the framework and the use of scripts to create stories, the time and effort it takes to develop this kind of systems have been improved (see Fig. 7).

After developing the Virtual Alhambra, which was the first VRF-based application, many other VRF-based systems have been developed for different application domains. This has demonstrated that framework components are highly reusable and scalable. Worthy of note are a number of scientific disclosure systems, such as mussel culture, sea bass breeding and feeding, gilthead fish breeding and feeding virtual recreations, demonstration systems for the building industry, museum and monument guided tour systems, etc.

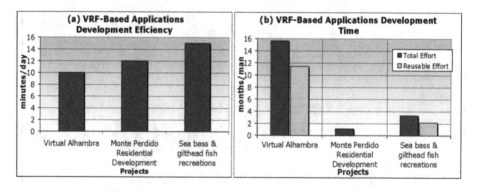

Fig. 7. Development Efficiency (a) and Time (b) using VRF in different projects

Fig. 7a and Fig. 7b. show a measurement of efficiency and the development effort, respectively, for three examples of projects of different complexity in terms of story duration and number of possible story branchings. Fig. 7a represents the measurement of efficiency calculated as the total duration of all the stories a story programmer can build per day using the script system provided by VRF. Fig. 7b shows that most of the development effort can be reused in future applications. Reusable effort consists of components development and component services development.

In conclusion, it can be said that VRF and specifically the Virtual Guides System provide an easy and efficient way of developing virtual guided tours, thanks in part to the reusability of the framework components.

References

1. Active Worlds: Home of 3D Chat, Virtual Reality Building Platform (2007), http://www.activeworld.com
2. Louvre: Another Way to Visit the Louvre. Virtual Tours (2007), http://www.louvre.fr/llv/muse/visite_virtuelle.jsp?bmLocale=en
3. Second Life: What is Second Life? (2007), http://secondlife.com/whatis
4. Djajadiningrat, J.P., Overbeeke, C.J., Wensveen, S.A.G.: Augmenting Fun And Beauty: A Pamphlet. In: DARE 2000. Proc. Designing Augmented Reality Environments, ACM Press, New York (2000)
5. Löckelt, M.: Action Planning for Virtual Human Performances. In: Subsol, G. (ed.) Virtual Storytelling. LNCS, vol. 3805, pp. 53–62. Springer, Heidelberg (2005)
6. Swartout, W., Hill, R., Gratch, J., Johnson, W.L., Kyriakakis, C., LaBore, C., Lindheim, R., Marsella, S., Miraglia, D., Moore, B., Morie, J., Rickel, J., Thiebaux, M., Tuch, L., Whitney, R., Douglas, J.: Toward the Holodeck: Integrating Graphics, Sound, Character and Story. In: Proc. Autonomous Agents Conference (2001)
7. Young, R.M.: Creating Interactive Narrative Structures: The Potential for AI Approaches. In: Proc. AAAI Spring Symposium in Artificial Intelligence and Interactive Entertainment, AAAI Press (2000)
8. Tarau, P., Figa, E.: Knowledge-based conversational agents and virtual storytelling. In: Proc. 2004 ACM symposium on Applied computing, Nicosia, Cyprus, pp. 39–44 (2004)
9. Abawi, F., Reinhold, S., Dšrner, R.: A Toolkit for Authoring Non-linear Storytelling Environments Using Mixed Reality. In: Göbel, S., Spierling, U., Hoffmann, A., Iurgel, I., Schneider, O., Dechau, J., Feix, A. (eds.) TIDSE 2004. LNCS, vol. 3105, pp. 113–118. Springer, Heidelberg (2004)
10. Theune, M., Faas, S., Heylen, D.K.J., Nijholt, A.: The virtual storyteller: Story creation by intelligent agents. In: Göbel, S., Braun, N., Spierling, U., Dechau, J., Diener, H. (eds.) Technologies for Interactive Digital Storytelling and Entertainment, pp. 204–215. Fraunhofer IRB Verlag, Darmstadt (2003)
11. Cavazza, M., Pizzi, D.: Narratology for Interactive Storytelling: a Critical Introduction. In: Proc. 3rd International Conference on Technologies for Interactive Digital Storytelling and Entertainment, Darmstadt, Germany (2006)
12. Fuertes, J.L, González, Á.L., Mariscal, G., Ruiz, C.: Aplicación de la Realidad Virtual a la difusión de la cultura: La Alhambra Virtual. In: INTERACCION 2005. Proc. VI Congreso de Interacción Persona Ordenador (AIPO), Granada, pp. 367–371 (2005)
13. AndalucíaWeb: La Alhambra de Granada. El monumento más visitado de España (2007), http://www.andalucia-web.net/alhambra_infos.htm

14. ArsVirtual: Espacio Virtual para la Difusión del Patrimonio Cultural. La Alhambra de Granada (2007), http://www.arsvirtual.com/p_espagnol/visitas_virtuales/otros_monumentos/alhambra/alhambra01.jsp

15. Reilly, P., Lockyear, K., Rahtz, S.: Towards a Virtual Archaeology. In: CAA 1990. Computer Applications and Quantitative Methods in Archaeology. BAR International Series, vol. 565, pp. 133–139. Tempvs Reparatvm, Oxford (1990)

16. Hoorn, J.F., Konijn, E.A., Van der Veer, G.C.: Virtual reality: Do not augment realism, augment relevance. Upgrade - Human-Computer Interaction: Overcoming Barriers 4(1), 18–26 (2003)

17. Wooldrige, M., Jennings, N.R.: Intelligent Agents: Theory and Practice. Knowledge Engineering Review 10(2), 115–152 (1995)

18. Habbo Hotel: Habbo (2005), http://www.habbo.com

19. Donikian, S., Portugal, J.-N.: Writing Interactive Fiction Scenarii with DraMachina. In: Göbel, S., Spierling, U., Hoffmann, A., Iurgel, I., Schneider, O., Dechau, J., Feix, A. (eds.) TIDSE 2004. LNCS, vol. 3105, pp. 101–112. Springer, Heidelberg (2004)

20. Göbel, S., Feix, A.: MuViPlan: Interactive Authoring Environment to Plan Individual Museum Visits. In: Trant, J., Bearman, D. (eds.) Proc. Museums and the Web 2005, Archives & Museum Informatics, Toronto (2005)

21. Flor, L., Fuertes, J.L., González, Á.L., Varela, J.I.: The "Activities Exhibitor": A way to build self-adapting tutoring systems. In: Proc. Third World Multiconference on Systemics, Cybernetics and Informatics (SCI 1999) and Fifth International Conference on Information Systems Analysis and Synthesis (ISAS 1999), pp. 379–386 (1999)

22. Frutos, S., González, Á.L., Martínez, L., Montes, C.: Adapting Computer-Human Interaction in Real Time. In: Proc. IEEE International Conference on Systems, Man and Cybernetics, pp. 1038–1043 (1998)

23. González, Á.L.: Modelo para la Generación y Gestión en Tiempo de Ejecución de Procesos de Interacción Hombre-Máquina a Partir de un Lenguaje de Especificación de Relaciones con el Usuario. PhD Thesis dissertation, School of Computing, Technical University of Madrid (2003)

24. Puerta, A., Eisenstein, J.: Towards a General Computational Framework for Model-Based Interface Development Systems. In: IUI 1999. Proc. International Conference on Intelligent User Interfaces, pp. 171–178. ACM Press, New York (1999)

25. Gudmundson, A.: LERUX: An XML-based language for user interface specification. Master Thesis, Technical University of Madrid (2004)

26. Hammerton, J., Osborne, M., Armstrong, S., Daelemans, W.: Introduction to Special Issue on Machine Learning Approaches to Shallow Parsing. JMLR Special Issue on Shallow Parsing 2(3), 551–558 (2001)

Behavior Modelling

What Gestures to Perform a Collaborative Storytelling?

Laurence Perron

FT R&D 2 Avenue Pierre-Marzin F- 22300 Lannion
Laurence.perron@orange-ftgroup.com

Abstract. The idea behind 3D multi-user worlds is to use virtual reality techniques to allow several people to "exist" and play in the same virtual environment. In this way, technologies around non verbal behavior: voice and body movement are essential to coordinate "speech acts", actions with other partners or objects, to share space (localization, displacement, proxemy) and to improve the awareness, telepresence... Our studies are mainly centered on the non verbal behavior in small groups and on command gestures. Our aim is to carry out some experiences and transfer the results in design of a Storytelling Collaborative Virtual Environment (SCVE) without intrusive devices. Briefly, this paper presents our approach to design digital storytelling game.

Keywords: non verbal behavior, command gesture, collaborative storytelling, multimodality, avatar, Collaborative Virtual Environment.

1 Introduction

Our aim is to carry out some experiences and transfer the results in design of a narrative digital environment. Our experimentations concern Human/Human mediated collaboration without intrusive and immersive devices [1-2]. Our recent studies are focused on collaborative storytelling games in small groups [3-4]. In these particular games, the users are represented by character or video in multimodal and collaborative storytelling platform. It is primordial to represent the user by in the way that they are supported by the Human communication especially non-verbal behavior: gestures, gaze, life sign, social attitudes, emotion, etc. Voice and gesture are both the basis of natural dialogue between players and the multimodal interaction support of the digital storytelling setup. This double function is very interesting for the users but remains a Human Computer Interaction (HCI) research field and more specifically new multimodal humanized interfaces [5-7].

In fact, we are focusing on non verbal behavior and particularly on gesture interaction because this modality would give the user more freedom to create and participate in the story narration. We are specifically interesting in Human behavior experiments in the creative storytelling task and the design of multimodal interactions. On one side, we investigate through several human behavior studies a way to permit the "natural" distant narration between users. For us, a narrative task is by essence a creative task and consequently, the non constraint interactions are essential. On the other side, we present several versions of storytelling setup called

M. Cavazza and S. Donikian (Eds.): ICVS 2007, LNCS 4871, pp. 77–88, 2007.

VIRSTORY that to take into account the results of studies and in particular, we explain the different manners that make it.

2 Narration Experimentations in Small Group

We focused on users engaged in a collaborative storytelling task in which gestures and speech were essential as a medium for the collective narration: the human communication and 3D objects manipulation in Collaborative Virtual Environment (CVE). We wished to determine how subjects interact in small group and what they do when they are utilised hand gesture or/and speech to communicate with the system or/and with distant partners. The aim is to improve multimodal interfaces supporting mediated collaboration and particularly human communication supported by autonomous characters.

2.1 Observations Before Game Design

In the beginning, we imagined a creative digital game for everybody –user without particular abilities- and we founded a narrative game "Once upon a time". This game uses cards to illustrate a piece of story e.g.: princess, wolf, etc. Each user must play with her/his pieces of story to tell a nice and coherent story with the other users. This game was the starting point of the VIRSTORY design. If the primary aim is to conceive a creative environment, the secondary aim is to understand Human behavior especially the non-verbal behavior like gaze, facial expression, postural body and gesture of hand to improve our collaborative and creative platform. Existing character animation techniques in CVE prompted us to study sensorial deprivation along two lines of reflection. We wished to establish how subjects interact in a trio, and what they do when they are deprived of a form of expression as the case with the intrusive device in CVE (cf. Fig. 1). For us, it's primordial that the users are also the improvisational narrators and particularly, in the storytelling context. It's the reason why the users create themselves the story even if we are helping us with some narrative pieces or rules. The second reason it that we think the narrative situations seems more similar at the process of collective making decision. The decisions are related to cube manipulation, narrative coherence. 18 subjects in 6 groups (12 men + 6 women - average age 24 - 5 years' higher education) participated in an experiment in which the instruction was to "create the most beautiful story".

Fig. 1. Four conditions: 1: without deprivation (normal) – 2: with masks to deprive subjects of facial expressions – 3: with very dark sunglass to deprive subjects of gaze modality – 4: with their hands under the table to deprive subjects of gesture modality.

Three subjects played together to make up a story with 18 cards. Each episode was based on one of the 18 cards which all had to be used. The control condition was always applied first and lasted 15 minutes. The others each lasted for ten minutes (with a break after two conditions).Each subject was filmed and the recordings processed by manually annotation each subject's gestures into mutually exclusive non-verbal categories.

2.2 Categorization of Gestures

In communicative and collaborative situations, our body is a powerful vehicle for information. Human studies [8-9] have concluded that more than 65 percent of information exchanged during a face to face interaction, is expressed through non-verbal means. The facial movements are difficult to reproduce. Subtle and fast changes can give very different results and express different facial expressions. In fact, the mimics can be understood in different manners by the users because the emotions are contextualized in the discourse, the situation and the culture [10]. Additionally, it is more difficult to reproduce and recognize emotion [11-12]. Real problems stay always how do you define what's a virtual human? And mainly, if you take in consideration a diversity of context: every day life, work and particularly imaginative game! Our idea is to improve the quality of the remote communication even if people can compensate verbally (as in the case of conference calls). The compensate mechanisms are parasite task that is added to the main task. We nevertheless believe that certain activities are far more affected by this additional task and the result should be insufficiency of communication or a real displeasure. We suggest a behavioural model centred on interpersonal communication and especially non-verbal within CVE. This suggestion has been formed on the basis of studies relating to the various functions of human gestures [13-17]. Our approach is an iterative and multidisciplinary approach based on the comparison of real and mediated group activities [18-20]. So, the result presented here concerns principally the non-verbal behaviour research. It mainly consists of the reproduction of the non-verbal part relative to gestures which include postural changes and other movements at a low level of awareness frequently made to feel more comfortable. We consequently set out to distinguish gestures in terms of their degree of correlation with language. Our assumption was that a degree of independence in relation to speech may be an indication of non-verbal repertories that could be constituted and reused without any user intervention. To quantify hand gestures, we used the DAMB non-verbal categorization [21]: **D**eictic (D), **A**daptator (A), **M**etaphoric[1] (M), and **B**eat (B).

Fig. 2. Deictic: designating gestures, useful for pointing designing to an object or a person in a physical or virtual space

---

[1] Metaphoric: it's a large category that includes gestures intended to illustrate speech content like iconic, symbolic or emblematic gesture.

Fig. 3. Adaptator or self-contact gestures: touching gestures resulting from behaviours learned for adaptation purposes, such as washing oneself or driving a car, but used in an interaction without these "adaptive" needs being present. They reflect emotions and the speaker's internal state and are less dependent on language.

Fig. 4. Metaphoric: gestures intended to illustrate speech content, e.g. oral = "big like" plus hand movement

Fig. 5. Beat (or Punctuator) which set the pace of the talk has the communicative aim of reaching the interlocutors

2.3 Variability and Omnipresence of Self-contact

The quantitative analysis of DAMB gestures revealed a high degree of variability among individuals, despite the homogeneity of the group. Apart from gestures related to handling the cards, DAMB gestures accounted for between 30 and 40 percent of the playing time. Adapters were predominant all the time, although there were up to twice as many in some cases compared to others (cf. Fig. 7). This phenomenon was observed not only in groups but also on an individual scale.

2.3.1 Self-contact Gestures

The large number of self-contact gestures or adaptators reflects the emotional charge related to the situation, which can range from withdrawal to the expression of feelings stemming from the ludic aspect of the game. Although it is difficult to identify the exact emotions behind adapters, their presence is evident. Since the game here consisted in making up and recounting a story, it alternately brought into play the imagination, eloquence, affects, persuasive force, negotiation, etc. Talking, communicating with someone else, also means sharing and showing emotions that non-verbal behaviour immediately reveals.

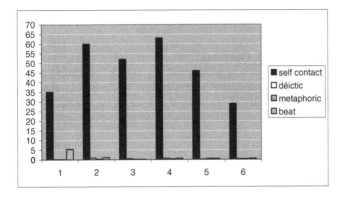

Fig. 6. DAMB categories/trio of subjects

2.3.2 The Punctuator: A Predominantly Feminine "Charm"

It seems that punctuators are used primarily by women. Only in Group 1, composed entirely of women, was a high rate of punctuators identified. In Groups 3 and 5 where all the subjects were men, the rate was very low. Although women punctuate more than men, some do so more than others, as shown by a subject in Group 1. When we examined her body movements we noted that she punctuated in all conditions, even when her hands were supposed to be handling the cards only. This non-verbal style subject seemed to be "beat". Punctuating movements could be considered as a way of proving to others one's capacity as a speaker and thus one's ability to convince. An analogy is lawyers who, rivalling one another in eloquence, wave their arms about dramatically. Other studies have also shown that politicians make extensive use of punctuators. It thus seems that verbal ease goes hand in hand with non-verbal accentuation or emphasis.

2.3.3 Non-verbal Dichotomy and Mutual Adjustment

For Group 1 consisting entirely of women (and especially for "without eyes" condition), the punctuator's body movements contrasted with those of the other two subjects who were essentially adapters. Punctuators and adapters have different communicative aims: the former are a way of enhancing the communication while the latter attest to lesser communicative intentionality. In short, one of the subjects speaks, forcefully signifying her words by an abundant use of punctuators, while the other two subject's consequent withdrawal is reflected by adaptators.

2.3.4 No Eyes, More Gestures

Each episode lasted ten minutes (except for the control which lasted 15), during which time the subjects were not interrupted by the experimenter. Some groups finished sooner, however, while others carried on playing even after being interrupted. Consequently the actual duration of the game varied. In the "sunglasses" condition playing time was longer than in the "control" condition. This seemed to result from the fact that the subjects needed more time to construct their story when they were unable to look at one another. The subjects also seemed to punctuate their talk more when they were unable to rely on the others' gaze. This lengthening of the duration of the task, coupled with the increased use of punctuators, highlights the role of the gaze in collaborative and cognitive processes.

2.3.5 With a Mask, Fewer Gestures

We noted an overall reduction in gestures in the "mask" condition where the players were deprived of facial expressions, compared to the "control" condition. The most noteworthy reduction was that of adapters, the percentage of which was lower only in the "no hands" condition. It seemed that the subjects no longer allowed themselves to move.

2.3.6 Without Hands They Still Move

Even with the instruction 'no hands' the subjects could not stop themselves from moving. Interestingly, the game lasted longer here, as if the fact of being prevented from moving, other than to handle the cards increased the time needed to make up a story.

2.4 Some Results…More Questions

Observations of this experiment showed that character can already be animated with recurring self-contact gestures. Moreover, gestures contribute to the feeling of presence that users expect when facing a character. Unfortunately, self contact seems not really support efficient communication between users. This non verbal behavior concerns more the internal sensation than the communicative intention. Self contact gestures are used to create animations library of that can be replayed by characters during same situation. One must nevertheless bear in mind the fact that mechanisms of mutual adjustment exist, from the point of view of non-verbal behaviour that cannot reduce a human's behaviour to that of an animated character.

3 Gestures, Interaction Style, and Iterative Design

Considering the immaturity of techniques, we have studied pragmatic animation models [22-23]. VIRSTORY integrates user's non-verbal and communicative behaviours. This "multi-users" platform is based on client/server architecture. Each client is responsible for rendering a single user's view. All users connected to the same embedded server see each other's remote users as an animated avatar with 3D articulated body. The entire interface is "multi-users" and in 3Dimension. (Fig. 7 & 8)

3.1 "Wizard of Oz" (WoZ) with VIRSTORY

We realized WoZ experimentation (cf. Fig. 9 & 10); the experimenter realized the user action and the user played with an associate partner. The role of associate partner is important because he plays with the subject and sometimes, he had encouraged the subject to use the vocal incentives. This experimentation (20 subjects: 9 males and 11 females, 16 adults and 4 children are participated) allows understanding the organization of the oral and gesture modalities of interaction between themselves, as a

Fig. 7. VIRSTORY: On the left, the first player with the second player's avatar and vice versa on the right when the user takes a cube, the distant user can see the character with the cube and the colour feedback on the cube. If the character is red then the cube is red, etc. On the bottom of a user's screen is displayed the *"private space"*, consisting of the cubes the user has not yet used in the story (the own cubes of the distant user are not visible). Only cubes already used by either user are visible by both users. These cubes lie on the yellow points that represent the common storyline. The first point is the beginning and the last point corresponds to the end of the story. When a user selects a cube from his private space and moves it to the storyline, this action is seen by both users. As a user moves a cube on the beginning of the storyline and tells "once upon a time", the second user finds a cube to continue the story and so on.

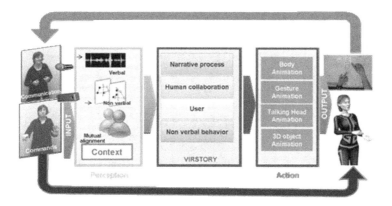

Fig. 8. VIRSTORY- Model of collaborative storytelling

function of the habits and competences of the subject (adult/child difference for example). One of the interests of multimodal interfaces is to let a user choose the way to interact as she/he prefers. If pointing with a laser is efficient when this tool is given to a user, the question remains open whether such efficiency is kept without a physical pointing device, for example with computer vision pointing gesture recognition.

The experimenter only reproduced gestures performed on objects of the storytelling setup, while other gestures such as wrist or arm rotation to turn a cube were interpreted. After a user moves a cube on the first location of the story line and tells "once upon a time", the second user finds a cube to continue the story and so on until the last cube is moved on the last location. In order to see one of the 3 faces of a 3D cube, or to move a cube on the storyline, a user must select this cube either with a pointing laser and/or with an oral command (figure 9-left). Pointing laser and oral commands are not recognized by the system, but it is the experimenter (in the foreground in figure 9-right) who observes the user's movement of the laser pointer, listens to the user's oral verbalization, interprets the user's intention and executes commands with a touch screen. The partner (in the background in figure 9-right) plays with the subject unaware that the partner uses a same screen and that his oral commands are fake. Each subject is shot and the recordings are processed by manually coding each subject's gestures and utterances into 4 categories: oral incentives (vocal hint by the partner), oral commands (vocal command/subject), pointing commands (laser pointer command/subject) and cube action by the experimenter (subject feedback action).

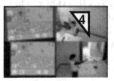

Fig. 9. 1: A child with a laser pointer. 2: The WOZ experimenter carrying the child's command 3: the partner playing with the child 4: video recording

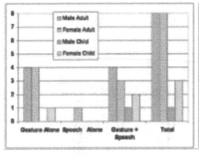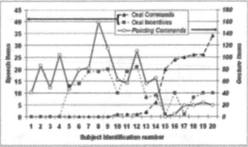

Fig. 10. Left: interaction styles as a function of sex and age. Right: number of interactions and oral enticements for the 20 subjects ranked according to the number of oral commands.

We observed (figure 10-left) few differences between males and females except for a woman who only used oral commands. It is surprising to observe how children easily used speech and gesture to interact with the objects. It may be hypothesized that children do not have stabilized interaction practices opposite to adults. It is important to pinpoint that the instructions were voluntarily vague on the means to interact. A user was given an experimental document with a drawing of a character with a laser pointer in one hand and a bubble with the written word ``prison'' as a suggestion. The number and the nature of user's action are described in figure 10-right. The number of pointing gestures is highly variable, ranging between 0 and 159, during the maximum period of 15 minutes allowed for the story-telling game. Among the 20 subjects, one never pointed, another pointed (4 times) only when oral commands failed and one subject only pointed (159 times). Users clearly have different preferences but are very consistent within them. Data suggest that it is simple to take a laser to point. The pointing gesture instrumented by the laser pointer was reinforced by several feedbacks: the action on the "on" state of the laser pointer, the sound of the click of the pointer on/off toggle, the green impact allowing seeing the pointed location. Concerning oral commands, it can be noticed that 9 subjects have used no oral commands and that 1 subject has used oral command only. The variability in the number of oral commands (ranging from 0 to 34) is less than for gesture command. Data show that only the subjects using voice responded to oral enticement and that the number of enticement had no effect on the different interaction styles that are observed:

- Subjects try to use oral commands in order to test their effectiveness.
- Subjects who utter to complete gesture.
- Subjects who are thought to wish to interact only with voice and who turn to another interaction modality after successive failures.

Among the 10 subjects using both gesture and speech, the two following interaction modes have been found:

- A subject completes the laser pointing with an oral command allowing turning the cube in order to see the other faces. Pointing gestures are followed by 3 oral commands `"*turn*" -these virtual cubes have only 3 faces (to minimize manipulation gesture and mental workload).
- A subject behaves as in the preceding case to turn a cube but also to move a cube on the storyline.

To conclude, such an experiment allows defining a spoken vocabulary, to observe, depending on the context, the importance of a given modality over other modalities. The most important lesson learnt from this experiment is that modality influences the type of cooperation. The more the subjects pointed and the lesser the story was built in a cooperative manner: the story was build by successive elements without real integration of the distant user.

3.2 VIRSTORY on the TABLE

In order to progress in the platform design, we realized a new experimentation with MERL DiamondTouch Table or DTT [24].

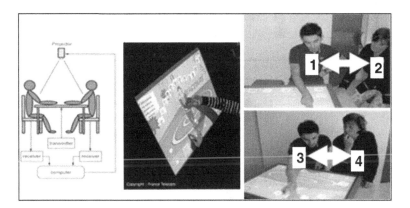

Fig. 11. Left: MERL DTT setup - Middle: VIRSTORY on the DTT -Right: Two experimental conditions (Top: ALONE in this condition, one gamer plays alone but the story is narrated together – Bottom: COPRESENCE, each gamer plays and tells the story). Each duo has narrated during 4 sessions represented by 4 numbers for 2 conditions counterbalanced). The place of each gamer on the DTT is counterbalanced too. In fact, this experience included 4 stories for 4 situations.

However, distant collaboration has to preserve as far as possible the advantages of "face-to-face" communication and the mutual awareness provided by co-presence. According to these principles, we focused on the gestures: tactile inputs and non verbal behavior as it conveys major information supporting mediated interaction such as intentionality (who is intending to do what), action identity (who is doing what) and pointing. 30 subjects have contributed to this experience randomly put in pairs. Each pair told 4 stories for 2 conditions: ALONE and COPRESENCE. Each pair was filmed and the recordings processed by manually coding -about 60 hours- each subject's gestures into non-verbal categories DAMB (see above). We also added three categories: "M: *Manipulation*" (touch inputs on DTT) "I: *Interactor*" e.g: gaze or gesture of one's hand which invites the other one to interact) and "C: *Collaboration*" e.g.: oral and explicit demand of collaboration.

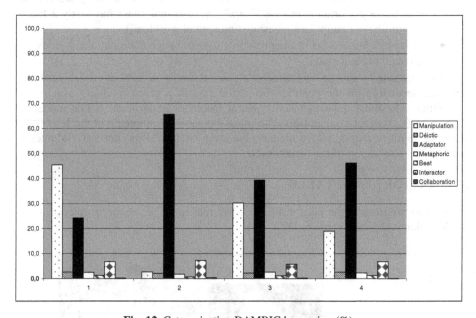

Fig. 12. Categorization DAMBIC by session (%)

Fig. 13. New version of VIRSTORY with synchronous multipointers

We observed the preponderance of self contact gesture or Adaptators. In fact this non verbal behavior is an indicator of activity but with a strong inter condition variability (min 20%-max 70%). The results are still during in the treatment. In the next experiment, the co-localized situation (side-by-side in front of DTT) vs. remote situation (virtually sitting face-to-face) will be studied. We aim at investigating how gestures affects mediated collaboration when remote gesture visualization of distant users and a synchronous multi-touch needed for interaction are provided.

4 Conclusion

This last experiment should serve as reference to another experiments (distant collaboration with DTT) and to design a new platform integrating several technologies: gesture inputs, synchronous multi-users and multi-pointers, visualization of remote gesture, optimization of finger interaction by the fusion of tactile and computer vision tracking...Finally, the lessons learned from the sensorial deprivation, WoZ VIRSTORY and VIRSTORY on DTT experiments are that the technical problems encountered during the design of a storytelling CVE should not shadow other questions: for which user, for which type of interaction or cooperation, what device used? The integration of several technologies: one hand, speech and vision gesture recognition and the other hand, an animation character module in our setup is in progress in our labs. This integration and the development of future behavioral module dedicated at the storytelling collaborative game VIRSTORY should be a help for continuing the work on the studies about the non-verbal in small groups interactions. Our objectives are also to explore steep by steep: the multimodal inputs in relation to character animation, the gesture recognition and her usability "in situ", the design of the setup with new form of co-manipulation... Our approach is indubitably interdisciplinary and pragmatic!

References

1. Le Mer, P., Perron, L., Chaillou, C., Degrande, S., Saugis, G.: Collaborating with virtuals humans. In: Blandford, A., Vanderdonckt, J., Gray, P. (eds.) People and computers XV - Interactions without frontiers. Joint proceedings of HCI 2001 and IHM 2001, pp. 83–103. Springer, Lille (2001)
2. Tapie, J., Terrier, P., Perron, L., Cellier, J.-M.: Should remote collaborators be represented by avatars? a study of an application used for collective medical decision-making. In: Special Issue: Collaborative distance activities: From social cognition to electronic togeherness, AI & Society (2005)
3. Perron, L.: An avatar with your own gestures. In: INTERACT 2005 Workshop Appropriate Methodology for Empirical Studies of Privacy. Communicating Naturally through Computers, Rome, Italy, September 12-16, 2005, pp. 12–16 (2005)
4. Kendira, A., Perron, L.: VIRSTORY: a Collaborative Virtual Storytelling. In: Harper, R., Rauterberg, M., Combetto, M. (eds.) ICEC 2006. LNCS, vol. 4161, pp. 20–22. Springer, Heidelberg (2006)
5. Buisine, S., Martin, J.C., Bernsen, N.O.: Children's gesture and speech in Conversation with 3D Characters. In: International Conference of Human Computer Interaction, Las Vegas, NV USA (2005)
6. Cavazza, M., Martin, O., Charles, F., Mead, S., Marechal, W.: Users acting in mixed reality storytelling. In: Balet, O., Subsol, G., Torguet, P. (eds.) ICVS 2003. LNCS, vol. 2897, pp. 189–197. Springer, Heidelberg (2003)

7. Oviatt, S., Cohen, P., Wu, L., Vergo, J., Duncan, L., Suhm, B., Holzman, T., Winograd, T., Landay, J., Larson, J., Ferro, D.: Designing the user interface for multimodal speech and gesture applications: State-of-the-art systems and research directions. In: Human Computer Interaction, ch. 19, MA, vol. 15, pp. 421–456, 263-322. Addison-Wesley Press, Reading (2001)

8. Kraut, R.E., Fussell, S.R., Siegel, J.: Visual Information as a Conversational Resource in Collaborative Physical Tasks. Human-Computer Interaction 18, 13–49 (2003)

9. Feyereisen, P., Van de Wiele, M., Dubois, F.: The meaning of gestures: what can be unterderstood without speech? Cahiers de psychologie cognitive - European bulletin of cognitive psychology 8(1), 3–25 (1988)

10. Ekman, P., Friesen, W.V.: The repertoire of nonverbal behavior: Categories, origins, usage, and coding. Semiotica 1, 49–98 (1969)

11. Cassell, J., Bickmore, T., Campbell, L., Vilhjálmsson, H., Yan, H.: Human conversation as a system framework: designing embodied conversational agents. In: Press, M. (ed.) Embodied conversational agents, pp. 29–63. MIT Press, Cambridge, MA, USA (2001)

12. Prendinger, H., Ishizuka, M.: Life-Like Characters: Tools, Affective Functions, and Applications. Springer, Heidelberg (2004)

13. Goldin-Meadow, S.: The role of gesture in communication and thinking. Cognitive Sciences 3(11), 419–429 (1999)

14. Pina, A., Cerezo, E., et Seron, F.J.: Computer animation: from avatars to unrestricted autonomous actors (A survey on replication and modelling mechanisms). Computer & Graphics 24, 297–311 (2000)

15. Kaur-Deol, K., Sutcliffe, A., Maiden, N.: Modelling interaction to inform information requirements in virtual environments. Interactions in Virtual Worlds, Enschede, Netherlands (1999)

16. Riva, G., Galimberti, C.: Galimberti Computer-mediated communication: identity and social interaction in an electronic environment. Genetic, Social and General Psychology Monographs 124, 434–464 (1998)

17. Pelachaud, C., Poggi, I.: Talking faces that communicates by eyes, ORALITE ET GESTUALITE: communication multimodale et interaction, Aix, pp. 211–218 (1998)

18. Whittaker, S., Geelhoed, E., Robinson, E.: Shared workspaces: how do they work and when are they useful? International Journal of Man-Machine Studies (1993)

19. Perron, L.: Non verbal et univers virtuels: comment collaborer via des clones, 15ème Conférence Francophone sur l'Interaction Homme-Machine, Caen (Novembre 25-28, 2003)

20. Carbini, S., Delphin-Poulat, L., Perron, L., Viallet, J.E.: From a wizard of Oz experiment to a real time speech and gesture multimodal interface. Signal Processing, Special issue on Multimodal Human Computer Interfaces (2005)

21. Masse, Laurence: La communication verbale et non verbale en situation d'entretien psychothérapeutique Thèse de doctorat en Psychologie - St Denis Université Paris 8 (1999)

22. Bouguet, A., Pavy, D., Le Mer, P.: Virtual Humans Animation in Collaborative Virtual Environment. In: CollabTech 2005, Japon (July 2005)

23. Kendira, A., Perron, L., Viallet, J.E., Carbini, S., Delphin-Poulat, L.: VIRSTORY: Using Human Behavior Studies to Design a Multimodal Collaborative Virtual Environment. In: Collab Tech 2006, Tsukuba Japon, pp. 114–119 (2006)

24. Pauchet, A., Coldefy, F., et al.: Mutual awareness in co-localized and distant collaborative tasks using shared interfaces. In: Interact 2007. LNCS, vol. 4662, pp. 59–73. Springer, Heidelberg (2007)

What Does Your Actor Remember? Towards Characters with a Full Episodic Memory

Cyril Brom[1], Klára Pešková[1], and Jiří Lukavský[2]

[1] Charles University, Faculty of Mathematics and Physics, Prague, Czech Republic
[2] Institute of Psychology, Academy of Sciences, Prague, Czech Republic
brom@ksvi.mff.cuni.cz

Abstract. A typical present-day virtual actor is able to store episodes in an *ad hoc* manner, which does not allow for reconstructing the actor's personal stories. This paper proposes a virtual RPG actor with a *full* episodic memory, which allows for this reconstruction. The paper presents the memory architecture, overviews the prototype implementation, presents a benchmark for the efficiency of the memory measurement, and details the conducted tests.

1 Introduction

Computer role-playing games (RPGs) typically feature virtual worlds large in size, lifetime and behavioural possibilities. These worlds, both in off-line and on-line RPGs, are usually inhabited by tens of virtual actors ("non-player characters", NPCs). An innate challenge of these games is to provide a player with a believable story. Though there is likely more narration in RPGs then in any other kind of commercial games, storytelling in RPGs is still far from novels or films.

The story generating in RPGs is a multi-dimensional problem—one cannot tackle it in a Façade-like style [11] for example, as the world is much more complex. One facet of this problem is unfolding the story and keeping it consistent when a player speaks with NPCs, i.e. letting the actors to tell believable stories about themselves. Imagine that while you are playing an RPG, you come to a medieval village, find an NPC shaman in her den and ask her (selecting a question from a template list):

Hey, I am the representative of the king Hromburac Pekelny, and you please tell me, what were you doing during the last week? And, please, summarise it in two sentences.

Well – she answers – *I was here every day, meditating and heeling toes, you know. Nothing interesting happened, except of Wednesday when filthy brigands came to rob me.*

To be able to answer such questions according to their personal histories, and not using a text written in advance by a designer, the NPCs must be simulated even if no player is around (at least to some extent), and they must be equipped with a *full episodic memory* and a *linguistic module* transferring the outcome of the memory to syntactically correct sentences. By "full", we mean a generic memory that stores more or less everything happening around the actor tagged with the actor's own relevance estimation, as opposed to an *ad hoc episodic memory* storing only the events specified in a hardwired fashion inside the actor's script or reactive plan (this kind of episodic memory is almost always present in current intelligent actors).

M. Cavazza and S. Donikian (Eds.): ICVS 2007, LNCS 4871, pp. 89–101, 2007.

A full episodic memory shall even allow the player to ask further, for example:

> *Ok, that sounds* interesting. *Please, summarise the same now in 15 sentences.* or *Please, focus on the filthy brigands.* or *Tell me more about Saturday evening.*

We have been developing actors with this kind of episodic memory as a part of our on-going work on a large educational storytelling game [1]. The issue of episodic memory agents in general has been recently tackled in literature, e.g. [14]. However, we are interested in a *full* episodic memory that is *special-purpose* in the context of RPGs emphasising a story—and this issue has not been addressed sufficiently yet.

Two aspects of the issue must be stressed. First, it must be assumed that the virtual world lasts for days or weeks and features tens of different actors (this contrasts with many applications of intelligent actors). Consequently, the highest attention must be paid to the memory size, to storage/retrieval speeds, and to the balance between them, as they present a sort of trade-off. Second, because of the novelty of this research field, an issue how to measure efficiency of the memory arises. Standards for comparable testing, i.e. benchmarks, have not been defined yet.

The goal of this paper is to present a new model of a full episodic memory for an NPC. To implement an entire actor presents a several man-years effort. Presently, about a half is done (especially, the linguistic module has not been addressed yet); however, we propose the whole architecture to facilitate thinking about the complete picture. A subgoal is to present a benchmark for measuring efficiency of the memory, detailing results of tests concerning size of the memory. Other tests are detailed in [5].

Section 2 analyses requirements of the memory, and Section 3 details related work. Section 4 presents our architecture contrasting what has already been done with what remains. Section 5 presents benchmark scenario, and discusses its construction. Section 6 describes the prototype implementation, reveals the experimental results and discusses them, and also introduces future work. Section 7 concludes.

2   Problem Analysis and Requirements

From the psychological point of view, *episodic memory* [17] represents personal history of an entity. Episodic memories are related to particular places and moments, and are connected to subjective feelings and current goals. Some psychological studies focus on so called *autobiographic memory*, which is similar to episodic memory but usually used in larger, i.e. lifetime, scope.

As our goal is to *imitate* human-like episodic memory, we need the actors to remember only what real humans would remember, and forget in similar way and extend as real humans would do. Unfortunately, there is no thorough functional description of human episodic memory from which we could derive our model. Thus, we are forced to derive the requirements only from case-studies of forensic psychology (e.g. [13]) and from our own phenomenological experience:

1. The memory should cope with complex tasks that include manipulation with several objects and apparently require human-level cognitive abilities, like cooking or merchandising, for they can be performed by an NPC. These tasks typically have hierarchical nature—they can be logically decomposed to sub-tasks, which can be divided to yet smaller tasks, until some atomic actions are reached. This point is fully implemented by the presented work, as detailed in Sec. 4.

2. The memory has to store and reconstruct personal situations: a) what an actor performed with which objects and why, and b) who was seen by the actor and what did the other actor perform (we remark, that presently only (a) is implemented, (b) is a work-in-progress). Time information, at least approximate, shall be also stored. The memory should be able to provide information like "where is something?", "when did the actor see x?", "what did the actor do from y to z?", "why did you do a?" and reconstruct stories like the abovementioned. The memory is expected to reconstruct information *on demand*, i.e. when a user asks, rather than automatically based on an environmental clue. This point is implemented, though the actors' answers are grammatically poor, see Sec. 6 for an example.

3. The memory should not store all available information; either external, or internal. In particular (a) neither all objects located around the actor, nor all activities of other actors should be stored. The objects used by the actor should be stored more often then the objects not used, but only seen. (b) Only important actions of other actors should be stored. (c) Generally, the way of choosing activities/objects to remember should be based on their relevance to the actor, on their attractiveness, and on the actor's attentional and emotional state. Presently, storing of actions of other actors is not implemented. Point (a) is achieved concerning the objects. Concerning Point (c), attractiveness (or saliency) of the objects and attention are implemented (Sec. 4). The emotional module has been implemented separately.

4. The memory operates in large time scale. As time passes, the unimportant details should be forgotten, until only a "gist" of what happened is kept. Different episodes should be forgotten in different rates based on their importance and emotional relevance. Several similar episodes can be eventually merged together. Forgetting is partially implemented, but not the merging of episodes (Sec. 4, p. 7).

5. Coherence shall be maintained, in particular if there are two contradictory records in the memory, i.e. an object x has been seen both at a and b, one of them must be marked as more trustful. This issue is a work-in-progress described in [4].

3 Related Work

In classical agent research, the issue of generic episodic memory is almost untouched, since the agents typically do not need to store more than a few episodes in an *ad hoc* memory for action selection purposes. This is also the case of most intelligent actors, though exceptions exist—see bellow. In robotics, Dodd [3] has recently developed a general memory system for a humanoid robot ISAC, which included also episodic memory working with emotions. An a-life example is the work of Ho et al. [7], who developed agents with various episodic memories aiming to investigate how different types of memories improve survival of the agents. Though these memories fit well for their domain, they are relatively low-level from the point of view of human-like actors, especially those from RPGs. For example, they are not designed to cope with complex, hierarchical tasks. This is also the limitation of most memories studied in the context of navigation in robotics. In the field of virtual actors, an implemented memory model was presented on ALOHA system [15]. It exploited to a great advantage division of the memory to short-term one and long-term one, but unfortunately stored records only about objects and groups of objects, but not actions. Another example is Steve [16], who employs an episodic memory [9] to explain himself after a given lesson, which lasts, however, only a couple of minutes. FearNot! actors are also equipped with a episodic memory [8], which is, however, similarly to Steve, relatively short term one.

In agent research, perhaps the most elaborate model of episodic memory has been developed by Nuxoll [14]. This model is intended to be a robust, general-purpose architectural extension of Soar with broader scope than the model of ours. This, however, means that our model may benefit from some domain-specific tricks, which may finally increase efficiency of the memory in our domain. In all cases, it will be interesting in future to compare this model with ours using our benchmark scenario.

4 Proposed Full Episodic Memory

This section outlines the architecture of our actor, and details its episodic memory. The memory has two parts: a short-term (STM), and a long-term memory (LTM). We start with presenting the behavioural representation of our actor, proceeding through the STM to perception-action loop and to the LTM.

Our actor employs classical cognitive architecture (Fig. 1). The dashed parts are not implemented (linguistic module, "other memories"), or implemented separately but not included in the prototype described in this paper (emotional module, drives).

The goal structure. The actor is driven by hierarchical reactive planning with behaviour represented by AND-OR trees. In general, in the context of action selection, the AND-OR tree metaphor deals with abstract *goals* representing what should be achieved, and *tasks* representing how to achieve the goals. Typically, every goal can be accomplished by several tasks, while every task can be achieved by adopting some sub-goals. An actor needs to perform only one task to achieve a goal, provided there is no failure (hence, OR nodes), but he needs to fulfill all sub-goals to solve a task (hence, AND nodes—Fig. 2). Usually, these sub-goals are being adopted depending on some conditions or priorities, which allows both for sequential as well as reactive behavior. The tasks that cannot be further decomposed are *atomic actions*, i.e. primitives changing world-state. In our case, every top-level goal has its *activity level* based on drives, external events, and a schedule. The most active top-level goal is called *active*, several nearly "the most active" are *preactive*. To be performed, every task may need several *resources*, i.e. objects (e.g. hammering is possible only with a nail and a hammer).

The important tenet of our approach is that behaviour of all actors in the simulation is represented in this way. Violation of this principle, e.g. in the case of the user's avatar, whose behaviour is not represented in this sense at all, is discussed later.

The STM. The STM has four parts: the perceptional field, the memory field, the own-tasks field, and the others-tasks field. The *perceptional field* (PF) can entail several *phantoms*, which are index-functional entities representing perceived externa objects, including their presumed state. The *memory field* is similar, but the phantoms in there refer to the LTM memory instead of the external world. The *own-tasks field*

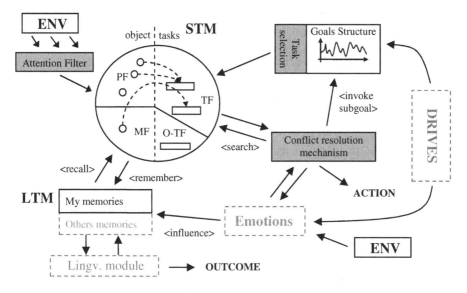

Fig. 1. The overall architecture of our actor. PF – phantoms of the STM. TF – own tasks of the actor. MF – records retrieved from the LTM. O-TF – others-tasks field. The dashed parts are not implemented, or they are implemented separately. See the text for further description.

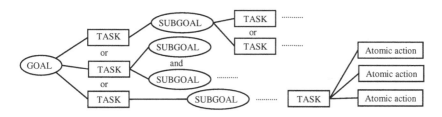

Fig. 2. Behavioural representation is based on AND-OR trees

(TF) entails tasks chosen to be performed or being performed (this structure is similar to so-called intentional stack from BDI architectures). Each phantom points at a parameter of a task *iff* it fits as a resource of the task. Each phantom can point at more tasks and more parameters of one task. The ***others-tasks*** field is not implemented yet. It is intended to represent tasks being seen as being performed by another actor.

The action selection mechanism (ASM). The action selection works as follows:

1. The activity level for each goal is calculated.
2. The task to be performed is chosen for the active goal (based on priorities) and passed to the TF. Sometimes, a task for a preactive goal is chosen as well.
3. The phantoms in the STM start to point to the added task.
4. If there is a task with a parameter at which no phantom points, a new *search task* on this type of resource is added to the TF.

5. The conflict resolution mechanism chooses a task to be performed from the tasks in the TF. If the task can be decomposed to a sequence of atomic actions (e.g. the search task), it is executed. If it can be decomposed only to subgoals, one of these subgoals is activated and the loop continues at step 1.

A search task works as follows: The actor looks around at the first place. If the required resource is not seen, the LTM is queried. If there is a record about the needed object, the most trustful record is put the memory field as a phantom, and the actor gets off to the presumed position of the object. When the object is seen, the phantom is moved to the PF. In case of no record in the LTM, a random search is initiated.

Perception. For the prototyping purposes, we have used a grid-world, where every object from the room the actor is located in can be seen (i.e. there are no obstacles). At every time step, just one object may pass through the attention filter and "become" a phantom in the PF. This is either an object looked for by a search task, or an object that has just captured the actor's attention because of its high *saliency*. Saliency is computed from a preset base saliency and from current activity of both active and preactive goals (e.g. a preactive "eating" goal increase saliency of eatable objects). If a new phantom of an attractive object appears in the PF, all tasks that can be performed with this object are put to the TF to compete with the tasks placed there by active or preactive goals. (The whole mechanism is based on the capacity model of attention [10]. Its thorough description is, however, out of scope of this paper.)

This mechanism helps us to achieve several things. First, the amount of objects passing to the PF is limited (as in the case of a real human). Second, an external object can attract the actor's attention, and invoke a new task, or activate a preactive goal via its task in the TF (step 3, the ASM)—e.g. an actor having active "playing" goal and preactive "feeding" goal may stop playing and start feeding when noticing food.

Concerning the others-tasks field, basically, the actor is intended to directly see tasks of an observed actor, e.g. that he is cooking (i.e. performing "cooking" task), and right now, he is stirring a soup ("stirring ›soup‹" subtask), provided the second actor declared his tasks as public. This is to be achieved either through the mechanism of attention in case of an attractive/dangerous task, or by intentional observation.

Decay. A phantom is decaying both in the PF and the MF until it eventually vanishes. The decay can be stopped or slowed down by looking at the object repeatedly (i.e. "rehearsal") or by using the object. Similarly, tasks decay in the TF if not being performed. Typically, a task from the TF disappears a moment after it has been accomplished. When a phantom or a task vanishes from the PF/TF, it **is** recorded into the LTM, as detailed later. Tasks from the others-tasks field are intended to be handled similarly. There is no exact limit on the size of the STM, but typically, there is up to 10 phantoms and 5 tasks, which is roughly consistent with human data [12].

The LTM. The fixed arrangement of the LTM is a tree-like structure comprising tasks (Fig. 3a). During remembering, two types of entities are added into this structure: phantoms, and so-called time pointers. The basic principle of remembering is to store everything that has just vanished from the PF or the TF (in future, we plan to add *activation* to each entity and to store only the entities above a threshold). Specifically:

1. If a phantom of an object that was seen by the actor, but not used has just vanished from the STM, its actual state, including the position, and the time of the decay are stored in the LTM, and the phantom is linked to all tasks where it can be used as a resource (Fig. 3b). Storage is done in constant time due to a hash map.

2. As soon as a task that is performed vanishes from the TF, a record is made about it using a time pointer. In the LTM, there is a set of *time pointers* that orders the tasks at every task layer of the LTM. When a new task is stored, a new pointer from the previous task to this new task is added at the appropriate layer (Fig. 3c). This pointer includes information about the time of the start and the end of the performance of the task, and a goal denoting why the task was carried out (if such a goal existed—a task could be generated without explicit active or preactive goal by an attractive object). Additionally, phantoms of the objects used as resources of this task are linked into the LTM. In case of a sequence of identical atomic actions, only their number and the pointer to the first different action are stored. In future, also a part of the motivational state of the actor that contributed most to the activation of the goal (e.g. hunger drive was high in the case of feeding goal activation), and the average emotional relevance over the time of task performance will be stored with the time pointers. Presently, the emotional relevance is determined manually for the experimental purposes.

3. The tasks performed by other actors are intended to be stored in the similar way as the own tasks (Point 2), except there will be no time pointers, but time-stamps, and no goal and motivational state will be stored (as they are not known for other actors).

Forgetting. Perhaps the most important feature of the LTM is that less emotionally interesting records are being deleted. Specifically, the emotionally less important episodes are being "bitten out" from the bottom of the LTM (Fig. 4). A *normalised importance* is computed first as: $i = e \cdot 1/h \cdot 1/d^{1/2}$, where h is the layer of the LTM structure, d number of days passed from the episode, and e is either the emotional relevance of a task (the cases 2, 3 above), or the saliency of an object (the case 1). i is low for the far-off, emotionally uninteresting, and fine-grained tasks. The time-pointers and phantoms of tasks with low i are then removed when the NPC "sleeps".

Retrieval. To increase memory retrieval speed, phantoms are (apart from the above-mentioned structure) hashed, and time pointers are indexed by days. Consequently, searching for an object, i.e. filling the memory field in the STM, is $O(1)$. The question "what did the actor performed at time t" is answered using time pointers in $O(n)$, where n is the average number of top-level tasks performed during a day.

The story reconstruction mentioned in the introduction is not implemented yet, but it will be built upon the already implemented question "what was the actor doing from t_1 to t_2". The answer to this question returns all tasks from the required layer of the LTM from t_1 to t_2. All what is needed additionally is to return the tasks from different layers to fit to the expected size of the story. Which tasks are to be chosen can be determined by their emotional importance similarly to determining which tasks should be forgotten (i.e. concrete tasks will be chosen only for highly emotional situations).

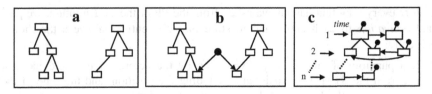

Fig. 3a. A fixed arrangement of the LTM, each box represents a task. 3b. Storage of a phantom, which was used in two tasks. 3c. The tasks are sorted by time pointers during storing.

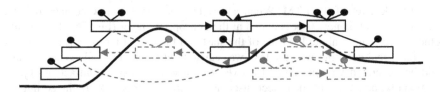

Fig. 4. Forgetting is schematically depicted. Phantoms and time pointers below a particular layer are removed with all information they included.

5 Benchmark Scenario

The trouble with measuring efficiency of a full episodic memory is that neither a rigorous testing methodology, nor a benchmark is available because of the novelty of the field. Hence, our subgoal was to create such a benchmark and to conduct preliminary tests to reveal basic characteristics of our memory and to make a first step towards laying a methodological ground. This section details the benchmark.

Any valuable benchmark scenario for an RPG must be "ecological plausible" with respect to this domain. There is no need to run a real RPG, but to model its most important features *just* to the extent that would allow for carrying out the experiments. At the first place, the scenario must feature situations in which a typical NPC can take place. Second, the scenario should last for several days. Third, it must seize a dynamic and a complexity of a typical RPG.

We have decided to exploit a five-day scenario world inhabited by a shaman NPC. The dynamic to be seized could emerge a) from the changing internal needs of the shaman, b) from her interaction with other NPCs or a player, and c) from the drama manager reasons. To model (a), during a day, the shaman is to carry out several *homeostatic* tasks like eating, sleeping, tidying up etc., one of which is a "parking" task performed when nothing more important is urging. To model (b, c), the shaman is to carry on *typical tasks*, e.g. voodoo doing, teeth extracting, as well as some *unexpected tasks* like extinguishing a sudden fire. In the abstract sense, these three kinds of tasks differ only in their timing. Every homeostatic can be performed several times a day, usually at least once, and more or less in the same time every day. A typical task can be performed anytime during a day. Unexpected tasks are carried less often, in case of this benchmark one per day. The concrete numbers used are given in Tab. 2.

For simplicity, we decided not to model other NPCs, but to imitate their presence. This is being done in two ways: first, by random changing positions of objects (i.e. "moving" them by an "NPC"), second, by invoking an NPC related goals operating with objects instead of NPCs (e.g. extracting teeth uses the object "teeth").

The former brings a problem with measuring the world *dynamic*. We decided to specify dynamic as n/m, where n is the number of changes of objects (because they were either taken by the shaman, or moved by an imitated NPC), and m is the total number of objects in the environment (i.e. dynamic can be greater than 1). Then, we measured performance of the memory in different dynamics.

To determine the exact setting and to allow for reproducibility, we decided to specify the course of activation of homeostatic goals in advance as a function of time, modelling presumed changing of drives (Tab. 1). Three typical tasks were performed once a day, and each day, one unexpected task was carried out; in both cases time being determined randomly (uniform distribution). This randomness models a random event, or an interference of a drama manager, or an interaction between the shaman and an imitated NPC. Average duration of each task was specified in advance as well, covering the intervals from minutes to hours (Tab. 1).

Complexity of RPGs further demands following:

1. The tasks have to be hierarchical, i.e. they must entail subtasks, and they may need more than one resource (e.g., extracting teeth needs both teeth and tongs).
2. There should be a plethora of different objects the shaman can use (Tab. 2).

Name	Type	Depth	Durat.	Activation
Sleep	hom.	2+2	7 hours	
Eat	hom.	2+2	1+1+1	
Wash	hom.	2+2	1+1	
Smoke	hom.	2+2	0.5	
Tidy Up	hom.	3+3	1.5	
Herborize	hom.	2+2	3	
Meditate	park.	2+2	24	
Make Voodoo	typical	2+2	0.5-2	random
Predict Future	typical	2+2	0.5-2	random
Cure	typical	2+2	0.5-2	random
Heal Tooth	typical	2+2	0.5-2	random
Smoke Signals	typical	3+3	0.5-2	random
Fight	unexp.	2+2	0.5-1.5	random
Resist Wind	unexp.	2+2	0.5-1.5	random
Extinguish Fire	unexp.	2+2	0.5-1.5	random
Kill Predator	unexp.	2+2	0.5-1.5	random

Nr. of individual objects/classes of objects	50/18
Nr. of top-level tasks in total/ performed in one day:	
homeostatic	7/10
typical	5/3
unexpected	4/1
Avg. nr. of objects for a task parameter:	4.5
Avg. nr. of tasks an object is a resource for:	2.17

Table 1. The top-level goals of the shaman. The depth is given in the number of goals+tasks. The x-scale of the activation is a one day scale.

Table 2. The basic parameters of the scenario

6   Implementation and Tests

We have prototyped the memory model and the benchmark scenario in Python. We are also implementing the memory into our large-scale project [3] for the purposes of our storytelling game [2]; but this is out of scope of this paper. We carried out two tests revealing the size of the memory and the efficiency of the actor (measured in time steps spent by searching for an object). For brevity, we detail in this paper only the benchmark and the first test. The second test is detailed in [5].

To abstract an RPG environment, we implemented a coarse-grained space model: a 3x3 grid of rooms, between which the can actor "jump" if there is a "door" (Fig. 5). Time was discretised: one time-step is 12 seconds, i.e. a day lasts 7200 time-steps. Every atomic action, including "jump", takes one time-step.

The shaman is equipped with a memory, a perception, and an action selection mechanism. The STM comprises perceptional field, memory field, and own-tasks field; the others-task field is unimplemented. The LTM allows for asking the following questions: "Where is a resource for task T?" (complexity of $O(1)$); "When did you do task T?" ($O(1)$); "Where was object X between t_1 and t_2?" ($O(m)$, where m are records concerning object X); "What did you do between t_1 and t_2?" ($O(n+m)$, where n is number of actions between t_1 and t_2 and m is time needed to find the first record from the interval, i.e. average number of top-level tasks performed during a day). The example of answer to the last question in the current implementation is:

> "I was doing SearchRandom for smokeability because of Smoke. I was doing go from room 1 to room 2 because of SearchRandom. I was doing look in environment because of SearchRandom. I was doing go from room 2 to room 5 because of SearchRandom. I was doing pick up Calumet1 because of Smoke. I was doing Smoke."

If there are two different records concerning the same object, the newer record is considered as more trustful. As already mentioned, the suggested linguistic module is out of our scope presently, hence unimplemented. The emotional module is implemented separately [1], i.e. not included in the prototype. Hence, LTM forgetting is implemented in an *ad hoc* manner; during a night (when it is "sleeping") the actor forgets the bottom level of time pointers and phantoms for the previous day for all tasks except of the unexpected one (which is considered as emotionally salient).

Setting. Two experiments were carried out on a 2 GHz Win-XP PC; the first one measuring the size of the memory without forgetting, and the second one with forgetting. We carried out 3 variants of each test; each with a different world dynamic (0.1, 0.5, 1). Ten runs were carried for each variant; each simulating 5 consecutive days. The position of all objects was randomised for each run. The saliency of the objects was switched off to reduce the amount of parameters of the simulation, i.e. only the objects the shaman used were remembered.

Results. The size of the fixed LTM structure was 140 items (tasks and atomic actions). Average number of phantoms and time pointers respectively in the LTM without forgetting for one day in dynamic 0.5 (over all runs and days) was: 90/277 comparing to 90/136 of the memory with forgetting. For comparison, *naïve memory* storing at every time step all objects in the room the actor was located in, stored 40.000 phantoms in one day on average. Fig. 6 depicts the change of the number of time-pointers stored in the memory with and without forgetting for dynamic 0.5 (average over 10 runs). We do not show the results for dynamics 0.1 and 1 for the tests showed the numbers are almost the same.

Discussion. A real-time RPG is a complex system with a vast amount of parameters. Any aspect of behaviour of memory can be understood only as a multi-dimensional, likely non-linear function over these parameters. To study complex, non-linear systems, scientists typically follow reductionism. We adopted this approach as well. We left the saliency effect of objects on attention out of account, we implemented forgetting without a real emotional importance, we avoided NPCs, and randomised objects' positions at the start of each trial (they should have been clustered by rooms instead—e.g. a spade typically can not be found in a bedroom). The world dynamic was calculated as if the probability that an object can be moved was same for all objects, disregarding that some objects are moving objects, some can change their state without changing the position, and some can be moved more often than others.

Still, after the reduction, the tests revealed several important observations:

1. Contrary to time pointers, phantoms are not being forgotten, since all of them are used as resources not only for atomic actions, but also higher-level tasks. Only if forgetting touches higher levels of the LTM structure, phantoms can be forgotten.
2. Our memory is far better than the naïve one, but still, given 200 B for an item, after 5 days, the shaman's LTM will possess 395 kB $(200 \cdot (140+5 \cdot (90+277)))$ without, and 254 kB $(200 \cdot (140+5 \cdot (90+136)))$ with forgetting. This fact and Point 1 suggest that forgetting, even deeper, is essential.
3. The memory size is independent on the world dynamic. The reason is that only tasks performed and their resources were stored, and their amount does not depend on the dynamic. Will the size become dependent when storing also salient objects?

Apart from this issue (Point 3), we plan to include real NPCs into the tests. It would be also interesting to compare other models of episodic memories, e.g. [14], using our benchmark. Besides directions of future trialling, there are some open questions concerning the model itself. First, trustfulness of the objects must be determined more plausibly. In worlds with high dynamics, the actor tends to search on wrong places, because the object in question has been already moved. The trustfulness issue is our work-in-progress [4]. This work also includes a better spatial representation of the environment for it is essential in determining the trustfulness. Second, actions of other NPCs are to be stored as well so that the reconstruction of *their* stories is possible. This is another work-in-progress. Third, equipping the actor with emotions and drives is needed to allow for implementing real forgetting. This will also elevate overall believability of the actor. Fourth, forgetting should be also augmented by a process of merging several similar or repeated unimportant episodes together (see the example from Introduction). Fifth, neither our actor currently can carry out two atomic actions in parallel (e.g. go and eat), nor is the memory optimised for task interleaving. These last two points presents future work. Finally, there is a sort of "holy-grail": guessing the goals of a user avatar. Contrary to the foreign NPCs, there is no available information about goals of the user. The NPC can only guess them from the sequences of atomic actions, hence create a sort of "theory of mind". We have an idea how to address this problem by bayesian learning, this is, however, a pie in the sky.

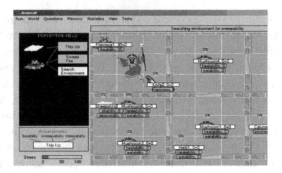

Fig. 5. A part of a screen-shot from the prototype. Left: the short term memory. Right: the grid world of the shaman actor (only 4 rooms from 9 are shown). The shaman is in the upper left room.

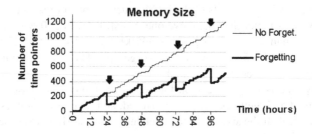

Fig. 6. Average nr. of time pointers stored in the memory during 5 days (over 10 runs; dynamic =0.5). The arrows denotes nights.

7 Conclusion

We have presented a full episodic memory for a non-player character from an RPG to allow for reconstruction of the character's personal history. The memory is widely optimised on effective storing and retrieval. Additionally, it enables to store episodes for a long time. These are the most notable features that make the memory applicable for RPGs. The model is portable to any other application featuring human-like actors provided it employs behavioural representations based on AND-OR trees.

We have also introduced the "5-day" shaman scenario aiming as a general benchmark for full episodic memory actors. Using this benchmark, we demonstrated that memory performs well concerning its size; however, forgetting was essential.

So far, the memory only stores actions the actor performed, and objects it used, and the emotional salience of the episodes must be determined manually. We are now connecting the memory to the emotional model [1], and implementing the storage of actions of *other* actors. Additionally, the issue of determining trustfulness of memory records is addressed [4]. The final actor will be ported to our large scale project [3].

Acknowledgments. This research was partially supported by the Project of the Ministry of Education of the Czech Republic No. MSM0021620838, and GA UK 351/2006/A-INF/MFF. Authors would like to thank to Andrew Nuxoll for answering questions on his work, and Tomáš Holan for general comments.

References

1. Bída, M., Kadlec, R., Brom, C.: Relevance of emotions for artificial beings (in Czech). In: Mind, intelligence and life, Vydavatel'stvo STU, Bratislava, pp. 158–172 (2007)
2. Brom, C., Abonyi, A.: Petri-Nets for Game Plot. In: Proceedings of AISB Artificial Intelligence and Simulation Behaviour Convention, Bristol, vol. 3, pp. 6–13 (2006)
3. Brom, C., Lukavský, J., Šerý, O., Poch, T., Šafrata, P.: Affordances and level-of-detail AI for virtual humans. In: Proceedings of Game Set and Match 2, The Netherlands, Delft (2006) (6.3.2007), http://urtax.ms.mff.cuni.cz/ive/public/about.php
4. Brom, C., Pešková, K., Lukavský, J.: Determining trustfulness of records in episodic memory by means of an associative network. In: ECAL 2007. LNCS(LNAI), vol. 4648, pp. 243–252. Springer, Heidelberg (2007)
5. Brom, C., Pešková, K., Lukavský, J.: Modelling human-like RPG agents with a full episodic memory. Technical Report No. 2007/4 of the Department of Software and Computer Science Education, Charles University in Prague, Czech Republic (2007)
6. Dodd, W.: The design of procedural, semantic, and episodic memory systems for a cognitive robot. Master thesis. Vanderbilt University, Nashville, Tennessee (2005)
7. Ho, W., Dautenhahn, K., Nehaniv, C.: Autobiographic Agents in Dynamic Virtual Environments - Performance Comparision for Different Memory Control Architectures. In: Proc. IEEE CEC, pp. 573–580 (2005)
8. Ho, W., Dias, J., Figueiredo, J., Paiva, A.: Agents that remember can tell stories: Integrating Autobiographic Memory into Emotional Agents. In: Proc. of AAMAS, ACM Press, New York (2007)
9. Johnson, W.L.: Agents that learn to explain themselves. In: Proc. of the 12th Nat. Conf. on Artificial Intelligence, pp. 1257–1263. AAAI Press (1994)
10. Khaneman, D.: Attention and Effort. Prentice-Hall, New Jersey (1973)
11. Mateas, M.: Interactive Drama, Art and Artificial Intelligence. PhD thesis. Department of Computer Science, Carnegie Mellon University (2002)
12. Miller, T.: The magical number seven, plus or minus two: Some limits on our capacity for processing information. Psychological review 63(2), 81–97 (1956)
13. Neisser, U.: John Dean's Memory: A case-study. Cognition 9, 1–22 (1981)
14. Nuxoll, A.: Enhancing Intelligent Agents with Episodic Memory. PhD thesis, The University of Michigan (2007)
15. Peters, C., O'Sullivan, C.: A Memory Model for Autonomous Virtual Humans. In: Proceedings of Eurographics, Ireland, pp. 21–26 (2002)
16. Rickel, J., Johnson, W.L.: Animated Agents for Procedural Training in Virtual Reality: Perception, Cognition, and Motor Control. In: App. Artificial Intelligence, vol. 13 (1999)
17. Tulving, E.: Elements of Episodic Memory. Claredon Press, Oxford (1983

BEcool: Towards an Author Friendly Behaviour Engine

Nicolas Szilas

TECFA, FPSE, University of Geneva,
CH 1211 Genève 4, Switzerland
Nicolas.Szilas@tecfa.unige.ch

Abstract. Virtual agents, to be expressive, not only need algorithms for displaying the subtleties of human behaviour, but also require environments and tools so that people can author them. Because powerful algorithms are sometimes difficult to author, a compromise has to be found between algorithmic sophistication and authorability. Our approach for providing expressive characters at the behavioural level is based on such a compromise. This paper provides a model for describing behaviours which is author focused, while enabling some interesting algorithmic features such as parallelism and inter-agent coordination. The model has been implemented and simulation results are displayed.

Keywords: Virtual characters, behaviour engine, expressiveness, authoring, authorability, interactive drama.

1 Agents' Expressiveness

The visual representation of agents in virtual worlds has raised the question of expressiveness. These agents are not only rational agents, being able to take decisions according to their goals and the environment [8], but they also need to exhibit some lifelike attitude, and in particular display emotions within their behaviours [10].

Within this general goal consisting of increasing the expressiveness of virtual agents, our research has followed a specific approach based on the two strong following assumptions:

- Expressiveness can be improved at a level which is independent of the visual realism of agents. An extreme but illustrative case is the art piece called "Pixel blanc" [9], which displays the movement of one single pixel on a screen. The programming of the movement is such as the pixel seems to have life, "hesitate" before moving then suddenly "takes the decision" to move forward, etc. The visual representation of the agent consists of one pixel yet it is expressive, and a similar algorithm could be applied to a more realistic agent, a virtual dancer for example. This higher level of expressiveness, that we denote the behaviour level, is the focus of this paper.
- To the question "where does the expressive behaviour come from", there are two answers: from the agent itself or from the human who created it. We chose the

M. Cavazza and S. Donikian (Eds.): ICVS 2007, LNCS 4871, pp. 102–113, 2007.

latter. In that sense, the role of the agent is to mediate some expressiveness between two sets of humans: the creators of the agents and the users of the virtual world containing the agent. Of course, this is quite a specific mediation, which requires sophisticated algorithms for the agents. But it should not be omitted that to be effective, these agents need some creative people to use them to express themselves. We call these people "authors". One could argue that many existing systems do not use authors. They are designed by researchers and they are efficient. However, in these cases the researchers or engineers do play the role of authors, explicitly or implicitly.

Given these two assumptions, our goal is to design a behaviour engine in such a way that it is easily handled by authors, who obviously are not necessarily fluent in programming. The authoring issue is considered, in this research, as a primary requirement for the design of a behaviour engine, which contrasts with more classical approaches in which the most efficient engine is created before considering how an author could use it.

The rest of the paper is organized as follows. In the next section, the notion of behavioural level is more precisely explained. Then a review of existing behaviours engines is presented. Then we introduce *BEcool*, the proposed behaviour engine, its implementation, examples and future research.

2   The Behavioural Level

From the various systems using virtual agents that have been developed so far, a general scheme emerges regarding the software architecture. The systems tend to be hierarchically structured into three components as far as movement is concerned: animation, behaviour and reasoning. Animation includes body part movements, facial animation, path planing, gaze control. The animation level is informed by the upper levels to generate appropriate animations. Note that the animation level is usually combined with the other modalities such as speech. Behaviours are larger units which contains one or several animations. Behaviour management includes triggering the animations, running animations in parallel, blending animations, synchronizing animations between several characters, managing failures, managing priorities between competing behaviours. Reasoning is related to higher levels of intelligence such as strategic planing, decision making, affective reasoning. It is highly dependent on applications. In our current research, reasoning is performed by a central narrative engine [12], but other applications could use AI-based agent architectures.

The division into three levels is not always clear cut. For example, mechanisms for re-planing a path after a failure are usually included at the animation level, but they could also be managed at the behavioural level. It is however quite useful to modularize the architecture because each module can be developed and worked on separately. Furthermore, in terms of authoring, various skills are required for different levels. For example, graphical skill is needed for the animation level, not for the upper levels. Drawing an analogy with the field of drama, animation requires the skill of an actor, behaviours the skill of a director and reasoning the skill of a screenwriter.

There has been a lot of work about the control of agents' behaviours, often derived from previous work on robotics. We focus here on some systems that emphasize the role of the authoring.

An early system for authoring characters' behaviours is the system called *Improv* [7]. It allows the description of behaviours in terms of scripts. Scripts are sequences of simple actions (animations). Scripts are described in text form, making it easy for an author to write behaviours. The scripting language allows for non-deterministic behaviours, parallel behaviours and conditional choice between animations.

Other systems such as *Hap* use a hierarchy of goals [5]. Each goal contains a series of simple actions or subgoals, triggered if some conditions are met. Actions or subgoals can be triggered in parallel. Hap has been later extended into *ABL*, to carry out joint behaviours, that is the coordination of behaviours involving several characters [6]. *Hap/ABL* requires writing a list of goals with sophisticated parameters. It is a form of programming, making it unsuitable for authors. *ABL* was used to write an Interactive Drama [11], which demonstrated its usability for a large scale project, but also confirmed the fact that it requires proficient programming skills.

Other systems are based on finite state state machines [1][2][4]: a behaviour is represented as a node (state) in a graph, while transitions between behaviours are represented by arcs. More advanced systems use hierarchical finite state machines, which allow a behaviour to be described in nodes which can themselves be represented by an entire graph. This simplifies the representation of behaviours and enables reuse of sub parts of behaviours. Several finite state machines can run in parallel.

In terms of authoring, despite the visual representation (graphs), these systems require programming. In [1] for example, the graph structure is written in a dedicated language called HTPS, which is itself compiled into C++. HTPS is far more usable than C++, but it stills requires programming skills.

Commercial systems tend to focus more on the authoring aspect of behaviour authoring. A graphical environment for authoring hierarchical finite state machines was released ten years ago by a company named *Motion Factory* (the technology is now part of the *Softimage* software). The system not only provides a graphical editor for drawing hierarchical finite state machines for characters, but it also enables real time monitoring of the execution of the finite state machines, highlighting which states are active. However because the system is quite generic (for example any node or any transition could launch an animation or send a message), it remains difficult for the user (the author) to easily coordinate several animations beyond the simple case involving a sequence of animations.

Virtools' is another example of an authoring tool for 3D applications which includes a behaviour engine. Behaviours are described as flowcharts: building blocks are connected through a data flow. However, once again, *Virtools* is hard to use for non experts, because the charts cover all aspects of programming, including complex calculation, environment sensing, user interaction.

This short review illustrates that most behaviour engines developed so far have been focused on performance rather than authorability. In the following, we describe *BEcool*, an authoring tool that was designed with the intention that it be easy to use by an author.

3 BEcool

3.1 General Specification

Our goal is to find a compromise between authorability and performance. In other words, *BEcool* is a behaviour engine which aims at being easy to author, departing from systems based on language programming, while proposing features beyond the simple sequencing of events. *BEcool* is based on three main principles:

- Behaviours are represented by oriented graphs, where each node in the graph is an animation and each arc is a transition. These graphs are meant to be visualized by an author.
- Two nodes belonging to two disconnected subgraphs can be active at the same time (parallelism).
- Animation coordination is managed by events generated by animation nodes.

Note that a similar approach is proposed in [15], but for the management of the entire narrative. The behaviour engine coordinates with two other modules, receiving data from the first, and feeding data into the second. The first module, in our case the narrative engine [14], launches the behaviours by providing the name of the behaviour and its parameters while the second module, typically a game engine, displays the animations triggered by the behaviour engine. The game engine is also responsible for sensing the environment by sending events to the behaviour engine.

Why do we expect this approach to provide an efficient answer to the issue of expressivity in behaviour authoring? First, while text-based scripts are intuitive for organizing sequences of events, they become programming as soon as parallelism is involved. Graphs on the other hand, with their two-dimensional nature, allow a more intuitive representation of parallelism. Furthermore, as argued by Wages et al. [15], graphs are becoming commonly used in software, making them more familiar to potential authors. Second, our approach does not try to represent any specific organization of animations within a behaviour. Contrary to other systems discussed above, which are substitutes for a general programming language, the behaviour description is highly constrained, allowing only a few types of node and links that the author can "play with" in order to describe a behaviour.

3.2 Behaviour Description

In order to introduce the various features of *BEcool*, successive cases are presented.

Simple sequencing: The sequence of animations is simply represented by a chain of nodes (Figure 1). The plain arrow between two nodes means that the target node is activated when the source node is finished. When a node is activated, it triggers the animation attached to the node. More precisely, it sends a message to the animation engine, which executes the animation and then sends back a message when it has finished. One of the nodes is a start node, which means that it is activated as soon as the behaviour is launched. One of the nodes is an end node, which means that it sends a message that the behaviour is finished to the module that called *BEcool*. In Figure 1 and those which follow, the caption of the figure contains the command that is sent to the behaviour engine to execute a specific behaviour, where variable parameters are prefixed with an interrogation mark. In the figures themselves, each node contains an animation also described by variables, which are instantiated during runtime.

Fig. 1. Simple Sequencing. *Inform1(?actor , ?addressee, ?text).*

Branching: In Figure 2, at the start of the behaviour, one of two animations is triggered, walk or run, depending on the distance between two characters. The triggering of one of the transitions rather than the other depends now on events, associated to the transitions (arrows). These events (*far* and *close* in the example) are managed as follows: the behaviour engine sends not only the animation name and the associated parameters to the animation engine, but also a list of "sensors", that is a list of events, that have to be sent back when some conditions related to the 3D environment are met. In the example of Figure 2, the *Init* node asks the game engine to send *far* as an event when the distance between the actor and the addressee becomes greater than 5 meters. Note that this sensor is specific to the node it comes from. If the conditions of the *far* event mentioned above are met when another node is active, no event is sent by the animation engine.

Parallelism: In Figure 3, the mechanism of event management is used for the synchronizing of two parallel subgraphs. While the *Walk* animation is launched by the

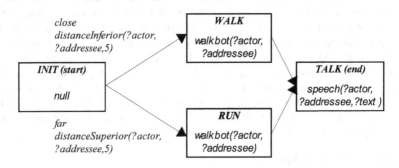

Fig. 2. Branching. *Inform2(?actor , ?addressee, ?text).*

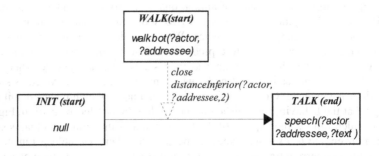

Fig. 3. Parallelism. *Inform3(?actor , ?addressee, ?text).*

first node, the event *close* is sent back by the animation engine as soon as the other character is at a distance smaller than 2 meters.

When this happens, this triggers another transition, in another subgraph, to activate the node *Talk.* this is represented by a dash arrow, pointing to the regular transition. This means that the target node is activated if both the source node is finished (here *Init*) and the event (here *close*) has been triggered.

Inter-actors coordination (joint behaviours): in order to coordinate several actors, we made the choice of a centralized authoring. One single behaviour is directing several actors, as if these actors were one entity. This approach is less general than an autonomous agent architecture [6], but it highly simplifies the architecture. In particular, no complex plan sharing is needed between two autonomous actors. More importantly, such an approach is more intuitive for an author, because it shares similarities with the activity of a stage director, who coordinates several real actors. In Figure 4, the behaviour is composed of two subgraphs, one for each of the two characters involved in the behaviour. The first subgraph means that the actor calls the addressee and then talks to him/her (when s/he gets close). The second subgraph means that the addressee walks towards the actor when s/he is beckoned and then listens to the actor. These two subgraphs are linked by two events, *end* (to notify that the call is finished) and *close* (to notify that the addressee is sufficiently close to start to talk).

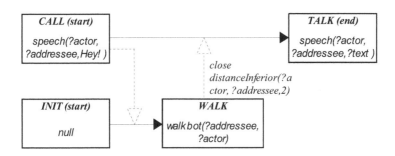

Fig. 4. Inter-actors coordination. *Inform4(?actor , ?addressee, ?text).*

3.3 Management of Multiple Behaviours

A behaviour is launched by sending a message to *BEcool* containing the name of the behaviour and a list of parameters.

When several behaviours are running at the same time, it might happen that the same actor is involved in two concurrent behaviours. A design choice has to be made between cancelling one of the behaviours, suspending one of the behaviours and restarting it later, blending the behaviours [3]. Again, a simple solution has been chosen, based on the priority affected to the behaviour when it is launched. When a character is involved in a running behaviour and a new behaviour involving the same character is asked to run (conflicting situation) the following rule is applied:

IF the priority of the new behaviour is equal to or greater than the priority of the running behaviour,
THEN cancel the running behaviour (*failure* message sent), without restarting and start the new one
ELSE send a *failure* message for the new behaviour.

In the current implementation, the fact that a character is involved in a behaviour is computed by checking if this character is one of the parameters of the behaviour. This is a clear limitation because even if a character only plays a peripheral role in a behaviour, it is considered as "busy" during the whole running of the behaviour. This could be improved in the future.

It has been mentioned above that there is no restart mechanism at the level of the behaviour engine. Thus BEcool does not take into account the continuous changes in the environments. But such mechanism can be implemented at the upper level, by the narrative engine in our case. In the whole architecture, that will be detailed below, the narrative engine might decide to relaunch the behaviour, if it is relevant from a narrative point of view (or a different point of view, if another type of module is managing the behaviour engine).

In some cases however, a behaviour might be interrupted by another behaviour, but it does not mean that the interrupted behaviour has failed. Suppose for example that John says to Mary: "I love you, I love you". If this behaviour is interrupted during the second utterance of the word "love", then an author should be able to decide that the behaviour is considered as successful, despite the technical failure. Thus we introduce two different messages:

–   the *success* message, which might be sent before the end of the animations;
–   the *end* message, which is sent when the last animation has succeeded.

If the *success* message is sent to the upper level, then the behaviour is considered as successful and the consequences of this can be computed, even if, later, the behaviour fails. If only the *end* message is sent to the upper level, then the behaviour is considered as both finished and successful. If the *failure* message is sent, then it is considered as a failure only if no *success* message has been received before. An example of such behaviour is depicted in Figure 5.

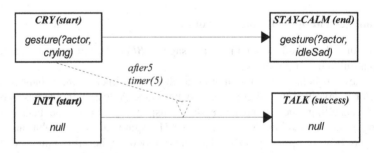

Fig. 5. Example of a behaviour which sends a *success* message before being finished

3.4 Programming Interfaces

A behaviour engine has two programming interfaces: one for the upper level (narrative engine for example) and the other for the lower level (animation engine).

At the upper level, a specific behaviour is launched by sending a launch message to *BEcool*, which contains the type of behaviour to be launched (*inform*, *gesture* for example) and the associated parameters. For example, the upper level would send the following data: *inform(john,mary,"Hi Mary!","did you know that Bill broke his arm?")*. In this example, there are two text messages in the parameters because the behaviour has two speech bubbles, one for greeting, one for the actual content of the information. Note that the actual string syntax is different (see Fig. 8 caption). *BEcool* then starts or tries to start the behaviour. During the execution, it sends back to the upper level a feedback among the following: *failure, success, end*.

At the lower level, *BEcool* sends messages containing the name of the animation (such as *walkbot, gesture, speech*, etc.), the associated parameters, which are either parameters of the behaviour sending the animation, or some hardcoded data and finally a list of events. For example, the following data could be sent: *walkbot(john,mary,(close,distanceInferior,john,mary,1))*, which means "launch the animation of john walking to Mary and during this animation send the *close* message as soon as the distance between john and mary is smaller than 1".

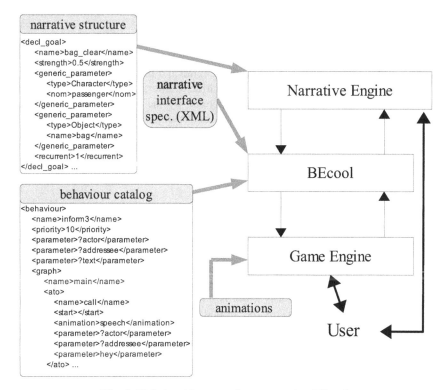

Fig. 6. Global architecture of a system using BEcool

3.5 Technical Architecture

In this section, the current implementation of *BEcool* is described, as well as its integration into a global technical architecture (see also [14] fore details). *BEcool* is developed as an independent program written in plain Java. No particular programming formalism has been used in the implementation. This program communicates with the two other modules via sockets. The upper module is either a narrative engine previously developed by the author [12][13] or a "tester", a simple Java program allowing the user to manually enter commands to be sent to the behaviour engine. Figure 6 represents the architecture, with the narrative engine.

The narrative engine is the *IDtension* program, fully written in Java. *IDtension* generates high level narrative actions such as "John informs Mary that Bob want to steal the money from Greg", or "John gives a letter to Mary".

The animation engine is a customization of *Unreal Tournament 2004*, a commercial game engine delivered with the eponymous game. The customization consisted in adding the socket communication and the event management, as described above.

Behaviours, as depicted in Figures 1 to 4, are coded in an XML file called the behaviour catalogue. The main elements handled by the grammar are:

- ato: node in the behaviour graphs (*ato* stands for *atomic behaviours*),
- link: simple link between nodes,
- conditionalLink: event-triggered link between nodes,
- event: specific event generated by a node when certain conditions are met,
- condition: condition related to an event.

The communication between the narrative engine and the behaviour engine is also specified with another XML file, called the narrative interface specification, in order to match the type of high level actions generated by the narrative engine (inform, encourage, dissuade, perform, etc.) to the behaviours. Typically, two different narrative actions can be played by the same behaviour. This XML file enables independence between the modules: there is no need to hard code within the narrative engine the names of the behaviours, neither the usage of their parameters.

4 A Complete Example

In order to better illustrate the behaviour engine discussed in this paper, we detail hereafter a full example of a behaviour. This behaviour is used whenever a non player character wants to convey an information to another non player character. In natural language, this behaviour can be described as follows: "the first character walks towards the other one (or just turns towards him if they are close), greet him when arriving at 2 meters – which makes the second character turns towards him – starts uttering the main message when arriving at 1 meter, and finally stops in front of the second character" while the main message is finishing.

This example is depicted in Figure 7. It involves linear sequencing, branching, parallelism, and inter-character coordination. It contains 8 animation nodes grouped into three subgraphs: one for the choice between walking or just turning, another one

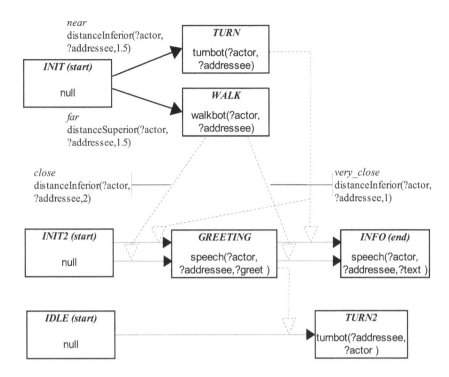

Fig. 7. A complete example of a behaviour: Inform_NPC(?actor, ?addressee, ?greet, ?text). This is an information transmission between two characters.

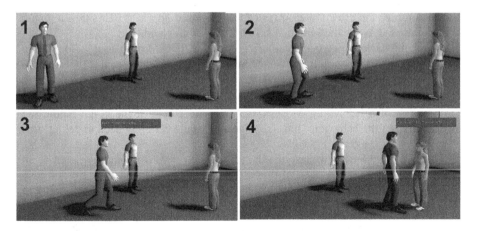

Fig. 8. Four successive screenshots of the execution of the behaviour depicted in Fig. 7. The string message sent to the behaviour engine is: "#launch::1234::inform_NPC::Bill::Kim::Good morning madam::May I see your passport?"

for the first character main speech sequencing and the last one for the second character's behaviour (turning). The dashed lines from the *TURN* and *WALK* nodes are designed to make sure that the end of these two alternative initial animations, the next animation in the speaker character is launched. The *WALK* node triggers two types of events, *close* and *very_close*, so that the *GREETING* and the *INFO* nodes are successively activated according to the distance between the two actors, in parallel to the walk animation. Figure 8 reproduces screenshots of the simulation of this behaviour, in the case where the two characters are far from eachother.

5 Conclusion and Future Work

In this paper, *BEcool*, an implemented behaviour engine has been presented. It has been designed to favour expressive authoring over agent intelligence. As a result, behaviours are fully described by visual graphs containing nodes for animations, arrows for sequencing, arrows' labels for environment's sensing (events) and dashed arrows for event-based animation triggering. This simple syntax allows sequencing, branching, parallelism and inter-characters behaviours.

The simplicity of authoring comes not only from the simplicity of this syntax, but also from the clear separation between levels. Behaviour authoring only involves the coordination of animations, not the "why" of the behaviours (reasoning), neither the "how" of the behaviours (animation level). In large scale production, these three levels would certainly involve three populations of authors.

The natural extension of this work is the development of a visual authoring tool. This tool would enable an author to directly draw the graphs within a dedicated software, without writing any XML line. This tool would produce the XML file needed by *BEcool* to run the behaviour (behaviour catalogue). The authoring tool development, that constitutes a considerable engineering work is a necessary step for the evaluation of the effective easiness of the proposed approach. This development has been initiated, using the Jgraph, a Java library for graph editing.

Beyond the lack of a visual authoring tool, is *BEcool* fully usable for a non programmer author? The graph depicted in Fig. 7 for example is not that easy to design. During our own usage of the graphs, we found that:

– It was easy to omit a case (a specific situation), resulting in a deadlock during the execution of a behaviour. Most of the time, we corrected the graph before the execution of the behaviour, but a regular user would certainly need to debug such cases.
– There is several ways to describe the same behaviour. This might be seen as an advantage, in terms of flexibility, but we find it problematic in terms of easy authoring. Indeed, an author should not waste time hesitating between possibilities for expressing a behaviour.

These remaining authoring difficulties suggest to define some graph templates, that is predefined graph structures that authors could reuse when writing a behaviour. These templates would guide the author by providing animation structures that occur recurrently in behaviours.

Despite the current limitations mentioned above, *BEcool* appears to be a promising tool for behaviour authoring, because it allows a totally visual representation of rather complex behaviours. Furthermore, its representation with graphs is quite compatible with the practice of storyboarding in the movie making industry.

References

1. Donikian, S.: HPTS: a behaviour modelling language for autonomous agents. In: Proc. of the fifth int. conf. on Autonomous agents, pp. 401–4082. ACM Press, New York (2001)
2. Granieri, J., Becket, W., Reich, B., Crabtree, J., Badler, N.: Behavioral control for real-time simulated human agents. In: Proc. of the 1995 Symposium on Interactive 3D Graphics, Monterey, CA, pp. 173–180 (1995)
3. Lamarche, F., Donikian, D.: Automatic orchestration of behaviours through the management of resources and priority level. In: Proc. of AAMAS 2002, Bologna, Italy, vol. 3, pp. 1309–1317 (2002)
4. Lau, M., Kuffner, J.: Behavior planning for character animation. In: ACM SIGGRAPH / EUROGRAPHICS Symposium on Computer Animation, pp. 271–280. ACM Press, New York (2005)
5. Loyall, A.B., Bates, J.: Hap: A reactive, adaptive architecture for agents. Technical Report CMU-CS-91-147, School of Computer Science, Carnegie Mellon University, Pittsburgh, PA (1991)
6. Mateas, M., Stern, A.: A Behavior Language: Joint Action and Behavior Idioms. In: Prendinger, H., Ishizuka, M. (eds.) Life-like Characters: Tools, Affective Functions and Applications, Springer, Heidelberg (2004)
7. Perlin, K., Goldberg, A.: Improv: A System for Scripting Interactive Actors in Virtual Worlds. In: Proc. of SIGGRAPH 1996, New Orleans, LA, pp. 205–216 (1996)
8. Russel, S., Norvig, P.: Artificial Intelligence: a modern approach, 2nd edn. Prentice Hall, Saddle River, NJ (2003)
9. Schmitt, A.: Le Pixel Blanc, http://www.gratin.org/as/txts/lepixelblanc.html
10. Smith, S., Bates, J.: Towards a Theory of Narrative for Interactive Fiction. Technical Report CMU-CS-89-121, School of Computer Science, Carnegie Mellon University, Pittsburgh, PA (1989)
11. Stern, A., Mateas, M.: Integrating Plot, Character and Natural Language Processing in the Interactive Drama Façade. In: Göbel, et al. (eds.) Proc. TIDSE 2003, pp. 139–151. Frauenhofer IRB Verlag (2003)
12. Szilas, N.: A Computational Model of an Intelligent Narrator for Interactive Narratives. Applied Artificial Intelligence 21(8), 753–801 (September 2007)
13. Szilas, N.: Interactive Drama on Computer: Beyond Linear Narrative. In: Papers from the AAAI Fall Symposium on Narrative Intelligence, Technical Report FS-99-01, pp. 150–156. AAAI Press, Menlo Park (1999)
14. Szilas, N., Barles, J., Kavakli, M.: An implementation of real-time 3D interactive drama. Computers in Entertainment 5(1) (January 2007)
15. Wages, R., Grützmacher, B., Conrad, S.: Learning from the movie industry: Adapting production processes for storytelling in VR. In: Göbel, S., Spierling, U., Hoffmann, A., Iurgel, I., Schneider, O., Dechau, J., Feix, A. (eds.) TIDSE 2004. LNCS, vol. 3105, pp. 119–125. Springer, Heidelberg (2004)

User Interactivity

Being There: Participants and Spectators in Interactive Narrative

Ruth Aylett and Sandy Louchart

MACS, Heriot-Watt University, Riccarton, Edinburgh. EH14 4AS, UK
{Ruth,Sandy}@macs.hw.ac.uk

Abstract. This paper considers the problem of evaluating interactive narrative and discusses the storification process through which a narrative is internalised. It establishes the range of roles that a user may take, and argues that the participant/non-participant distinction has a key role in storification. An experiment carried out as part of a larger test of a double appraisal approach to the creation of more dramatic characters is discussed. The results show that spectators and participants mark different stories as the most interesting, showing that this role difference does indeed impact their assessment of a narrative experience. The implications for story evaluation are discussed.

1 Introduction

This paper reports work carried out as part of an investigation in *emergent narrative* [2]. By this we mean the creation of story-like experiences in real-time using interaction between intelligent synthetic characters as a generative mechanism. The motive for this work is an attempt to resolve what we have described as *the narrative paradox* in which pre-authored plot structures conflict with the freedom of action and interaction characteristic of the medium of real-time interactive graphical environments. The central idea is that if a narrative experience can be generated without specifying a detailed plot in advance then the user can, alongside intelligent synthetic actors, jointly take responsibility for the unfolding of the story, and the user's actions become a positive contribution to the narrative experience rather than a potential obstacle to it.

An argument against this approach is that it cannot guarantee narrative structure because allowing characters to interact in real-time does not necessarily generate events that are experienced as narrative. One may respond to this position in a number of ways. For example, table-top and live-action role-play stand as empirical counter-arguments given that these are precisely generated by the role-playing activity of human participants as supported and shaped by the human game-master [14, 21]. One may also derive theoretical arguments from the game-master's pre-game work in designing a storyworld and rich characters capable of supporting the later jointly shaped narrative experience [16]. Fruitful analogies can be made with other art forms in which pre-authored structure and presentation-time improvisation are combined, as in a number of 20thC classical music pieces ('In C' by Terry Riley, the progenitor of minimalism, is one example).

M. Cavazza and S. Donikian (Eds.): ICVS 2007, LNCS 4871, pp. 117–128, 2007.

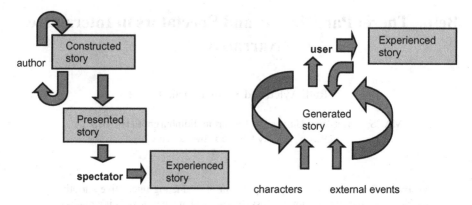

Fig. 1. Conventional narrative   **Fig. 2.** Interactive narrative

Finally one may respond practically by building and evaluating systems embodying the emergent narrative approach, as in the FearNot! interactive drama on the theme of education against bullying [1]. The last approach is often seen as the most convincing – 'the proof of the pudding is in the eating' - but it raises a further important question: how can one tell if an emergent narrative is successful?

There is in fact no agreed evaluation methodology for interactive narrative in general [20] and formidable problems must be faced in deriving one. Narratology has taken an analytical approach to its field, but analytical decomposition of the story artefact rarely attempts to answer the question of how 'good' a story is, though it may be used post hoc as a theoretical justification for a positive or negative aesthetic judgment. However both aesthetic judgement and supporting structural justifications are closely tied to the existence of a single narrative artefact with separate phases of authoring and presentation as illustrated in Fig. 1. It is an approach that invests heavily in the concept of audience – whether reader or spectator - as an objective evaluative vantage point from which *the* narrative artefact can be considered. Indeed, a classic view of authorship incorporates such a perspective as the author's desired effect, and while the more recent attack on the priority of author intentionality (the Foucaultian 'death of the author') undermines this linking evaluative function between authoring and presentation phases, if anything it puts still more emphasis on the narrative artefact itself ('the text').

Once interactivity is introduced, this position becomes untenable in our view. If interactivity means anything then the reader/spectator must be translated into the *user* (for want of a more generally agreed term), who, from the conventional perspective, is able to change the narrative artefact as it is presented, destroying its singular identity. Which then is the artefact that is to be evaluated? One must move from narratology to psychology and consider not *the* narrative artefact but the process through which the user engages with it and internalises it as a narrative experience – a process we have referred to as *storification* [2]. Figure 2 illustrates the process-oriented structure of interactive narrative. Within this framework, evaluation becomes subjective, contingent and process-oriented rather than objective, universal and artefact-oriented. Translating this into computing terms, the specific user experience and level of satisfaction must be considered, as argued in the case of Façade [12]. In principle, it is the storification process itself that ought to figure in evaluation, though accessing it is of course problematic.

2 Participative Narrative and Storification

The literature on narrative psychology focuses more on the impact narrative has on the overall psychology of the subject [9], and in particular whether it has lasting affective or cognitive impact, rather than on the process of storification itself. However it has increasingly been argued in the recent period that narrative thinking represents a fundamental structuring of human experience, both individual and collective [22] and that the internalisation of the individual's own past can be represented as an autobiographical memory [4], holding stories about the self.

It is tempting to see in this perpetual storification of individual life-experience the roots of external narrative as a way of socially restructuring autobiographical memory. A consequence of taking autobiographic memory as the basis for storification within narrative experiences, as distinct from ordinary life experiences, is a stress on the primacy of the self and its own actions within storification. The development of a theory of mind (ToM) which allows an individual to in some sense put themselves in the shoes of someone else is one way in which the self-oriented construction of autobiographical memory could be extended into a process engaging with the stories of others. The identification with a story character that is often felt by a spectator when they are narratively engaged might represent evidence of this extension.

However the existence of autobiographic memory as a more primitive structure, supplemented by ToM in order to process narrative as a spectator, suggests strongly that participating in a narrative experience might be experienced quite differently from spectating. Putting it into the context of an interactive narrative, spectating puts the user into the meta-narrative universe where participating forces them to commit to actions as a character within the narrative. As a spectator, characters are observed and ToM is used to infer inner state, for example emotion and motivation. As a participant, the motivation and emotion specific to the character must be felt, at least in imagination, in order to decide upon actions, so that the participating user *experiences* a commitment to act. From an evaluation perspective then, a story might have quite a different impact on storification and thus on evaluation in these two cases.

A further angle on this difference can be derived from work on systems of thought, originating in analysis of child development and learning [4]. Bruner identifies three specific such systems: enactive, in which a child uses action to manipulate objects; iconic, in which a child employs mental images which are primarily visual or otherwise sensorily-based; and symbolic, using language, reasoning, and other systems of meaning. In a participative narrative, these three systems are coupled very closely by the sense, reflect, act cycle required to act in the story-world, linked by the perspective of the specific role being played. In a spectating role, the input to these systems of thought is quite different, with a much greater importance for perceiving and reflecting over a range of characters, and little or no use of enactive systems.

3   Modes of User Engagement

Having considered in abstract the impact of participation as against non-participation in the story-world, it seems worth examining the actual roles that users play in relation to the narrative experience. Here, it would be a mistake to see interactivity in narrative as a binary attribute rather than a spectrum. At the non-interactive end is the conventional spectator or audience. At the completely interactive end is the participant user in a generative – or emergent - narrative. In between one can distinguish different degrees of coupling with the story-world at presentation time. The table below lists intermediate positions on this spectrum, each of which can be seen in specific software systems built by researchers as well in other media.

Table 1. User roles across a spectrum of interactivity

Degree of interactivity	Example
None	Conventional audience/spectator
Non-participant control	Conventional authoring
Non-participant influence	Forum Theatre spect-actors; Deus ex machina; many God games
Participant control points	Branching narratives
Freely participating character	LARP, Emergent narrative

Non-participant control is merely the reverse side of the audience/spectator: the author does not appear within the narrative experience but rather determines it with a control reaching variably down an abstraction hierarchy from overall theme, through abstract action sequences to details of character behaviour [2]. Film is the most extreme example given that the director may control even the detailed expressive behaviour of actors through the use of multiple cuts and editorial composition of the final artefact. Multi-media authoring typically also belongs in this class.

Non-participative influencing allows the user to retain the objective aspects of the audience while simultaneously taking a degree of authorial responsibility for the overall narrative experience and typically interleaves interactive and non-interactive phases. It covers a variety of forms in which the user does not directly participate in the narrative experience but nevertheless lacks full control over its unfolding, either because events outside of their control are simulated, or because characters have a degree of autonomy. 'God-games' such as The Sims are one example of this user role, but an interesting variant can be found in the spect-actors of Forum Theatre [3]. Here a section of the audience is allocated a character in the unfolding drama – the actor, playing in role – and meets with them to discuss what has happened in the previous episode and what they ought to do in the following episode. The actor will take the advice of their audience section unless it conflicts with their role, and is also allowed to halt an episode if it seems that further advice is needed. A version of this approach was implemented in the anti-bullying FearNot! system [1], in which episodes are generated as emergent narratives by synthetic characters but the user interacts with a victimised character between episodes and advises them.

It is also possible to act as a non-participant influencer by generating events exogenous to the characters [5] that impact their goals and force re-planning, by, for example, removing resources required by their current plan. The game-master of role-playing games may adopt either of these approaches: their use of non-player characters is well short of participation since they are essentially disposable vehicles for influencing the human players in specific ways.

Branching narrative can be seen as a minimally interactive form of participation. It allows a set of pre-authored possibilities to be navigated through decisions by the user at specific choice points, thus isolating interactive possibilities from non-interactive story-elements. This distinction becomes very clear in computer games in which entirely scripted cut scenes are interleaved with interactive choices which may themselves not result in much, if any, narrative structure. It has however been used effectively in pedagogically oriented systems [17] where meeting educational objectives may require this degree of authorial control at the expense of interactive freedom.

As one moves from the interleaving of interactive and non-interactive narrative components in a branching narrative, to the emergent narrative framework, interactivity becomes the determining influence on the user experience. For this reason, there are in principle as many stories as there are characters, since when dramatic interest is generated by character interaction, if every character has a narrative experience then by definition a participating user playing the role of any character will have one.

4   An Experiment in User Role and Evaluation

We have argued above that the participant and non-participant roles result in basic differences in the storification process. If true, then it must be taken into account in evaluating interactive narrative since the invisible internal structures that are being evaluated may well differ. In order to establish whether this is so in practice, we conducted an experiment using an emergent narrative system based on the FatiMA agent architecture [6] used in the FearNot! application already mentioned – see Fig. 3.

FatiMA is an autonomous agent architecture driven by cognitive appraisal, which generates internal emotional states using the OCC taxonomy [18] and links these to coping actions [13] generated both as emotionally-driven reactions and emotionally-driven planning [7, 8]. The detail of this architecture is not germane to the evaluation reported here but has been reported elsewhere [1]; it supports emergent narrative generated by interaction between characters each with a separately-configured instance of FatiMA as their 'mind'.

An entirely new scenario was created involving a group of characters with sharply conflicting goals exploring an Egyptian pyramid that turns out eventually to contain an alien spaceship. Although a graphical visualisation system can be linked to FatiMA characters, as was the case in FearNot!, in this instance a text-based visualiser was used to avoid the considerable effort involved in generating graphical assets.

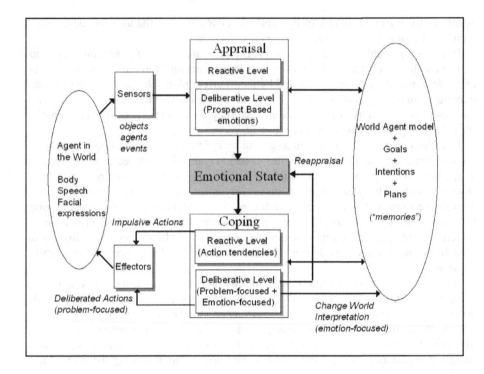

Fig. 3. The FAtiMA agent architecture

Two variants on the architecture of Fig. 3 were developed. In the first of these, characters were given the ability to evaluate the emotional impact of the set of actions they were considering by assuming that other characters would react as they did themselves. This involved relabelling actions as events and running them a second time through the agent mind as if they had happened to the character rather than being carried out by the character – a double appraisal approach. This allowed the action with the greatest emotional impact to be chosen. In the second variant, double appraisal was carried out using the actual minds of other characters in the scene – possible in a graphical world as it is not in the real world.

Different stories using this scenario (identical set and initial character definitions) are generated by the system on different occasions depending on which FAtiMA variant is implemented in the agent minds, due to the impact this has on the actions selected by characters. A further element of indeterminacy is added by the stochastic outcome of some physical actions, so that for example a character who is shot may be killed or may be just wounded. To take these variations into account, and also in order to prevent the user interface design from affecting results, the system was used to exhaustively generate all possible versions of a single short scene to be used for evaluation. This turned out to produce five distinct stories in the form of sets of language and non-language actions. The language actions were turned into text by hand by manually applying a standard templating approach used within FearNot! Of the resulting stories, number 3 and number 5 can be seen below in Appendix 1.

As previously mentioned, the evaluation of stories is an open research question. To date, apart from an interview-based study for a non-implemented system by Kelso et al [11], very little has been done in order to assess the intrinsic quality of a story. Much of the evaluation work for interactive storytelling systems has instead been oriented towards character believability or user interest in replaying stories [20, 12]. This study aimed to provide results that robustly support comparison with other work in the field and as a result sought to establish the statistical significance of those results. The one-Way-ANOVA approach was selected from other possible statistical approaches, as it is generally suitable for tests with similar data ranges to the ones in this study. The assumption was made that the differences between samples were normally distributed. Results have been subject to an analysis of variance (ANOVA) and are statistically significant to a 0.1 range[1] within the evaluation test batches. The probability of insignificance (p) and degree of significance (%R) are indicated for each result.

46 subjects (M 32 F 14) carried out a number of ranking and marking exercises with the five stories, of which two are the subject of this discussion. The table below details the participants' distribution.

Table 2. Participant distribution

	Male	**Female**	**Total**
Interactive	22	8	30
Non-interactive	10	6	16
Experts	10	1	11
Non-Experts	22	13	35

The evaluation plan designed for this application was composed of 5 different tests that aimed towards assessing the dramatic values of the stories generated by the system. T1 and T2 aimed to assess stories from a spectator perspective by presenting the user with a set of stories and asking them to mark and rank them by order of preference. Although T1 and T2 displayed the same stories to their test audience, these were slightly modified in T2 so that all stories contained the same amount of actions and therefore were of equal length. This was to establish whether the length of stories plays a role in the marking or ranking by the user. The actions used to lengthen the stories did not influence the appreciation of stories as none of them were reported as being either interesting or meaningful. The final three tests (T3, T4 and T5) aimed to assess stories from a participative perspective and presented the users with a role to play by making decisions for the game-master (T3) and one character (T4, T5) in every cycle. The user was presented with scenario situations and was asked to make decisions, which influenced the outcome of the overall story. Therefore, the users determined from their decisions, the story they experienced. These stories were also marked by users.

---

[1] Note that the 0.1 range is a non-standard statistical measure. However this approach suited the work carried out in this study.

Test A (T1/T2): Subjects read the set of stories generated by the system
Test B (T4/T5): Subjects played the role of the colonel and took decisions for him
In both cases, subjects:
  a.   Marked each on a scale 1-5 for dramatic interest and ranked them
  b.   Marked a certain number of actions for their meaningfulness (1-10 scale)
  c.   Marked a certain number of actions for their dramatic interest (1-10 scale)

The results can be seen in Fig.4 below (Participation 46 Male (32) / Female (14) – p= 0.091 / 90.9 %R)

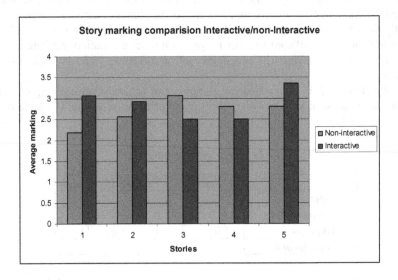

Fig. 4. Non-interactive and interactive marking of stories 1-5

Stories 1, 2 and 5 benefited from interactivity, and presented interactive markings that are significantly higher than their non-interactive counterparts. On the other hand, stories 3 and 4 display the inverse trend. Story 3 presents the best average in non-interactive marking, but only scores joint fourth in interactive marking. Story 5 presents the third best average in non-interactive marking but is first in interactive marking.

The effect of participation as against non-participation is clear in this experiment, though it is not at all clear exactly what in the stories causes this difference. The colonel takes more actions in story 5 including killing one of the party, and it may be that having to take the decision to do this increases the feeling of responsibility for what happens in the scene on the part of the user, or produces more highly emotionally-tagged elements in autobiographical memory. We have not yet found any experimental work in psychology that might clarify this finding, but modelling autobiographical memory, as has been done within FearNot! characters, though not within the scenario discussed here [10], suggests that very different structures would result from carrying out such an action and from observing it. The results cited do however make it clear that, as we argued above, if the experience of the user is seen as a key evaluation criterion, participative narrative must be evaluated through participation and not through spectating.

5 Conclusions and Further Work

In this paper we have reported an initial experiment in assessing the impact of participation in an interactive narrative on its evaluation. We have hypothesized that this result is related to the differences in the storification process we would expect to find in these two cases, especially if we relate storification to the construction of autobiographical memory. A further search of literature in psychology is required to establish whether existing experimental work can help to explain this result.

Another avenue could be explored by incorporating autobiographical memory into the characters, comparing the changes in a character that carries out an action and a character that observes it. This approach may provide interesting indications of the weight specific story-elements might have in the human mind, but one must add that it does not take account of the element of projection and imagination in the human engagement with narrative – the user is well aware that this is indeed narrative and not real life.

The result of the experiment described does however suggest very clearly that evaluating a participative narrative by observation is likely to provide very misleading results and that there is no alternative to trying to assess the experience of the participating user. Physiological monitoring, already used for evaluation of interaction with conversational synthetic characters [19] might be worth investigating here.

References

[1] Aylett, R.S., Louchart, S., Dias, J., Paiva, A., Vala, M., Woods, S., Hall, L.: Unscripted Narrative for affectively driven characters. IEEE Journal of Graphics and Applications 26(3), 42–52 (2006)

[2] Aylett, R., Louchart, S.: Towards a narrative theory of VR. Special issue on storytelling. Virtual Reality Journal 7, 2–9 (2003)

[3] Boal, A.: Theatre of the Oppressed. Theatre Communications Group, New York (1979)

[4] Bruner, J.: The Narrative Construction of Reality. Critical Inquiry 18(1), 1–21 (1991)

[5] Cavazza, M., Charles, F., Mead, S.J.: Character-Based Interactive Storytelling. IEEE Intelligent Systems 17(4), 17–24 (2002)

[6] Dias, J., Paiva, A.: Feeling and Reasoning: a Computational Model. In: Bento, C., Cardoso, A., Dias, G. (eds.) EPIA 2005. LNCS (LNAI), vol. 3808, pp. 127–140. Springer, Heidelberg (2005)

[7] Elliot, C.: The Affective Reasoner: A process model of emotions in a multi-agent system. PhD Thesis, Illinois (1992)

[8] Gratch, J., Marsella, S.: Tears and fears: Modeling emotions and emotional behaviors in synthetic agents. In: The Fifth International Conference on Autonomous Agents (2001)

[9] Green, M.C., Strange, J.J., Brock, T.C. (eds.): Narrative Impact: Social and Cognitive Foundations. Lawrence Erlbaum, Mahwah (2002)

[10] Ho, W.C., Dias, J., Figueiredo, R., Paiva, A.: Agents that remember can tell stories: integrating autobiographic memory into emotional agents. In: AAMAS. Proceedings of Autonomous Agents and Multiagent Systems, ACM Press, New York (2007)

[11] Kelso, M., Weyhrauch, P., Bates, J.: Dramatic presence. PRESENCE: The Journal of Teleoperators and Virtual Environments, MIT Press 2(1) (1992)

[12] Knickmeyer, R., Mateas, M.: Preliminary evaluation of the interactive drama facade. In: Conference on Human Factors in Computing Systems 2005 (2005)

[13] Lazarus, R.: Emotion and adaptation. Oxford University Press, NY (1991)

[14] Louchart, S., Aylett, R.S.: Solving the narrative paradox in VEs - lessons from RPGs. In: Rist, T., Aylett, R., Ballin, D., Rickel, J. (eds.) IVA 2003. LNCS (LNAI), vol. 2792, pp. 244–248. Springer, Heidelberg (2003)

[15] Louchart, S., Aylett, R.S.: Evaluating synthetic actors. In: Proceedings, AISB Symposia 2007, University of Newcastle, April 2007, pp. 439–445 (2007)

[16] Louchart, S.: Emergent Narrative – towards a narrative theory of Virtual Reality. PhD thesis, University of Salford (2007)

[17] Marsella, S., Johnson, W.L., LaBore, C.: Interactive Pedagogical Drama. In: The 4th International Conference on Autonomous Agents (2000)

[18] Ortony, A., Clore, G., Collins, A.: The cognitive structure of emotions. Cambridge University Press, Cambridge (1988)

[19] Prendinger, H., Becker, C., Ishizuka, M.: A study in users' physiological response to an empathic interface agent. International Journal of Humanoid Robotics 3(3), 371–391 (2006)

[20] Riedl, M., Young, R.M.: An objective character believability evaluation procedure for multi-agent story generation systems. In: Panayiotopoulos, T., Gratch, J., Aylett, R., Ballin, D., Olivier, P., Rist, T. (eds.) IVA 2005. LNCS (LNAI), vol. 3661, pp. 278–291. Springer, Heidelberg (2005)

[21] Tychsen, A., Hitchens, M., Brolund, T.: The Game Master. In: Proceedings of The Interactive Entertainment Conference 2005, Sydney, Australia (2005)

[22] Young, K.: The Neurology of Narrative. SubStance - Issue 94/95 30(1&2), 72–84 (2001)

Appendix 1 – Story 3 and Story 5

Speaker	Story 3 and Story 5 are identical to start with
Colonel	Let's be clear about what we are all about to do! No one has ever been down there! Our intelligence reported this site has a potential threat to our land security! We all know why we are here today! The technology possibly hidden in there is all that matters to us. In the unlikely event of an encounter of any type, we are to wipe this place down and make sure no one or nothing ever come out of this temple! Dead or alive!
Colonel	God bless you all. Military personnel in formation, the others behind me, keep an eye for traps, and do not lose sight of each other. All right, let's go!
Lieutenant	Yes Sir!
Sergeant	Following your order Sir!
Professor	Yes sir, yes!
Doctor	OK Sir!
Researcher	Following your order Sir!
	Colonel – Explores temple; Lieutenant - Explores temple; Sergeant – Explores temple; Professor – Explores temple; Doctor – Explores temple; Researcher – Explores temple

Speaker	Story 3		
Researcher	Colonel!, Here!, Here come here.. I have something odd here; it looks like a metal door with strange writings on top of it!
Colonel	Lieutenant! Have you got any idea what these inscriptions might mean?
Lieutenant	Colonel, these seem to be the same symbol set we recovered in New-Mexico. I couldn't translate it into the details but it seems to refer to some sort of farm land or exploitation next to a digit symbol by the look of things!. The last line reads the sun must meet the eye! Not sure what that means!
Researcher	I think I got it Colonel!! If you look down the diagram, it is not an eye, although it looks like it, but a hole in an eclipse type shape. Just like this door and the small round shape it has there in the middle. Let me orient the beam of light from my electric torch directly towards the hole!
	Door opens!

Speaker	Story 5
Doctor	Colonel, everyone, I have something strange there. There are some writings on this stone. A strange drawing and some hieroglyphs!
Doctor	Oh my god, this is fascinating, my grandfather was right all along! These are the four element guardians, they represent ancient gods, prior to the ones to which most of Egyptian mythology is based upon!. If the predictions are right they shall return within 7 days of their temple being penetrated! By entering this chamber we have provoked their return! The infidels will all die and I shall trust them with my life! This family talisman should revive the sacred guardians! Statues start to be animated and move towards the party
Colonel	In the chest, Fire at the red light in the chest! Fire! Fire!
	Statues are not stoppable Statues kill Lieutenant

Colonel	You stupid weirdo! (to Doctor)
	Colonel – Kills Doctor Statues stop and break into pieces
Colonel	OK nothing to worry about here!. Come on everybody; remember what we are looking for, a sort of entrance to another chamber!
Colonel	Here!, Here come here.. Hell man, I think this thing might be real after all.
Colonel	Professor! Do these hieroglyphs there above the door say anything of what might be behind it?
Professor	Hum Yes Colonel!, Well, this is strange, these do not appear to be conventional hieroglyphs! There are actually two sets of text there. One that can be interpreted as a death threat to any mortal disturbing the lizard gods, no idea whose these can be! The other one although it looks like Egyptian hieroglyphs contains many symbols I have never encountered and does not make any sense to me I am afraid!
Colonel	This is a door, therefore it should open one way or another, look for clues on the structure of the door and the wall!
	Colonel accidentally orients the light beam onto the door and triggers the opening of the door - End of scene!

Linkin TV4U: Text-Based Production and TV-Like Representation for Hyperlinked Video Blogging

Narichika Hamaguichi[1], Hiroyuki Kaneko[1], Mamoru Doke[2], and Seiki Inoue[1]

[1] Science and Technical Research Laboratories, Japan Broadcasting Corporation (NHK)
1-10-11, Kinuta, Setagaya-ku, Tokyo, 157-8510 Japan
{hamaguchi.n-go,kaneko.h-dk,inoue.s-li}@nhk.or.jp
[2] NHK Engineering Services, Inc.
1-10-11, Kinuta, Setagaya-ku, Tokyo, 157-8540 Japan
douke@nes.or.jp

Abstract. This paper considers various schemes for implementing hyperlinks between video programs, and proposes a way of representing hyperlinks inspired by the TV industry that is well suited to video content. By representing links in a TV-like manner, we found that hyperlinks could be incorporated in a way that does not detract from the fundamental nature and appeal of video media. In addition to proposing a new way to implement hyperlinks, the paper also describes a prototype system with a full range of hyperlink-handling capabilities including a link description format, a link creation function for the script production environment, a link representation function for the playback environment, and a link management function for the distribution system.

Keywords: Video Blogging, Hyperlink, TV4U, TVML.

1 Introduction

The phenomenal global penetration of the Internet can be largely attributed to the simplicity and popularity of various schemes for incorporating hypertext in the World Wide Web, HTTP, HTML, and Web browsers that were adopted from the very beginning of the Internet era. While capabilities used to be confined to text and still images, the Internet has now evolved to the point where its ability to handle video, audio, and the whole range of multimedia content is taken for granted. But even though the Internet has embraced multimedia, there has been little progress in hypermedia beyond traditional hypertext, and even for handling video content for video sharing services over the Internet, no hyperlink standard has been established.

A key reason, we believe, that hyperlinking has not developed for dealing with video content is that so far no generally accepted method for representing video hyperlinks has been developed. For example, in the case to hypertext, links in text on a Web browser are generally displayed in underlined blue text, and if the cursor is moved over a hypertext hot spot, the cursor changes to a pointing finger icon. A familiar click sound is heard when a user clicks on a hypertext link (behavior differs somewhat from browser to browser). This method of representing hyperlinks is extremely simple yet

M. Cavazza and S. Donikian (Eds.): ICVS 2007, LNCS 4871, pp. 129–138, 2007.

powerful, and has been universally adopted so that everyone recognizes hypertext links at a glance when they see them.

This paper focuses on how hyperlinks are represented in video material, and we try to define the best way for implementing hyperlinks in video content. In addition, the paper also describes a prototype system incorporating all the basic functions needed to support hyperlinks: a hyperlink description format, a link creation function for use in writing scripts, a hyperlink representation function for the playback environment, and a link management function for the distribution system.

2   Conventional Ways of Representing Hyperlinks in Video

Although ordinary hypertext still has not been surpassed, there have nevertheless been many attempts to develop a hyperlink scheme specifically for video. Figures 1-3 illustrate some of the classic methods for representing hyperlinks, and we have highlighted the attributes and drawbacks of each approach.

Fig. 1. External link approach: With this method, links are provided outside the video content. For example, this approach might be used to provide links to data broadcasts from digital TV [1] or to combine banner ads with video distribution services [2]. The association between the main content and the link information is significantly weakened by the fact that they are separated on the screen, and the overall uniformity as a medium is also weak. In some cases, the visual effect is unsightly or jarring.

3   TV-Like Hyperlink Representation

Based on our brief survey of attributes and shortcomings of different ways of representing hyperlinks in video, and based on a comparison with hypertext, we have identified a number of hyperlink requirements. Hyperlinks for video should

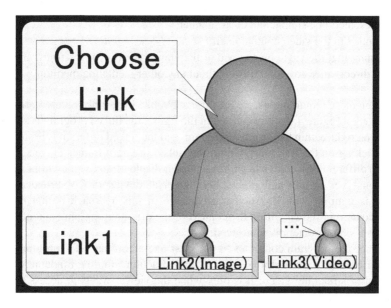

Fig. 2. Interactive approach: In this approach, the video is actually stopped and the viewer is presented with the option of selecting a link. For example, this is the case in flash content and multi-story games [3]. Because this method interrupts the temporal flow of the video and requires the viewer to perform an action, this approach tends to detract from the fundamental nature and appeal of streaming video.

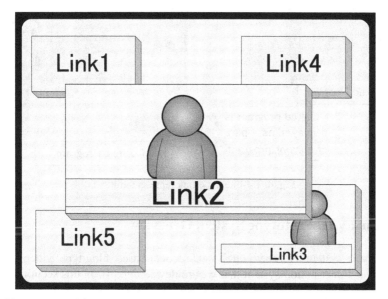

Fig. 3. List approach: Links are arranged on the screen to enabling viewers to quickly grasp the full range of available options. This is common approach in implementing graphical interfaces for video or image databases. While this provides a good overview of various video resources that are available, it represents more of a simple database viewer than video content per se.

- be represented in a simple and clear manner,
- be included in the video content itself,
- not require that the video be stopped or the viewer perform any actions, and
- permit direct video-to-video links without any other mediating medium.

Based on these requirements, we propose a TV-like hyperlink representation model as illustrated in Figure 4. As one can see in the figure, the linked program is shown in a small screen right within the original program, and the linked program is brought to the fore by clicking on the link mark within the linked program frame. This technique of showing a different broadcast site within a smaller display frame right within a program is traditional yet simple and practically universal device of TV broadcasting, so everyone is familiar with it. Another advantage of this approach is that the linked program content is shown within the context of the original program content, so sense of unity as a single content is reinforced.

And since the program continues to play just like an ordinary TV program without the viewer having to do anything, there is no distraction from the fundamental nature and appeal of streaming video. It is only when the viewer wants to access the linked program that an action—clicking on the linked program—is required. This immediately takes the viewer to the linked program accompanied by a sound effect and visual effect of being drawn into the linked program screen.

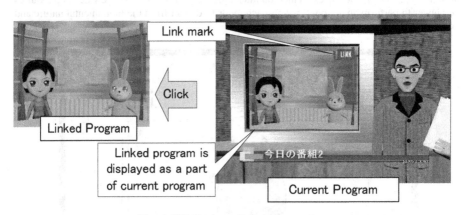

Fig. 4. TV-like hyperlink representation

4   Linkin TV4U Prototype System Overview

The prototype system is based on TV4U, a text-based blog-type video content production and distribution system that we are developing [4]. In this section we will examine all the functional capabilities of this prototype system from content production and link editing on the Script Editor to video production and distribution on the server side and video playback and link presentation of the client side.

4.1   Script Editor: Video Production and Link Editing

This system features a script editor called TV Creator shown in Figure 5, that makes it extremely easy for production users to create their own video content. TV Creator has an intuitive interface very similar to a word processor, and production users create scripts by simply writing spoken lines and defining actions on a simple form, pasting in

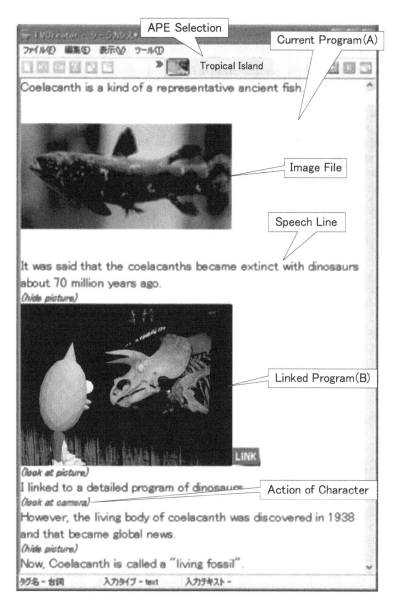

Fig. 5. TV Creator

still images and other types of materials, and choosing an appropriate APE direction style sheet [5] (see the Appendix). User-created scripts are converted to XML scripts, which are then made freely available to others via the Internet by uploading the scripts to the TV Server, as described in the next section.

TV Server provides an index of all clips and video content previously produced and made available by other users. One can easily embed a link to this other content by accessing TV Server from TV Creator, selecting the material you want to link, and pasting the linked content right into your own script like any other kind of material content at the place you want the link inserted (Linked Program (B) in Figure 5).

4.2 Server Side: Video Creation and Distribution

The primary functions of the TV Server are to manage XML scripts and to provide a public site where programs can be freely accessed. It also features a system (TV Renderer & Encoder [6]) on the back end that renders and encodes video based on XML scripts uploaded to the TV Server, so content produced by production users can be made available in movie file format. In other words, when linked programs are inserted by TV Creator as described in the previous section, the files converted to movies are inserted when linked programs are invoked and played back.

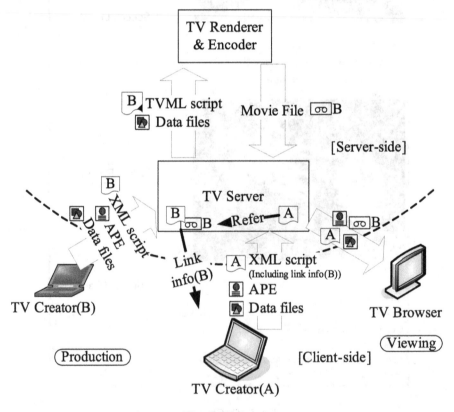

Fig. 6. TV Server

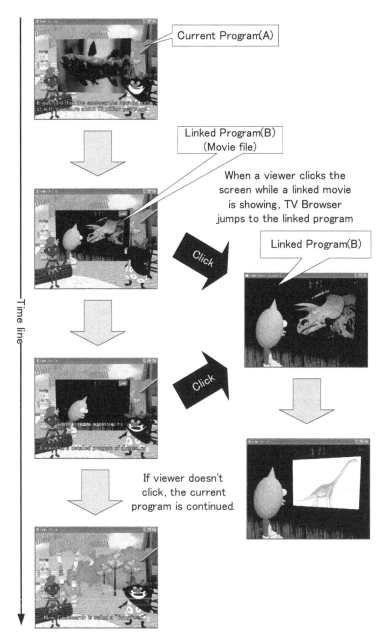

Fig. 7. TV Browser

Figure 6 shows the typical flow of data through the system. XML script (B) created by TV Creator (B) is converted to TVML script (B) [7] (see also the Appendix) by the TV Server, then sent to the TV Renderer & Encoder. The TV Renderer & Encoder produces Movie File (B) based on the TVML script and the data files, and returns the file to the TV Server. Then if a production user creating a script on TV Creator (A) wishes to embed a link to video content (B), he acquires URLs for the XML Script (B) and Movie File (B) from the index on the TV Server, embeds the link information in XML Script (A), and uploads the script to the TV Server where it can be accessed by others. For example, if someone wants to view Program (A) that has now been made available, he downloads XML Script (A), the APE style sheet, other data files, and Movie File (B) that is linked to the program. The program is then synthesized and played back on the client side.

4.3   Client Side: Video Playback and Link Presentation

Special playback software called TV Browser is used to play the video programs. To play a program, the viewer accesses the TV Server with TV Browser and downloads the set of elements making up the program—the XML script, the APE style sheet, and any additional material. The set of elements is then converted to a TVML Script which is played by the browser embellished with computer graphics effects, synthesized voices, and so on (see the Appendix).

Figure 7 illustrates how a program is viewed on the TV Browser. In this example, a link to Program (B) is embedded in Program (A). The linked movie can be inserted anywhere in the current program, and as shown in the figure, plays within its own linked screen in the current program with a Link Mark widget displayed in the upper right corner of the small screen. If the viewer clicks on the screen while the Linked Program (B) movie is playing, TV Browser jumps to the actual Linked Program (B) and begins playing the Program (B) from the beginning. On the other hand, if the linked program appears to be uninteresting and the viewer continues to watch Current Program (A) without doing anything (i.e., without clicking on the browser), the Linked Program (B) movie abruptly ceases within five seconds, while Current Program (A) continues. Since the viewer does not have to do anything in this process, it is essentially the same as ordinary TV watching.

5   Conclusions

We surveyed the basic ways in which hyperlinks are represented in video, and highlighted the drawbacks associated with each approach. Based on our observations and comparison of successful hypertext approach, we identified the requirements for representing hyperlinks in a way that is most suitable for video, proposed a TV-like scheme for representing hyperlinks, and constructed a prototype video production, distribution, and viewing system that implements the proposed scheme.

When hyperlinks were incorporated in video materials such as multi-story games in the past, the producer(s) had to create all of the linked video content as well as the main program. Production costs thus increased as the number of links increased, and it was not a very efficient approach. The system we propose here leverages distributed production of content by many production users in much that same way as hypertext on the World Wide Web, so we have avoided the inherent inefficiency of the multi-story game by enabling production users to freely incorporate links to other users' content.

Considering the remarkable user friendliness of the Linkin TV4U production system with its simple and intuitive approach to script writing and description, we believe that the addition of the new linking capability described in this paper could lead to a vast network of hyperlink-interconnected video content.

For representing hyperlinks, we have come up with a scheme that is simple yet powerful based on a long-established technique of TV program production and that is analogous to the way hypertext links are formatted and presented in Web browsers. We anticipate that, once this kind of linked representation becomes more generalized and catches on, it will lead to the emergence of a dynamic hyperlink culture linking and cross-referencing all kinds of video material. We plan to conduct field trials to verify the viability and effectiveness of the proposed methods formatting and representing embedded links in video content in our future work.

Appendix: APE Direction Style Sheet and TV Program Making Language TVML

Overall program direction style is very easily defined in this system by selecting an APE (Automatic Production Engine) direction style sheet in much the same way that bloggers choose a design template. Figure 8 illustrates how video programs are generated based on the APE style sheets. The production user first writes a script using the wordprocessor-like TV Creator described earlier. TV Creator outputs the script in XML format. The XML script interworks with APE to produce a playable program implemented in a script language called TVML (TV program Making Language).

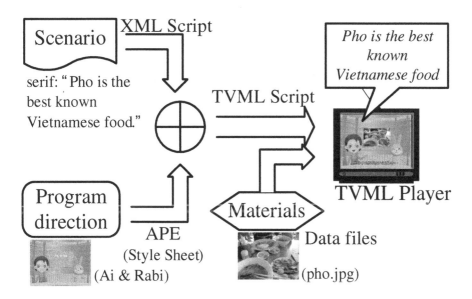

Fig. 8. Flow of program production based on APE direction style sheets

TVML is a self-contained language that can represent every aspect of a TV program including computer graphics characters, cameras, lighting, sets, props, background music, movie playback, superimposed effects, titles, and so on. When a TVML script is input to TVML Player (a software component installed on a PC), a TV-like video program is produced on the screen that is replete with computer graphics and the characters speaking in synthesized voices. APE is essentially a program direction style sheet with a set of TVML templates, and through conversion, the program directions are output as a TVML-encoded script. The TV Renderer and TV Browser then use TVML Player component to generate and display the TV-like video program.

References

1. http://www.nhk.or.jp/digital/en/digitalbroad/04_2_data.html
2. http://www.youtube.com/
3. http://www.mystworlds.com/
4. Hamaguchi, N., Doke, M., Hayashi, M.: Internet-Based Personal TV Station Enabling Individuals to Produce, Distribute, and View TV Programs. In: The IADIS International Conference WWW/Internet 2005, Proceedings, Lisbon, Portugal, vol. 1, pp. 52–60 (2005)
5. Hayashi, M., Doke, M., Hamaguchi, N.: Automatic TV Program Production with APEs. In: 2nd Conference on Creating, Connecting and Collaborating through Computing, Kyoto, Japan, pp. 20–25 (2004)
6. Hamaguchi, N., Doke, M., Hayashi, M., Yagi, N.: Text-based Video Blogging. In: WWW 2006. Proceedings of the 15th International World Wide Web Conference, Edinburgh, Scotland (2006)
7. http://www.nhk.or.jp/strl/tvml/

Anime Blog for Collecting Animation Data

Kaoru Sumi

National Institute of Information and Communications Technology,
3-5 Hikaridai, Seika-cho, Soraku-gun, Kyoto 619-0289, Japan
Kaoru@nict.go.jp

Abstract. We introduce an anime blog system that enable users to create blogs containing animation by searching for and selecting animations or images from a database by using simple words. This system collects animation or image data using consumer-generated databases, in the manner of Web 2.0. If users cannot find appropriate data, they can easily upload new data that they have created. Our animation database, Animebase, correlates natural language with three-dimensional animation data. When an animation is uploaded, the system applies motion data of this model to other models and generates new anima-tions, which are then stored in Animebase. Our basic concept is that the animation data corresponding to natural language is useful for enabling novice users to create content. We discuss the difficulty of this approach to collecting anima-tions and mention future work.

1 Introduction

We have developed an anime blog system that collects three-dimensional (3D) animation data using consumer-generated databases, such as those expected to ap-pear on Web 2.0. Users have indicated a need for a more appealing way to create animation in blogs. Animation data, such as models and motions, contained in the animation data-base called Animebase, is linked to natural language data, such as subject, predicate, and object, to enable users to create 3D animation data. In the system's interface, a subject is treated as a character, and a predicate is treated as an action. An object is treated as a character, article, or background picture. Users who are interested in using animations in their blogs can register and use animations not previously stored in the database.

In this system, a user inputs a scenario based on a pair of subject and predicate, or a pair of objects, and then selects an appropriate animation from an overview for the scenario. Then the user can select an appropriate animation from the overview. If there is no appropriate animation, the user can create one and upload the animation data. The system has several animation characters and background pictures. Once a user uploads a new animation, this motion can also be applied to all the other char-acters, and any user can create other new animations by reusing the uploaded motion data. We think that, from the perspective of collecting large animation data corre-sponding to natural language, it is highly significant that our system can be used for content generation easily and its wide application.

M. Cavazza and S. Donikian (Eds.): ICVS 2007, LNCS 4871, pp. 139–149, 2007.

2 Background

The e-Japan 2002 program called "Promoting content distribution" was estab-lished as a government policy to increase the number of creative resources available to people who create TV programs, movies, animations, and so on. The committee of content special examination focused on establishing professional skills by creating an educational (university based) industrial complex, and the Ministry of Public Management focused on increasing the number of people, such as creators and producers. Other countries have a variety of policies: a national system of content protection exists in the USA and Canada, promotion of export content occurs in the UK, and promotion of creation occurs in France and Korea.

However, actually creating content is currently very time consuming and expensive. This limits users' creativity in doing trial and error and practicing. In this paper, we report developing a system that enables novice users to create contents using Animebase, which corresponds 3D animation data, such as models and motions, with natural language data, such as subjects, predicates, and objects.

Attempts to transform natural language (NL) into animation began in the 1970s with SHRDLU [1], which represents a building-block world and shows animations of adding or removing blocks. In the 1980s and 1990s, more applications [2][3][4] appeared, in which users operate human agents or other animated entities derived from NL understanding. Recently, there has been research on the natural behavior of life-like agents in interactions with users [5][6][7]. The main theme in this line of inquiry is the question of how to make these agents as human-like as possible in terms of dialogicality, believability, and reliability.

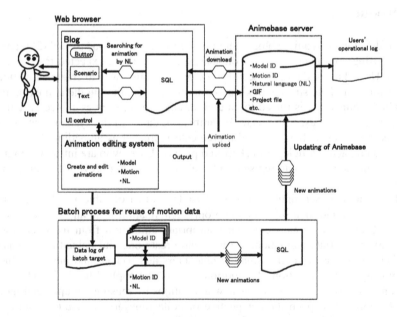

Fig. 1. Overview of Process Flow for the anime blog system

WordsEye [8] is a text-to-scene generation system that includes spatial data. In contrast, our system generates animations but not scenes.

Our main approach is to generate animation content by separating animation data into parts and re-forming it to create new animations by reusing these parts stored in a consumer-generated database.

There have been some successful trials using consumer-generated databases. For example, Wikipedia[1] is an encyclopedia that enables users to edit Web pages. You-Tube[2] is a free video access site that lets users view and upload videos freely. Yaku-shite-net[3] is a framework that generates and edits dictionaries for translation engines (Japanese and English) by letting users manage their own areas of expertise.

The anime blog system that we have developed is a consumer-generated database based on natural language. It was developed to enable novice users to generate content easily by combining natural language with animations.

3 Anime Blog System

The process used in the anime blog system is outlined in Figure 1. When a user inputs a subject and a predicate as a scenario and selects search, the system searches the animation database called Animebase for animations based on the entered sce-nario. When the user inputs objects or a background as a scenario and selects search, the system searches Animebase for images based on this entered scenario. The sys-tem then displays lists of animations or images as search results. If the users cannot find appropriate animations in Animebase, they can register animation data using an animation editing system. They can also upload image data as animation background. Regardless of their experience, users can easily use the animation editing system to provide alternate sources of data. When they upload new animation data with natural language expressions (predicate) developed using this system, batch processing auto-matically occurs at predetermined times. After the batch processing, the system creates more animations using the newly uploaded animation motion and natural language expression (predicate) and then stores them in Animebase by reusing the motion data of the new animation and applying it to the motion of other characters.

The following sections describe data selection by scenario, animation data regis-tration using the animation editing system, and animation data reuse in Animebase.

3.1 Animation Data Selection by Scenario

A snapshot of the system is shown in Figure 2. When the user inputs a scenario as a subject, an object, a background, or a predicate and selects animations and images, a scene is created. A full story in a blog contains one to ten scenes and can be reviewed continuously. Free text input areas, like those for a regular blog, can also be dis-played.

Essential input items include a subject and a predicate. There are free text areas for subject and predicate. The Japanese case particles "ga" and "ha" (which are case

---

[1] http://en.wikipedia.org/

[2] http://www.youtube.com/

[3] http://www.yakushite.net/

particles of a subject) can be selected using a toggle. In Animebase, a subject corresponds to a character, and a predicate corresponds to a motion. After a user inputs these things and selects search, the system searches Animebase for animations based on these entries. The user can manually select the most appropriate animation from lists of animations displayed as a result of searching. The user-input predicate must be entered in the basic form to avoid using inappropriate forms of the verb.

In addition, the user can input two complements—an object as an article or an object as a character—and a background. The case particles, "wo", "de", "to", "ni", "kara", "yori", and "he" in Japanese (which are case particles of complements) are prepared and users can select one from a list. In the case of background, after the user inputs free text, selects a case particle and selects search, the system searches Animebase for images based on these entries. The user can select an appropriate image from the lists of images displayed as the search result. In the case of an object as an article, the user can select search by articles from Animebase. In the case of an object as a character, the user can select search by animations from Animebase.

These animations and images are presented as transparent GIF files. A scene is created by continually overlapping the animations and images. The duration of one scene may be from a few seconds to up to ten seconds. Presenting all the scenes enables the whole story to be reviewed. A text area for free input by users can be copied from the scenario area at the user's request. One piece of work in the user's blog contains the text of scenarios (a minimum of one and a maximum of ten) with animation and blog-free text. The user can search these works, and those of other users, from the database by entering a word corresponding to the animations or images or the author's nickname.

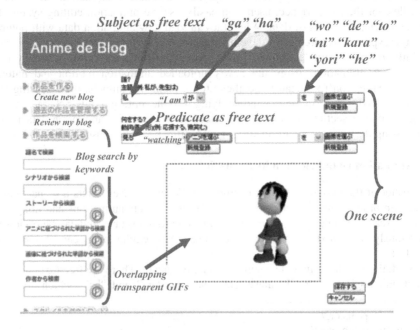

Fig. 2. A snapshot of the anime blog system

3.2   Animation Data Registration

When users create an anime blog and are unable to find any appropriate images or animations in Animebase, they can upload images or animations that they consider suitable. When users upload images and animations, they register some words corresponding to the uploaded information. For images, a word is corresponds to a background, and users can upload GIF files that they have prepared. Each file must be less than 60 MB in size. For animations, a word is a predicate, and the system provides the animation editing system at the anime blog system's Web site. The system recommends file formats with 320 * 240 pixels.

In the animation editing system, even novice users can instinctively create animations using the spatial keyframing[9]. This method uses animation data to record a user's realtime operations. As Figure 3 shows, the user set keys (yellow balls), and based on each key, he or she sets key poses ((1),(2),(3), or (4)). If the user only changes the position of the handle using the pink ball, he/she can easily create a complicated animation.

When the user creates animations using our animation editing system, a project file is created. This project file includes a virtual reality modeling language (VRML), animation file, a file of the position of the model, a file of the primary position of the model, a file of the cursor position, a file of the camera's parameters, and a file distinctive of the model.

The animation editing system is a Java applet using Java3D, so it is easy for users to use without downloading a program.

New characters can also be uploaded. The hierarchy structure among the characters must be the same because of the function for reusing the motion data for other characters. Our system has two types of hierarchy structure data as a human model (cartoon type and real type), and the system can reuse motions among characters of the same hierarchical type.

Fig. 3. Four snapshots of the animation editing system

3.3 Data Reuse of Animebase

The project file is created by using the animation editing system. When the animation project file is uploaded by a user, batch processing of an animation reusing a motion assigned to other characters automatically occurs at predetermined times.

Each record in Animebase contains a character's ID to identify each character, a motion ID to identify each motion, natural language information based on the mo-tion or the image, a project file, and a GIF animation for displaying in the blog page.

When a new motion ID for the motion is registered by new animation being stored in Animebase, the motion will be added to the other characters. First, the system creates new VRML motion files using the original VRML motion file. After that, the system creates each project file using the original project file and GIF animation for displaying the animation in the blog page using Java3D rendering. Finally, the files are registered in Animebase with national language information. This reuse batch process runs only among character models of the same hierarchy.

4 Application of Animebase: Interactive e-Hon System

Animebase is applicable to education, marketing, communication support, and research areas. It will make content generation by novice users richer and easier. As an example, this section introduces the interactive e-Hon system, which helps children to understand content.

We have developed a system that translates text into animation called Interactive e-Hon (*hon* is the Japanese word for book) [10]. This system helps children understand difficult content through the use of animation. Our idea is that visual data attracts a child's interest and that the use of actual examples, like metaphors, facilitates understanding because each person learns according to their own unique mental model [11][12], formed based on their background.

Interactive e-Hon is a fully automatic word translation medium that provides expression through the use of 3D animation and dialog explanation to help users understand Web content or any other electronic resources, such as news, novels, and essays. For a given content, animation and a dialog explanation spoken using a voice synthesizer are synchronized.

The system framework of Interactive e-Hon is shown in Figure 4. Interactive e-Hon generates documents with semantic tags (.tag files), morphological and dependency structure information (.morph files), and animation files (.ehon files), based on the .x file format of DirectX. Initially, the system attempts to reduce long, complicated sentences to simple ones. One animation and one dialog are generated for each sentence and then played at the same time.

The semantic tags consist of items concerning time, space, weather, and objects (from one to many objects).

The items are subdivided as follows:

time (season, date, time),

space (continent, country, region, scene),

weather

object (name, category, feature, position, action (name, category, feature, target (name, category, function, feature)))

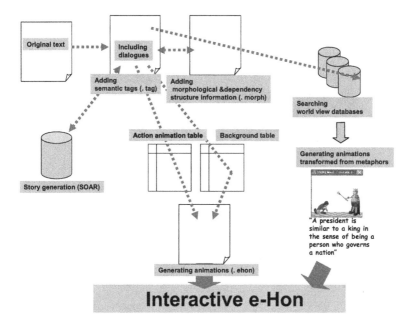

Fig. 4. Framework for Interactive e-Hon

	subject	predicate	object
①	president	go	hunting
②	president	meet	bear
	bear	is met (passive)	bear
③	president	shoot	bear
	bear	is shot (passive)	
④	president	refuse	to shoot
⑤	president	help	bear
	bear	is helped (passive)	

Fig. 5. Example of the devided sentences

To look up semantic categories, the system uses both the Japanese morphological analyzer and the Japanese lexicon, as mentioned above.

An animation is selected based on the action animation table and the background table. The action animation table includes an action's name, category, and modifier; an object's name, category, function, and modifier; and a priority score. If these registered patterns correspond to the pattern in the sentence, a registered animation is selected.

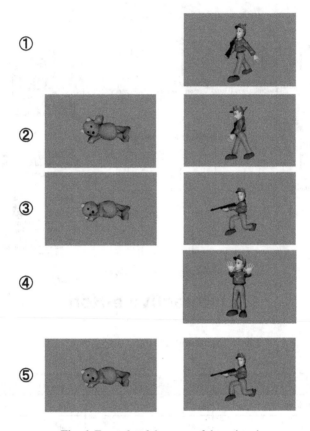

Fig. 6. Example of the parts of the animation

The background for the animation is selected from the background table. The table includes a scene ID, season, year, month, day, hour, minute, continent, country, region, scene, weather, and priority score. If these registered patterns correspond to the pattern in the sentence, a registered background is selected. This depends on the registration in the table.

Basically, the registration is as follows:

- a subject word corresponds to a character.
- an object word corresponds to a character or an object in the animation.
- a predicate word corresponds to a motion in the animation.

For example, if the sentences are divided into a list (Figure 5), the system picks models and motions based on the words (Figure 6). The models, motions, and background picture are then combined to generate a single animation.

Figure 6 shows a list in which each sentence has a subject, predicate, and object.

(1) Picking the President model using the words "go hunting", entering "go" as the motion (Figure 6-(1)), and using the background from the animation database generates an animation.

(2) Picking the President and dying bear models, entering "President, meet, bear" and the passive expression "bear, is met" (Figure 6-(2)), and using the background JPG file from the animation database generates an animation.

(3) Picking the President and dying bear models, entering "President, shoot, bear" and the passive expression "bear, is shot" (Figure 6-(3)), and using the background JPG file from the animation database generates an animation.

(4) Picking the President model, entering "refuse" as the motion (Figure 6-(4)), and the background from the animation database generates an animation.

(5) The system then generates the next animation of "president, help, bear".

Picking the President and dying bear models, entering "President, help, bear" and the passive expression "bear, is helped" (Figure 6-(5)), and using the background JPG file from the animation database generates another animation.

Our experiment indicated that Interactive e-Hon is an effective and powerful tool that assists child understanding. However, the system needs more detailed contents linked to each word to be able to create appropriate animation. Animebase will be helpful for providing storage as a rich animation database linked to several words.

5 Discussion

The anime blog system we developed gathers animation and image data (model, motion, background) corresponding to natural language information (subject, predicate, background, and object) and stores it in Animebase. Our evaluation of the system indicated that the animation content promotes user understanding and fixes user attention. However, creating the animation content is time consuming and expensive, so it is difficult for novices to create animation. This difficulty indicates the level of difference between novice and more-experienced animation creators. Animebase provides a user-friendly means for novices to create animation contents by simply entering text.

Some researchers have used motion archives or databases, for example, ballet[13], Japanese folk dance[14], and sign language[15]. However, the aims of those studies and the motions used were different. For example, traditional performing arts only use natural language corresponding to motion to express the motion type. Our expression is not motion type but the image of the motion. In the case of the sign language database, the natural language corresponding to the motion might also be the motion image, but this motion is not useful for regular animation. We could not find any research in which animation data was collected for the purpose of creating content for novice users.

At this time, our system is limited in that the position and layout are sometimes strange because the displayed animation is simply GIF files laid over each other when the user first creates the blog's animation. The user can re-edit the animation by using the animation editing system, but this may be bothersome for users because they may want to create a blog by only selecting an animation and images. This problem can be avoided by creating rules for the layout and positions. For example, the subject is always to the right in the image and the layout is always looking to the middle. Developing an interface for editing and creating rules for default positions and layout is the basis of our future work.

When people make creations, their mental images of the creations are very different from each other. In our approach, we can select each part of the animation content by ourselves and re-form them using the reuse function. We cannot always create content that precisely matches our own imagination, but we come close by using our approach and large animation databases.

We think that Animebase will enable novices to create content by offering an environment in which information can be shared freely. It will be useful for the following situations: education; e-learning based on digital content; understanding and learning assistance for children or elders; business; transmission of information that appeals to individuals and its services; advertising and marketing for using digital content; communication support; visual communication support for different regions, cultures, or background knowledge; research use; and free use of digital content.

We expect that new research and business opportunities will be created and new areas of information science will be discovered by allowing academic and business access to the database. Analyzing processes to increase the use of the databases by various users will also be a basis for our future work.

6 Conclusion

We have developed an anime blog system and Animebase, a consumer-generated database, and the framework for information transmission. Animebase enables novices to generate attractive and understandable animation contents. At the same time, we can gather a lot of animation and image data with natural language information, benefiting from the anime blog system.

References

1. Winograd, T.: Understanding Natural Language. Academic Press, London (1972)
2. Vere, S., Bickmore, T.: A basic agent. Computational Intelligence 6, 41–60 (1990)
3. Bolt, R.A.: "Put-that-there": Voice and gesture at the graphics interface. In: International Conference on Computer Graphics and Interactive Techniques. Proceedings of the 7th annual conference on Computer graphics and interactive techniques, ACM Press, New York (1980)
4. Badler, N., Phillips, C., Webber, B.: Simulating Humans: Computer Graphics, Animation and Control. Oxford University Press, Oxford (1993)
5. Cassel, J., Vilhjalmsson, H.H., Bickmore, T.: BEAT: the Behavior Expression Animation Toolkit. In: Prendinger, H., Ishizuka, M. (eds.) Life-Like Characters, pp. 163–187. Springer, Heidelberg (2004)
6. Tanaka, H., et al.: Animated Agents Capable of Understanding Natural Language and Performing Actions. In: Prendinger, H., Ishizuka, M. (eds.) Life-Like Characters, pp. 163–187. Springer, Heidelberg (2004)
7. Marsella, S., Gratch, J., Rickel, J.: Expressive Behaviors for Virtual World. In: Prendinger, H., Ishizuka, M. (eds.) Life-Like Characters, pp. 163–187. Springer, Heidelberg (2004)
8. Coyne, B., Sproat, R.: WordsEye: An Automatic Text-to-Scene Conversion System. In: SIGGRAPH 2001. Proceedings of the 28th Annual Conference on Computer Graphics, Los Angeles, California, USA, ACM, New York (2001)

 9. Igarashi, T., Moscovich, T., Hughes, J.F.: Spatial Keyframing for Performance-driven Animation. In: ACM SIGGRAPH / Eurographics Symposium on Computer Animation (2005)
10. Sumi, K., Tanaka, K.: Automatic Conversion from E-content into Virtual Storytelling. In: Subsol, G. (ed.) Virtual Storytelling. LNCS, vol. 3805, pp. 262–271. Springer, Heidelberg (2005)
11. Johnson-Laird, P.N.: Mental Models. Cambridge University Press, Harvard University Press, Cambridge, Mass (1983)
12. Norman, D.A.: The Psychology of Everyday Things. Basic Books (1988)
13. Soga, A., Umino, B., Longstaff, J.S.: Automatic Composition of Ballet Sequences Using a 3D Motion Archive. In: 1st South-Eastern European Digitization Initiative Conference (2005)
14. Nakamura, M., Hachimura, K.: An XML Representation of Labanotation, LabanXML, and Its Implementation on the Notation Editor LabanEditor2. Review of the National Center for Digitization (Online Journal) 9, 47–51 (2006)
15. Sagawa, H., Ohki, M., Sakiyama, T., Ohira, E., Ikeda, H., Fujisawa, H.: Pattern Recognition and Synthesis for a Sign Language Translation System. Journal of Visual Languages and Computing 17, 109–127 (1996).

Invited Session: Related EU Projects

Experiments with the Production of ShapeShifting Media: Summary Findings from the Project NM2 (New Millennium, New Media)

Doug Williams[1], Ian Kegel[1], Marian Ursu[2], Nico Pals[3], and Andra Leurdijk

[1] BT Research and Venturing, Adastral Park, IPSWICH UK IP5 3RE
[2] Goldsmiths, University of London, New Cross, London SE14 6NW, UK
[3] TNO Information and Communication Technology, P.O. Box 5050, 2600 GB Delft, The Netherlands

Abstract. Summary results of the assessment of new tools for the generation of reconfigurable screen media (ShapeShifting media) and of eight experimental ShapeShifting screen media productions covering genres including news, documentary and drama, are presented from the project New Millennium, New Media. The new tools for creating interactive and reconfigurable narratives depend upon a Narrative Structure Language which is briefly described. Evaluations suggest that whilst not all the productions could be marketed as they are, all the production formats have commercial potential. The tools, whilst presenting some difficulties in use in their current state, offer a control over the development of narrative found in no existing commercial software.

Keywords: ShapeShift, media, screen, narrative, broadband, tools.

1 Introduction

This paper is written at the end of a three year experiment into interactive narrative carried out within the project NM2 (New Millennium, New Media). It is intended to provide an overview of the project, and to provide a digestible summary of its purpose, design, methodology and findings, as well as acting as a clear pointer to the ways in which those involved in the development of interactive narrative for the screen can build upon the outputs of this project.

As a summary paper its scope is wide and its depth will be limited. However it is liberally referenced. The paper will highlight both successes enjoyed and problems encountered during the NM2 project, and will indicate briefly how some of these challenges were met and how, on occasion the ambitions of the project proved too great for the given resource and time available. The intention is to be pragmatic and transparent, so that others can see, share and learn from these experiences.

2 The Project

The overall objective of NM2 [1] was to enable the creation of new media genres through developing the tools necessary for its cost-efficient production and delivery.

M. Cavazza and S. Donikian (Eds.): ICVS 2007, LNCS 4871, pp. 153–166, 2007.
© Springer-Verlag Berlin Heidelberg 2007

The tools developed should, the project stated, facilitate the creation of compelling, potentially profitable, nonlinear interactive narrative-based content.

The targeted achievements for NM2 were as follows:

- Robust and easy-to-use production tools that can be integrated in today's production environments.
- Delivery systems targeted towards widely available consumer entertainment platforms, including set-top boxes, PCs and games consoles.
- Seven productions[1] covering a wide scale of forms and formats, which will provide tested models.
- A software language for expressing and generating meaningful interactive narratives.

2.1 Project Design

New media forms need a name. The term ShapeShifting media, first introduced to a wider audience in 2006 [2] has emerged from NM2 and it has become a useful shorthand way of describing screen media in which the story told adapts to the inferred or expressed preferences of the viewer or to chance operations within the narrative. Names are important; but new media forms also need new technologies to enable their creation. Just as Charles Dickens work needed the printing press and Stephen Spielberg needed the movie camera and the editing suite, ShapeShifting media needs tools to facilitate its creation.

New media forms also need to prove themselves not through being technically feasible but being engaging as stories. Pixar needed to create short but appealing computer-generated movies before they earned the right to produce full length computer generated animation films like 'Toy Story'.

NM2 set out to address both the technology and the content issues within one project. To address this effectively, NM2 was designed to be production-centric; the team believed that by doing so the emergent tools would have functions and capabilities informed by needs of producers and not by the whims of technologists. This project design was also chosen as it was believed that impressive innovative productions were the best possible advertisement for the NM2 technology being developed in the project and hopefully exploited beyond it.

The genres of the NM2 productions, all intended initially for broadband delivery, ranged from news, through documentary to drama. This was another deliberate decision intended to enable the development of a more generic NM2 System with a proven capability in many different media genres. At this stage it was not clear where the best production opportunities lay so it was important to hedge bets and develop a generic system that did not close off too many subsequent exploitation paths. The project required a wide diversity of skills, including market insight, software design, scriptwriting and narratology. To deliver these skills a consortium was formed including 13 partners from 8 different countries across Europe. The impetus for this collaboration was the EU 6th Framework IST programme.

---

[1] During the first year of the project, an eighth production was included in the work plan.

3 Description of the Eight Experimental Productions

At the heart of the project were eight experimental productions. All the production were described in simple treatments in the opening few months of the three year project. These treatments were developed through iterative assessment of the art of the possible by the technologists and the producers. The productions were subsequently developed during the project with ambition and possibilities being refined in response to the capabilities of the NM2 systems required for their realisation.

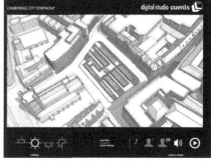

Cambridge City Symphony [3,4] is an experimental interactive production that updates the montage-based genre of the 1920s. The production allows visitors to explore the city of Cambridge, through their own choice of topic, length and time of the day. (Photo by CUMIS)

Gods in the Sky Choice [5] is an experimental interactive documentary about the science and mythology of ancient cultures. Using a remote control, viewers select 'Sit-back Entertainment', 'Education' or 'Information' mode, choosing topic, depth and length. (Photo by CUMIS). The production uses, with permission, the Gods in the Sky programmes produced by Wag TV for Channel 4.

Accidental Lovers [6] is a participatory black comedy about love, for television, mobile phone and Internet. The engagers can affect in real-time the unfolding drama of the unlikely romantic couple, Juulia in her sixties and Roope in his thirties. (Photo by Heli Sorjonen)

Interactive Village [7] presents a reconfigurable portrait of life in the Czech village of Dolni Roven. Movies are compiled dynamically to reflect engagers' choices of place and topic, made via a picture-based interface. (Photo by University of Ulster)

Gormenghast Explore [8,8,10,11] is an experimental, spatially-organised, interactive dramatisation of BBC TV's adaptation of Mervyn Peake's Gormenghast novel. Visitors explore the 2D environment of the castle to gain access to the stories of different characters, each freshly reconfigured at every visit. (Photo by CUMIS)

Runecast fortune-telling offers visitors their own personal access to the authentic myth world of the Vikings [12]. Real-time layering, oral storytelling and musical structure and techniques, combined with chance operations, make every visit unique. The ambition of this production, in terms of the demands it made from any prospective delivery system were enormous. (Photo by CUMIS).

MyNews&SportsMyWay is a digital interactive archive that allows engagers to discover, select and recombine news and sports items into stories which meet their individual tastes [13]. (Photo by Malmö University).

A Golden Age [14] is a configurable documentary for television, exploring the arts of the Renaissance in England. The engager determines the aspects of this subject which are of most interest. (Photo by Illuminations).

4 Description of the Narrative Structure Language

Early conversations about the productions, together with introductions to non-linear narrativity led to a set of requirements for the Narrative Structure Language (NSL), a new computational language [15,16,17] that supports the representation of non-linear narrative structures and that was subsequently used with the NM2 system to develop the later productions in the project.   The process also started conversations about workflow, production economics and the role of automatic content recognition[18] in the tagging of media items that have continued throughout the project and will, no doubt continue for years to come.

A key step in the development of the NM2 tools was the abstraction, from the many discussions about narrativity, of a minimal set of primitives that can be used to describe the interactive narrative structures required in the planned productions. These consist of a primitive object, the Atomic Narrative Object (ANO) [15], and three basic primitive aggregation structures [17], the link, layer, and selection group structure. Structured narrative objects are made from atomic narrative objects and other, less complex, narrative objects by means of these aggregation structures. The structures are fully recursive in that they can be combined to any level of depth.

Authors create a *narrative space* using the narrative structure language. This is an artefact on whose basis the NM2 system can construct, automatically, the *narrative threads* corresponding to each user interaction.

The logic of interaction is modelled as an inherent part of the part of the narrative space. Narrative objects can be annotated with interaction, in which case they become interactive narrative objects. Currently, NSL supports only Interactive atomic narrative objects.

The specification mechanisms that accompany NSL's aggregation structures make use of expressions that employ user input and context variables. In the current incarnation of NSL these expressions replicate to some extent the Prolog syntax, because the inference engine for NSL is implemented in Prolog. However, this does not make NSL tightly coupled with Prolog.

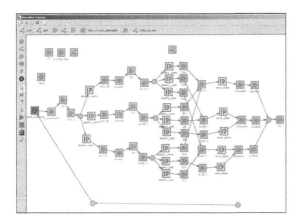

Fig. 1. Excerpt from the narrative canvas for Accidental Lovers, from which can be discerned the outline of the over arching 3-act structure

4.1   Description of the Emergent Tool Set

The Narrative Structure Language was a key step in developing the NM2 tools. These software tools had to enable users to build narrative structures using graphical abstractions of the narrative structure language primitives. To enable this, the concept of a narrative canvas was developed, upon which the graphical representations of narrative objects may be placed and decision rules defined.

The graphical elements are shown below and an example of a section of a narrative canvas, in this case depicting a portion of the 'Accidental Lovers' narrative is shown.

4.2 Method - The Evaluations

Each production became the subject of in depth evaluation. These were used to evaluate both the concept of ShapeShifting media and the tools developed for their creation. The evaluation methodology was developed [19] by framing the relevant issues against two axes. These axes were perspective of the user (an individual or a business?) and the article (the tools or the media production?). This analysis highlighted the following questions:

- Are the NM2 tools useful, economically feasible and are they valued by producers?
- Are the NM2 productions engaging, economically feasible and are they valued by end users?

The approach leads to four research domains as shown in the figure below.

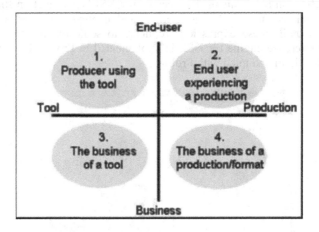

Fig. 2. The four research domains for the evaluation of NM2 experimental productions

To be successful NM2 must perform at a reasonable level in all these domains and preferably excel in a few of them. For each of the experimental productions, evaluation questions were defined and tested along these four domains. Not every evaluation covered all four domains. Evaluations were carried out using a range of techniques, sometime using media professionals, and, on occasion, using the reaction of 'ordinary' people. Both structured and unstructured interview techniques provided the input to the evaluation. For Accidental Lovers, which was broadcast in Finland, viewing and texting statistics were also available.

5   Results

The results are presented using the axes for evaluation developed within NM2. So production results are considered separately from the evaluation of the NM2 tools.

5.1   Production Results - General Comments

The evaluations suggested that whilst not all NM2 productions could be sold on the market in their current form, all the formats underlying the productions have the potential to be exploited commercially. Many suggestions were made by both experts and end-users on how the productions could be exploited in different markets and on different display devices.

It was recognised that improvements would need to be made to all the productions with respect to the aesthetics and usability of their interfaces. Another general point of concern is the need for a more fluent and transparent interaction. The user wants to know how they are interacting with the production and what the consequences of their actions are.

Some of the productions can be exploited for educational purposes, others for entertainment and gaming. For exploitation in entertainment and gaming markets it is important to take into account that the interaction should not be obtrusive because immersion in the storyline is essential for this kind of production.

In delivering the production to consumers it is important to consider the consequences of choosing a particular type of media and device. When users interact with the TV through a remote control, their posture and location relative to the screen suggests a more relaxed mode of interaction. A desktop PC typically affords a greater level of interaction and immersion. A mobile device provides a personal experience, whereas a TV is more suitable for a social experience.

A final remark that has to be made is that during the evaluations there were not many comments on how the interaction should be altered or extended. The interaction itself was not a point of discussion, but the design, in terms of usability and visuals of the interaction were. In discussing the production for exploitation it was mostly suggested how the type of interaction designed in the program could be translated into other areas, rather than that the subject matter used in the production should have been presented in a different way, with other interaction possibilities. Hence is seems that the production formats can be applied for multiple kinds of subject matter.

Results – Cambridge City Symphony and Gods in the Sky choice

The two earliest productions Gods in the Sky Choice and Cambridge City Symphony [3,4] were not able to use the NM2 system (since it had not been built) and had to use the first generation media tools previously developed by BT [20]. Their functionality had to be more constrained because of this. All the user interactions had to come before the programme started to play for example, whereas for later productions it was possible to build dynamic interactivity within the flow of each programme. The earliest productions were therefore designed to provide a menu of preferences from which the user could choose and it was these preferences that then determined the programme playlist that was executed.

These experimental productions helped in the articulation of the project vision but also became the first to highlight some key challenges: the interface metaphor and media asset management. With regard to the latter, it was essential to ensure that all the media files were present and correctly named and referenced by the system. Furthermore, the system required that play-lists were created representing all the different possible permutations and combinations of user choices, and these had to be correctly associated to the selection options made within the user interface.

City Symphonies suffered perhaps the most from the media management challenge; evaluators could not easily see a clear relation between the choices that they made and the images in the clip. This (obviously) made the production less pleasurable for them to watch and more difficult to understand. It is quite possible that this was caused by errors in the naming and referencing of files.

Gods in the Sky Choice appeared to work much better and many observers suggested that the format could be important for educational purposes more than pure documentary. In this context people who viewed the production felt it could be used to create a powerful online multimedia encyclopaedia.

The remaining productions all used the emergent NM2 system to define the non-linear narrative form within the production, but each worked with a slightly different release of the experimental systems and each was experimentally demonstrated using different forms of media delivery system.

Results - Accidental Lovers

Accidental Lovers was broadcast on Finland's premier public service broadcasting channel YLE1 in the winter of 2006/07. Through 4 broadcast events, 12 iterations of the story between the two lovers were broadcast, each story different and each responding to the text messages sent in via viewers' mobile phones. The production was successful, and this success was very important on account of its inevitable high profile. En route it also absorbed significant project resource, arguably to the detriment of individual other productions, but to the overall benefit of the project. As a broadcast production a number of unique capabilities were required within the delivery system:

- A means for collecting, moderating and choosing the text messages that were to be shown.
- A way of delivering a dynamically-changing playlist to a broadcast play-out system with minimal delay
- A narrative form and dialogue had to be established to enable viewers and interactors to understand the relationship between the displayed text messages and the way the story evolved.
- A mechanism was required to overcome any potential disappointment viewers may feel if their text messages were not shown and did not, therefore, visibly affect the emerging narrative.

The text moderation system allowed incoming text messages to be stacked and reviewed. The human moderator then chose which messages should be passed to the narrative, at the same time providing information about the character to which it should apply and whether the mood of the message was positive or negative. The PubliTronic Indigo broadcast play-out system was chosen to render the dynamically-changing play-lists. Indigo is a highly-flexible multi-processor unit which is commonly used to automate music television channels. For Accidental Lovers, the NM2 system provided a software control layer that enabled audio and video layers to be changed very quickly, within 4 seconds of broadcast, resulting in a fast response cycle between incoming text messages being chosen and ultimately affecting the emergent story. During the programme an unseen character Rane guided the audience through on-screen messages explaining what the audience had to do to affect the plot but also indicating the aggregated sense of the audience messages at the end of each act ("It seems you have made Roope's heart cold towards Juulia"). This signalled to the audience the effect of their message and of the likely story evolution in the next act. To help all those that sent messages to become more involved in the plot, irrespective of whether their messages had been screened or not, each text message received a scripted reply. This was chosen by the NM2 system through word matching to best answer the sense of their message.

Results - Interactive Village
The Interactive Village production was designed for the web, presenting a dynamic user interface (developed in Adobe Flash) within a web browser. It employed a map as a spatial metaphor, through which viewers could access video sequences pertinent to different locations within the village. The interface also provided thumbnail images which were dynamically chosen to reflect images of the scenes that the viewer could watch. By clicking on these, the viewer could jump to a new scene should the image entice them so to do. Because Interactive Village was the first production to require an internet-based version of the NM2 delivery system, a number of problems were encountered with the Content Synthesiser, the software component which dynamically renders play-lists into a continuous media stream. The team discovered that the Microsoft DirectShow development kit used by the Synthesiser did not provide them with sufficient control to guarantee a reliable output. The result was that this first-generation system proved incapable of adequately rendering the image, which often froze or simply failed. These failures in its technical performance made a complete assessment of the production difficult, though enough work was done to explain the concept. The assessment by media professionals was positive about the format of *Interactive Village*. They especially valued the way in which it offers viewers different perspectives on village life, and enabled different viewing modes, thereby enlarging its potential audience. There was some criticism on the interface, arguing that the map, which was used as a navigation tool, occupied too much screen space. A further criticism was that viewers needed a better indication of the choices being offered and of the likely results of making a particular choice. Encouragingly, the experts believed *Interactive Village* potentially represented a new way of making documentaries or of presenting other forms of factual audiovisual information (educational films, presentations in museums and archives) to viewers.

Results - Gormenghast Explore
The chosen interface for Gormenghast Explore was based on a 3D space (developed using open-source graphics engine Ogre3D) within which different video stories could be found. The ideal scenario would have seen interactions taking place within the 3D space being sent to the NM2 delivery system, and subsequently influencing an audiovisual stream which is rendered within the 3D space. This complexity posed problems that were not resolved in the project. Because this ambition was not realised, the team had to be creative in order to convey the concept. They opted to combine an illustration of the 3D space with pre-complied "new" stories, derived from the BBC work by restructuring the original content. The assessments of the

navigation in the 3D space was intriguing, there seemed to be consensus about the value of using space to navigate, as this allowed the viewer to enter the story and to discover it rather than simply being offered choices which would, it was felt, interrupt and interfere with the experience of the story.

Results – MyNews and SportsMyWay

MyNews&SportsMyWay was a very important production experiment for two reasons. Firstly it was one of only three that involved significant involvement from commercial production units (Accidental Lovers and A Golden Age being the other two) and it was the only production experiment that depended on an open ended pool of media content. All the other experiments involved constrained sets of media elements, the various reconfigurations of which could, in principle, be tested prior to delivering the service to a TV screen over a broadband connection. The news, however, is continuously changing and new content is being edited and added to the broadcaster's asset management system on a continuous basis. The challenge was to build narrative structures that would access and choose appropriately from this ever expanding pool of material. The production worked very hard to bridge the gap between traditional news broadcasting and a new personalised news genre by presenting a new option called "My News" among a number of pre-defined topic selections (such as Sport, Entertainment and Economy) which were composed mostly of traditional pre-edited newscasts. This helped the producers to deflect the anticipated concern that My News would fail to fulfil the role required of it in a free society.

This production highlighted some new issues related to metadata. It was important for metadata of sufficient quality to be rapidly associated with media clips, but there was also a need, not explored in this experiment, to adapt and redefine metadata over time. Old news stories can take on new meanings and once-disconnected news stories may become linked by the adoption of new terms like "the war on terror". Technically this is not difficult but it would require new workflow practices so that descriptions of news items could be updated as necessary.

Results - Runecast

The creators of Runecast chose a method they called "molecular accretion" to drive the narrative, based on chance operations from the casting of runes. The runes had associated characters and invoked different moods which could be represented by the imagery, music and story presented in the video. The ambition of the project was to dynamically apply colour filters to selected image files and assemble these in montage style, often using track mattes (a multi-layer masking effect[21]). These would be dynamically rendered by the Content Synthesiser together with reconfigurable music, again assembled according to rules dictated by the choice and chance based selection of the runes. Each of these components and principles was demonstrated and the overall appearance of the montage was also displayed. The complexity of the video and audio rendering which is required by Runecast has meant that the integrated version of the production has yet to be realised. However, a major revision of the Content Synthesiser software was undertaken in the final months of the project and it is hoped that this will make it possible to perform these exacting operations with enough efficiency to be delivered using affordable PC servers.

Results - A Golden Age

A Golden Age was ambitious and important because it sought to develop, from the script and production planning stages forward, a long form of reconfigurable narrative that would have the same aesthetic value as television and would create stories that, whilst assembled on the fly, were intellectually cogent. The experiment, like Runecast, chose an associative model for the narrative, with preferences expressed by the viewer resulting in the playlist being assembled by collating the media items that most closely matched the viewer's emergent profile. Uniquely, this profile was allowed to change with time: as more and more preferences were expressed the relevance of older choices was allowed to decay so their impact on the emergent narrative was played down. After every interaction opportunity, the delivery system recalculated the forthcoming playlist to ensure the programme better reflected the responses received from the viewer. The production also chose the simplest of interaction interfaces, a full screen television image at all times with modest and simple keyword prompts inviting an expression of interest, captured through pressing a single button on the remote control. Each keyword prompt related to a particular aspect of the Arts in Elizabethan England, and was directed by the narrative to be synchronised with video sequences in which that topic was explicitly discussed. Delivery of A Golden Age required the capabilities of the second-generation Content Synthesiser, which was capable of seamlessly rendering a continuous full-screen video stream. Difficulties were experienced with managing the synchronisation of the keyword prompts with particular events in the video. This was due to the variability of buffering and network delays when streaming video over the Internet. A solution to this was derived and this allowed the production to be tested. Real-time scalable content synthesis remains an active topic for research.

5.2   Results - Prototype Tools for Interactive Narrative Production

The tools generated by the project are research prototypes which were under development throughout the project, and so assessments of the software must be considered in that light. Two key issues raised by the tools' prototype nature are as follows:

- The software is not built to the same standard as commercial software, with the result that it contains bugs and may not always be stable in operation.
- The software represents an entirely new way of approaching narrative construction and does not fit tidily into established roles in the media production chain. There are no natural users of the software as its functionality appears to demand input from those with story making and editing skills. Most users of the tools were in one dimension at least out of their comfort zone

In spite of these limitations, the tools were found to be exciting and thought-provoking and enabled producers and scriptwriting teams to develop approaches to narrative creation that were not possible with any media tools available in the market today.

The production teams all found the NM2 Tools difficult to use. This was caused by the new way of thinking required for interactive production, and also, in some instances, due to the design and implementation of the tools themselves. This resulted in a production process that was more time consuming and less cost effective than a production process which depends only on familiar, industry-standard media production tools. For the tools to be commercially exploitable, their usability would need to be improved. One possible way to achieve this would be by integrating their most important and unique functionality with existing professional media tools. Products from Avid, Apple and Adobe currently focus on media manipulation rather than the assembly of media clips based upon rich, structured metadata. The ability to annotate media and design complex interactive narrative structures by means of a graphical interface would extend the applicability of such broadcast-orientated tools to novel broadband formats.

The development of the tools should be adjusted to suit the intended end-user. The optimum design would depend on whether the target was professional or amateur users. On the one hand it was suggested to make the tools available for free, to be used and improved by talented amateurs, but on the other hand it was also suggested that they could be used by professionals to make complex reconfigurable and interactive media productions.

The exploitation possibilities for the NM2 tools have been explored with reference to future scenarios [19]. The scenario approach allows key market uncertainties such as the demand for interactive media and the relative commercial strength of different roles in the media value chain to be flexed. Using this analysis a number of different roles for the NM2 Tools, where they offer different value propositions to different players in the value chain, have been identified.

6 The Way Ahead

As the project closes, a new web site, from which the tools can be downloaded and used, is being built. The web site www.shapeshift.tv , apart from being the repository of the NM2 software tools the site also aims to be a key resource for the community of people interested in developing ShapeShifting stories. Examples of ShapeShifting media productions will be hosted on this site and users will be able to experiment with the tools and develop new story structures of their own. The site will host training manuals, user guides and provide community tools allowing users of the tools to help each other with problems they may encounter.

Some of the ideas developed will be adapted for use in the user generated content domain under the new EU collaborative project TA2 (Together Anywhere, Together Anytime).

7 Conclusions

The NM2 project has developed a software tool set based on requirements set by eight different productions ranging from news through documentary to drama. The tools, whilst not as stable or as easy to use as commercially available software, deliver capabilities that are not found in commercially available software. They use a narrative structure language to define reconfigurable story structures and have been used in the safe execution of an interactive story broadcast on YLE1, the public service broadcaster in Finland and of an internal trial within the news rooms of Swedish Broadcaster SVT.

Evaluations of the productions developed within NM2 have universally supported of the format ideas they embody and have been generally positive about the idea of programmes whose stories can be shaped by the viewer, to adapt to their preferences whether stated explicitly or implicitly.

Acknowledgements

The authors acknowledge all the people who worked on NM2 for their hard work and contribution to the progress made, the EU 6th Framework IST Programme which part funded the research and all the partners institutions of NM2 for supporting this work.

References

1. Williams, D., Kegel, I., Ursu, M.F., et al.: NM2, New Media for a New Millennium. In: Hobson, P., Izquierdo, E., et al. (eds.) Knowledge-Based Media Analysis for Self-Adaptive and Agile Multi-Media. Proceedings of the European Workshop for the Integration of Knwoledge, Semantics and Digital Media Technology, EWIMT 2004, London, UK, November 25-26, 2004, QMUL 2004 (2004), ISBN 0-902-23810-8
2. Williams, D., Cook, J.J., Engler, M., Kegel, I.C., Lohse, L.C., Stevens, T.S., Ursu, M.F., Wyver, J., Zsombori, V.: ShapeShifted TV: A Real Opportunity for Broadband. In: International Broadcast Convention (IBC) 2006, pp. 401–409. IBC06 Conference Publication (2006)
3. Alifragkis, S., Penz, F.: Constructing the Image of the Ideal Socialist City: Dziga Vertov and the Cinema of the Russian Avant-Garde. In: Ioannidou, A., Voss, C. (eds.) Slavic Studies after the EU-Enlargement: Challenges and Prospects (Proceedings of the First Interdisciplinary Slavic Studies Conference University of Macedonia: Salonica, 29/9-1/10/2006), Berliner Slawistische Arbeiten, Peter LangVerlag, Berlin (2007)
4. Alifragkis, S., Penz, F.: Spatial dialectics: montage and spatially organised narrative in stories without human leads. Digital Creativity 17, 221–233 (2006)
5. Lohse, Ludvig, Thomas, M.: Storytelling for the Small Screen: Traditional TV vs. Interactive Entertainment – Authoring and Producing Reconfigurable Screen Narrative for sit-back Enjoyment. In: Subsol, G. (ed.) Virtual Storytelling. LNCS, vol. 3805, Springer, Heidelberg (2005), http://www.springerlink.com/content/j09m2l2t8820/
6. Tuomola, M.L. (director), Saarinen, L.E. (writer), Nurminen, M.J.: Accidental Lovers ("Sydän kierroksella"), Crucible Studio, Helsinki University of Art and Design Finland. Broadcast on Channel TV1 by YLE, The Finnish Broadcasting Company (2006/2007)
7. Wright, Terence: 'Dolní Roveň': Visual Ethnography and Interactive Narrative. Webcast Les Archives Audiovisuelles de la Recherche en sciences humaines et sociale (The Audio-visual archives of research in the human & social sciences). In: FMSH (Maison des Sciences de l'Homme), Paris (2007), http://semioweb.msh-paris.fr/AAR/FR/ video. asp?id= 901&ress=2883&video=32851&format=22#11552
8. Sussner, J., Thomas, M.: Interactivity and Digital Environments: Designing a Storymap for Gormenghast Explore. In: Subsol, G. (ed.) Virtual Storytelling. LNCS, vol. 3805, Springer, Heidelberg (2005), http://www.springerlink.com/content/j09m2l2t8820/
9. Sussner, J., Lohse, L., Thomas, M., Garcia, G., Alonso, I., Munoz, A.: 3D Navigable Interface for Interactive Movie Gormenghast Explore. In: AXMEDIS. Second International Conference on Automated Production of Cross Media Content for Multi-Channel Distribution IEEE Proceedings Leeds UK, pp. 242–250. IEEE Computer Society, Los Alamitos (2006), www.informatik.uni-trier.de/ ley/ db/conf/ axmedis/ axmedis2006. html

10. Sussner, J., Thomas, M., Richens, P.: Patterning reconfigurable narrative: interactive cinema as architectural elevation within 3D interactive digital environments. Digital Creativity 17, 243–256 (2006)
11. Lohse, Ludvig, Sussner, J., Thomas, M.: Gormenghast Explore: iTV Drama. In: Lugmayr, A., Golebiowski, P. (eds.) Interactive TV: A Shared Personal Experience. TICSP Adjunct Proceedings of EuroITV 2007, pp. 181–182. Tampere International Center for Signal Processing, Tampere (2007)
12. Thomas, M.: Playing with Chance and Choice – Orality, Narrativity and Cinematic Media. In: Bushoff, B. (ed.) Developing Interactive Narrative Content: sagas/sagasnet reader. High Text, Munich, pp. 371–442 (2005)
13. Larsson, H., Lindstedt, I., Nilsson, T., Reimer, B., Topgaard, R.: MyNews& SportsMy-Way. K3, Arts and Communication, Malmö University (DVD, restricted access) (2007)
14. Wyver, J. (producer/director), Conrad, L. (associate producer), Hart, M. (ed.): A Golden Age, Produced by Illuminations, Experimental Media Production (2007)
15. Ursu, M.F., Cook, J.J., Zsombori, V., Zimmer, R., Kegel, I., Williams, D., Thomas, M., Wyver, J., Mayer, H.: Conceiving ShapeShifting TV: A Computational Language for Truly-Interactive TV. In: Cesar, P., et al. (eds.) EuroITV 2007. LNCS, vol. 4471, pp. 96–106. Springer, Heidelberg (2007)
16. Ursu, M.F., Cook, J.J., Zsombori, V., Kegel, I.: A Genre-Independent Approach to Authoring Interactive Screen Media Narratives. In: The Proceedings of the AAAI Fall Symposium on Intelligent Narrative Technologies, November 9-11, 2007, Westin Arlington Gateway, Virginia, USA (to be published, 2007)
17. Ursu, M.F., Cook, J.J., Zsombori, V., Kegel, I., Williams, D., Hausenblas, M., Tuomola, M.L.: ShapeShifting Screen Media: A Declarative Computational Model for Interactive Reconfigurable Moving Image Narratives. In: AIIDE 2007. The Proceedings of the AAAI Artificial Intelligence and Interactive Digital Entertainment Conference, Stanford, USA, pp. 101–104 (2007)
18. Williams, D.L., Thomas, M.: The Perceived role of Automatic Content Recognitions Systems in the Production of Personalised Audio Visual Media, pp. 359–366
19. Leurdijk, A., de Boer, J., Esmeijer, J., Limonard, S., Mevissen, F., Pals, N., van der Duin, P.: NM2 deliverable "D7.12 Envisioning the future for ShapeShifted media – scenarios for 2012" (2007), www.ist-nm2.org
20. Lohse, Ludvig, Thomas, M.: Flexible Media: producing character-based reconfigurable drama. Digital Creativity 15(2), 98–109 (June)
21. Mattes, T.: http://www.mographwiki.net/Track_Matte

Day of the Figurines: Supporting Episodic Storytelling on Mobile Phones

Martin Flintham[1], Gabriella Giannachi[2], Steve Benford[1], and Matt Adams[3]

[1] Mixed Reality Laboratory, School of Computer Science, University of Nottingham
[2] Centre for Intermedia, Department of Drama, University of Exeter
[3] Blast Theory, Brighton, UK

Abstract. Day of the Figurines (DoF) is a pervasive game for mobile phones that uses text messaging. DoF is driven by a strong scripted narrative that is combined with various interactive elements to create a shared experience. It is also a slow game, unfolding over twenty four days of its players' lives, requiring them to send and receive only a few messages each day. Our experience of staging multiple performances of DoF to more than seven hundred players revealed key issues concerning the design and experience of time in such a pervasive game. Most players engaged episodically, raising issues of how to manage reengagement with the game and sustain social relationships. Our experience has led us to propose a framework for how to design time in shared interactive narratives in which five distinct layers of time – story time, plot time, schedule time, interaction time and perceived time – are mapped onto one another.

1 Pervasive Games and Episodic Storytelling

Pervasive games that use players' own mobile phones to deliver storytelling experiences raise new challenges for the design of time in relation to interactive narrative. Mobile phones enable players to interweave an unfolding story with the ongoing patterns of their daily lives in a fine grained way. Players can quickly dip into and out of a story, for example in the downtime between other activities. At the same time, the story can try to interrupt them as they go about these activities. The net result is a tendency towards highly episodic play, with players frequently disengaging and then re-engaging again sometime later on. We shall argue in this paper that this raises new challenges for how we design time in such experiences, specifically how we manage the pacing and synchronization of different players' experiences. We illustrate how these challenges play out in practice by drawing on our experience of designing, staging and studying a long-term text messaging game for mobile phones called Day of the Figurines, illuminating the nature of episodic participation and revealing the challenges involved in designing pervasive interactive narratives.

2 An Introduction to Day of the Figurines

Day of the Figurines is a narrative-driven text messaging game for mobile phones (a full description of the experience can be found in [4]). Players send and receive SMS

M. Cavazza and S. Donikian (Eds.): ICVS 2007, LNCS 4871, pp. 167–175, 2007.

to control a 'character' – their figurine – as it lives through a day in the life of a fictional town, visiting destinations, observing events, using objects, responding to dilemmas, undertaking missions and chatting with others. DoF balances pre-scripted narrative with interactivity. The game is fundamentally narrative driven, following a pre-scripted storyline. Players are refugees who are dropped off in the town in the early morning. As the day unfolds they experience a sequence of scheduled events including a fete at the recreation ground, two dead lovers being found at the cemetery, a riotous gig at the Locarno nightclub, and an army sweeping into town. These scripted events are interspersed with interactive elements such as multiple-choice dilemmas and missions that require players to visit destinations, find and use objects, and maintain their health.

Players control their figurines by sending SMS text messages to the game server, receiving further messages in return that tell them what their figurine sees, hears and experiences. The game supports a small set of predefined commands and each SMS message that they send has to begin with a recognised command name:

- **GO <destination>** – move to the named destination
- **SAY <message>** – sends this message to nearby players
- **FIND <player>** – checks whether the named player is at the current destination and if they are moves this player to be within talking distance of them
- **PICK <object>** – picks up the named object
- **DROP** – drops the currently held object
- **USE** – uses the currently held object, triggering its particular effect
- **UPDATE** – tells the player which other players and objects they can currently see nearby and reminds them of their current health status
- **HELP** – returns a message directing players where to find online help and also logs a help request in the system for operators to deal with later on
- **LEAVE TOWN** – quits the game for this player

Players can visit fifty distinct destinations. Each time they arrive at a destination they receive its description. Depending on the current game time, destinations may be open, in which case players receive its 'inside the destination' description, or closed in which case they receive its 'outside the destination' description.

Each player has a health score that reflects their overall status in the game. Players change their health or the health of others by finding and using objects. For example, using food and drink objects will often increase their health whereas the pool cue is essentially a weapon. A player's health can deteriorate to the point where they become incapacitated, meaning that they cannot move or hold objects and can only talk to other nearby players. These players may help them by using various objects, most notably the defibrillator which restores incapacitated players. If a player's health diminishes further then they will die and their game is over. It is possible to kill other players by repeatedly using a weapon object on them.

As well as chatting to one another, players interact with various kinds of pre-scripted content. **Events** are authored SMS messages that are associated with a set of destinations and that are sent to players at predetermined times, providing the game with a basic underlying narrative of action that unfolds over time. **Dilemmas** are events that demand a multiple choice response that in turn triggers a subsequent response message and also a change to the player's health level. Finally, **missions** combine multiple events, dilemmas, destinations and objects into more complex longer-running narrative structures.

The following example fragments of interaction (taken from the game of the figurine called 'Floss') show how DoF balances pre-scripted content with interactive game-play. We begin with her introduction to the game.

Received **03:02** GMT Wed 06 Dec	06:00am, welcome to Day Of The Figurines. FLOSS has been dropped by a truck at the edge of town. You are feeling OK. Where do you want to go?
Sent **09:49** GMT Wed 06 Dec	Go kaths
Received **09:54** GMT Wed 06 Dec	06:41am, a cloud passes; a chill runs through you; in the distance shouting. Do you A: Continue on to a street corner B: Rest a moment?
Received **10:29** GMT Wed 06 Dec	06:45am, you carry on; a group of men, pre-occupied with a figure on the ground, are shouting. They notice you. The shouting changes. You keep moving.
Received **10:38** GMT Wed 06 Dec	06:46am, you've arrived at Kath's Cafe, brickies demolish white food. There are many steaming hot mugs of TEA here. You are feeling OK.

Next we see her during the mission to free the dogs from the Rat Research Institute.

Received **09:01** GMT Sun 10 Dec	10:36am, the fence is high. A passing workman gazes up at that high fence: Gor blimey, guvnor, you ain't getting over that without a step ladder, so you isn't.
Sent **09:05** GMT Sun 10 Dec	Say hey everyone, i found a load of stepladders at the lock. Let's see if they get me in.
Sent **09:06** GMT Sun 10 Dec	Use stepladder
Received **09:08** GMT Sun 10 Dec	10:36am, You are feeling OK.
Received **09:11** GMT Sun 10 Dec	10:37am, you nip up the steps and jump down inside the yard. Fantastic work, liberator! Wait for a second to catch your breath.

Received 09:36 GMT Sun 10 Dec	10:39am, now do you A: Run across the car park in a crouch to reception B: Creep around the perimeter to a fire exit C: Smash a slot window at basement level?
Sent **10:01** GMT Sun 10 Dec	A
Received **10:06** GMT Sun 10 Dec	10:42am, you stumble on a patch of greasy substance, alerting a guard in reception. Task failed. You head for the exit and come across a SICK DOG. Pick it up.

Finally, we rejoin her at the end of her game as she is carried away from the town in helicopter.

Received **10:09** GMT Fri 29 Dec	05:45am, soldiers shove you onto a metal ramp and into the back of the helicopter. It's a crush: HALO, MIMIMOMO, SAMANTHA and PUPPET are here.
Sent **10:14** GMT Fri 29 Dec	Say Looks like this is the survivors party. At least i hope so
Received **10:18** GMT Fri 29 Dec	05:45am, SAMANTHA said: "i hope this is not a one way ticket to the concentration camp..."
Received **11:18** GMT Fri 29 Dec	05:52am, the metal door of the helicopter slams shut, plunging you into darkness apart from a tiny port hole. Through the scratched perspex you can see grass.
Received **12:07** GMT Fri 29 Dec	05:57am, with a roar the chopper sways and takes off. Below in the town you see scattered refugees stranded as you bank away into the grey dawn light.
Received **13:17** GMT Fri 29 Dec	06:04am, dawn rises over the town as refugees flood the streets. 75 people have died but some have survived. The day is over. Thank you for playing Day of the Figurines.

3   The Nature of Time in Day of the Figurines

In order to accommodate the distinctive nature of SMS (slow, costly and infrequent messages), DoF adopted a distinctive treatment of narrative and time:

- The twenty four hours of virtual game time are mapped onto twenty four days of real time. Unlike most computer games in which game time is accelerated relative to real-time, in DoF game time is slowed down so as to deliberately create a slow game that unfolds in the background of players' ongoing lives, perhaps only involving the exchange of a few text messages each day.
- DoF is delivered as an event-based touring artistic performance, being booked to run at hosting venues for fixed periods of time. Each performance runs for twenty four days, between set start and end dates, opening for ten hours a day (while the venue is open), with the game being suspended outside of these times.

To date, DoF has been performed in Berlin, Singapore and three times in the UK, being experienced by over 750 players. Overall, the game has been well received; over 70% of the 100 players who responded to our post-game questionnaire said that they would pay to play again and were generally positive about the idea of a slow narrative-driven game played using text messaging. However, the experience of playing the game did reveal some interesting issues with regard to its temporal structure.

- The majority of players played episodically, dipping in and out of the game, sometimes not actively engaging for several days before becoming active again. Over half of our questionnaire respondents reported that they played 'occasionally' as opposed to 'regularly' or 'seldomly'.
- Messages could be delayed for hours before being delivered to players due to network congestion, lack of coverage, or phones being switched off. Some players were irritated by the sudden flood of messages that could arrive as they switched their phone back on after a long break.
- Players reported being frustrated by talking to others and receiving no reply (perhaps because these others were no longer engaged) and it could be difficult to maintain long term social relationships.
- Some players reported frustration with playing across time zones as this led to a mismatch between the game's scheduled opening hours and their own waking hours. For example, UK players in the Singapore game would tend miss the first half of each day's play and consequently suddenly become very active towards the end.

This combination of delays, episodic engagement and multiple time-zones made it difficult for players to engage in conversation and maintain social relationships and a common complaint was that of being ignored by other players.

In short, while the idea of a slow narrative-driven pervasive game is appealing to players, it also raises some new challenges with regard to how to manage their episodic interaction, especially with how to manage disengagement and re-engagement and also how to maintain social relationships between players who frequently disappear and then reappear sometime later.

4 Designing for Five Layers of Time

We propose that this challenge of managing episodic engagement with an ongoing pervasive experience requires a new holistic approach to the design of time in interactive narrative. A great deal has been written about the nature of time and narrative by scholars of literature, drama, film, television and interactive media and so we now turn to this existing body of work in order to develop such an approach. We introduce an overarching framework for describing time in shared interactive narratives that comprises five layers, each of which addresses a different aspect of temporal structure, ranging from the nature of time in the fictional universe of the author's imagination through to the way in which time is ultimately constructed in a player's imagination. Between, lie three intermediate layers that address the temporal aspects of narration, scheduling and interaction.

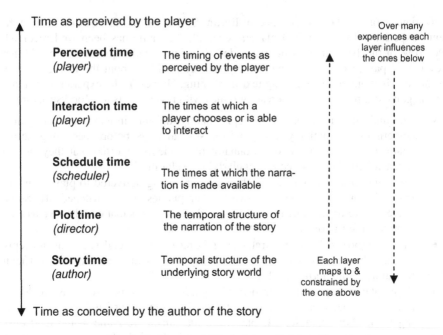

Fig. 1. Five layers of time in interactive narrative

Story time is determined by the author of a story and describes the structure of time in the underlying imaginary universe in which the story is set, much of which may be implied rather than ever being explicitly specified. Aspects of story time discussed in literary and drama theory including the historical epoch in which the story is set, the fictional span of the story, and whether time is cyclic or linear (see [8] for further discussion). In turn, games involve their own distinct temporal structures, including the distinction between 'result time' (games played until someone wins) versus 'set time' (games played for a fixed period of time when a winner is declared) [9]. For example, DoF's story time is set in modern times, is defined as a linear sequence of twenty four hours in the life of a virtual town and operates to a 'set time'.

Adopting the terminology of [8], **Plot time** (which might also be called discourse or narration time) describes the temporal structure of the narration of the story, i.e., the timing and ordering of events as they are presented by the narrator. This need not be the same as their timing and order in story time. For example, many plays adopt so-called 'open' structures which compress story time into a shorter plot time so as to omit unnecessary details, although some others assume 'closed' structures in which the span of plot time matches the underlying story time. It is also common for film and television narration to compress time ('ellipsis') and to alter the ordering of events as they are narrated (e.g., 'flashbacks') [1]. In turn, interactive media have introduced their own distinctive structures in the form of multi-threaded hypertext plots [5,7] and the looping structures of computer games [6] which may be combined with more traditional filmic elements. Adopting film terminology, the structure of plot time is determined by the director (who may be the same person as the author). DoF is a rare example of where plot time expands story time, mapping 24 hours of the former onto 24 days of the latter.

Schedule time describes the times at which the narration is made available to players, be they readers, viewers or players. All media involve a schedule time (books are published and plays and films are shown at set times), but it is in television that schedule time, through its relationship to channels and advertising sponsorship, takes on a particular significance to the point where it strongly influences the form of the underlying story and plot, as seen by the rise of TV series and serials [1]. Schedule time is controlled by the scheduler (or publisher). As an example, DoF is scheduled to be performed for ten hours a day beginning on set 'opening days', although this can vary due to local circumstances such as a venue being closed.

Interaction time describes the times at which players engage with the story once it has been made available, either as a matter of choice (playing at times that suit them) or as a result of technical constraints (such as network availability and delay). Interaction time is primarily controlled by the player. HCI research has produced various accounts of interaction time in narrative experiences including studies of how players' engagement with long-term mobile games adapts to the ongoing patterns of their daily lives, for example their commuting [2]. More generally, HCI has produced many studies and discussions of the temporal aspects of interaction in more general applications as we shall consider later on. Interaction time in DoF is characterized by largely episodic patterns of play, with players frequently disengaging and reengaging.

Perceived time refers to the way in which the timing of events is perceived by individual players. For example, players may experience the passage of time differently when they enter a 'flow state' during the playing of a game or similar intense pleasurable experience [3]. In a similar vein, inspired by Husserl's phenomenology, Francisco Varela talks about experienced time as having a three-part structure based on now, retention and protention [10]. Retention is described as belonging to the past even though it is happening now, whereas protention is 'the expectation or the construction of the future'. Whereas 'flow' indicates a perception of time experienced as duration, the 'now, retention and protention' structure point to the possibility of an experience based on tenses or trajectories.

The complexities of designing and managing time in DoF can then be understood in terms of this framework. In Dof, the author establishes a strong and distinctive sense of story time and a mapping of this onto plot time – twenty four hours of story time are mapped onto twenty four days of plot time. However, individual performances of DoF are then scheduled to take place on set days and at set times, which gives rise to potential problems with playing across time zones as noted previously. Next, players try to fit this particular schedule time with their own interaction times, which in the case of a mobile phone based pervasive game are highly variable and episodic, which gives rise to problems with floods of messages on reengagement and maintaining social relationships. Finally, players then have to reassemble their interactions (sent and received text messages) into a coherent story in their own imaginations.

We therefore propose that designing a complete treatment of time in an interactive narrative experience requires giving appropriate structures to plot, schedule, and interaction time so as to establish a coherent and effective mapping between story time and perceived time. Put another way, a powerful interactive narrative experience requires an understanding of how story time can be related through plot time, which in turn is affected by a schedule, and then by patterns of interaction, and finally by the ways in which players perceive time.

Finally, we suggest that there is longer-term 'back-pressure' between the layers in the sense that our emerging understandings of higher layers ultimately shape the nature of the lower ones. We have already seen how television theorists attribute the rise of new story and plot forms (series and serials) to the impact of TV schedules [1]. In the longer term, we predict that a growing understanding of interaction and perception time will lead to new schedule, plot and even story time structures. For example, DoF was deliberately designed to accommodate episodic play through small 'bite sized' scripted events and dilemmas which were responsively allocated to players whenever they chose to engage.

5 Conclusion

In summary, pervasive storytelling experiences such as DoF raise significant new challenges for how we structure time in shared interactive narratives. DoF shows how players engage with such experiences episodically, fitting the scheduled times of the experience with their own personal availability as they move from setting to setting. As a result, we have proposed that the complex temporal structure of shared interactive narratives needs to be designed with an understanding of five distinct layers of time – story time, plot time, schedule time, interaction time and perceived time – and how these map onto one another.

Acknowledgements

We thank the EU for supporting this work through IPerG, the Integrated Project on pervasive Games (www.pervasive-gaming.org). We also thank our colleagues from Blast Theory, Sony Net Services and the Fraunhofer institute for their work on Day of the Figurines that has inspired this work.

References

[1] Allen, R.C.: Channels of discourse, reassembled: Television and Contemporary Criticism, 2nd edn. Routledge, London (1992)

[2] Bell, M., Chalmers, M., et al.: Interweaving mobile games with everyday life. In: CHI 2006, Montréal, Canada, pp. 417–426. ACM, New York (2006)

[3] Chen, J.: Flow in Games (and everything else). Communications of the ACM 50(4), 31–34 (2007)

[4] Flintham, M., Smith, K., Capra, M., et al.: Day of the Figurines: A Slow Narrative-Driven Game for Mobile Phones Using Text Messaging. In: Pergames 2007. Proc. 2007 International Workshop on pervasive Games, Salzburg, Austria (April 2007)

[5] Landow, G. (ed.): Hyper/Text/Theory. The Johns Hopkins University Press, Baltimore, London (1994)

[6] Manovich, L.: The Language of New Media. MIT, Cambridge (2001)

[7] Murray, J.: Hamlet on the Holodeck The Future of Narrative in Cyberspace. MIT Press, Cambridge (1997)

[8] Pfister, M.: The Theory and Analysis of Drama (English translation). Cambridge University Press, Cambridge (1998)

[9] Thomson, P.: Games and Plays – An Approach to Ionesco. Educational Theatre Journal 22(1), 60–70 (1970)

[10] Varela, F.J.: The Specious Present: A Neurophenomenology of Time Consciousness. In: Petiot, J., et al. (eds.) Naturalizing Phenomenology: Issues in Contemporary Phenomenology and Cognitive Science, pp. 266–314. Stanford University Press (1999)

INSCAPE
An Authoring Platform for Interactive Storytelling

Olivier Balet

Virtual Reality and Simulation Department
CS Systèmes d'Information
5 Rue Brindejonc des Moulinais
BP 15872, 31506 Toulouse Cedex 5 - France
Olivier.Balet@c-s.fr
http://www.inscapers.com

Interactivity is a key feature of new multimedia content and services. However, the storytelling of these non linear forms of content requires today not only artistic skills but also expertise in specific technical tools, even including software programming. Whatever the form, be in theatre, movie, cartoon, video-games, training and simulation, the process for creating interactive content poses new challenges for authors and production teams. Indeed, this process calls for the combined knowledge of different domains such as cinema, 2D or 3D modelling, animation, cognitive and computer sciences.

The INSCAPE system, which is developed in the frame of the European Commission's sixth research framework programme, proposes an innovative approach for planning, authoring and experiencing interactive stories. This visual system tightly integrates state-of-the-art components developed by a consortium of fourteen European partners in close collaboration with end-users coming from different sectors (live art, television, simulation, cartoon…).

INSCAPE features an unprecedented collection of tools enabling the rapid and intuitive creation of interactive stories and making this complex authoring process accessible to any category of user.

With INSCAPE, the user can initiate the creation process by authoring a traditional storyboard with textual and pictorial elements. These elements can define scenes, actors, comments, dialogs, motions, as well as pictorial sketches of the story environment.

The acquisition modules can be used to reconstruct virtual environments from panorama pictures and capture motions from movies of real performers. The editing modules enable both the creation and configuration of 2D or 3D story elements such as characters, props, backgrounds as well as their different animations. Also, INSCAPE enables the creation and manipulation of sound assets containing dialogs, music, sound effects that can be, in the next creation steps, automatically mixed, specialised and blended according to both the story scneario and atmosphere.

Then, the user can associate graphical elements to each bit of the storyboard using an object browser that features an ontology based knowledge querying system. The author populates the story environment mixing 2D or 3D models, edits the behaviours

M. Cavazza and S. Donikian (Eds.): ICVS 2007, LNCS 4871, pp. 176–177, 2007.

of virtual characters and props, adds dialogs, music, sound and visual effects. Thus, he can progressively and intuitively set-up a complex scenario. The interaction and behavioural schemes can be edited by drag-and-dropping and configuring predefined templates; the INSCAPE interface enables the author to customize scripts or to create new ones using visual programming techniques, or for the most expert users, using the Lua scripting language.

With the story graph editor, the story can finally be visually split in different storylines with interdependencies and sequencing constraints. This graphical representation of non linear structures enables the easy definition of the interactions between the story elements and user inputs and the different possible ways to unfold the scenario according to user inputs and character interactions.

The innovative approach of interactive storytelling proposed by INSCAPE offers radically new possibilities for end-users to express their creativity and quickly transform their mental images into stimulating content. In the end, INSCAPE's challenge is to deliver a system that will stimulate and support creative people in building compelling interactive narratives to engage audiences and stimulate both imagination and skills.

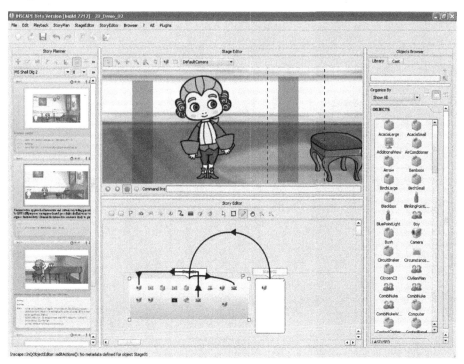

INSCAPE Beta version

Poster and Demo Session

RCEI: An API for Remote Control of Narrative Environments

Federico Peinado and Álvaro Navarro

Departamento de Ingeniería del Software e Inteligencia Artificial
Universidad Complutense de Madrid
c/ Profesor García Santesmases s/n, 28040 – Madrid, Spain
email@federicopeinado.com, alvaro.nav@gmail.com

Abstract. The proposal of this research project is to develop a standard connection mechanism to make narrative environments and the external systems that control them interoperable. Thanks to a new communication interface called RCEI, different knowledge-based storytelling systems will be able to perform interactive drama using different narrative environments that were available. The controller has a reasonable level of granularity, being the only additional requirement the development of valid adapters for both extremes of the connection. Open source implementation of this protocol and language is provided in order to save extra parsing and serializing efforts and make software more interoperable.

Keywords: Game Based Interfaces, Interactive Digital Storytelling, Virtual Environments and Intelligent Medias.

1 Introduction

Interactive Digital Storytelling (IDS) applications differ very much in their presentation to the user. Most of them use some kind of virtual environment with narrative or dramatic qualities, such as visual capabilities for showing text dialogs, representing 2D or 3D characters, objects and locations, giving feedback to the user through game-like HUDs, etc. These virtual environments are, of course, interactive, so their states are continuously changing, frequently in real time, depending on the interactors' actions and the behaviours implemented in the environment (logical or physical reactions, autonomous and proactive agents, hard-coded events, etc.). These environments also differ between applications and usually the integration with the final application is an expensive task in terms of time and effort.

This paper describes the proposal of a standard communication protocol and language designed for connecting bidirectionally a narrative virtual environment and a remote controller system in a generic way, abstracting low-level details relative to the composition of the multimedia effects of the virtual environment and the internal representation of the whole model that the controller uses privately. This toolkit receives the name of Remote-Controlled Environments Interface (RCEI [1]).

The development of this interface is part of a bigger project called Knowledge-Intensive Interactive Digital Storytelling system (KIIDS [2]), a framework and a

M. Cavazza and S. Donikian (Eds.): ICVS 2007, LNCS 4871, pp. 181–186, 2007.

library of domain-specific components for developing directed-IDS applications with the possibility of representing the drama in a RCEI-compatible environment.

The paper is divided in these sections: Section 2 presents a short overview of the related work on this topic. Section 3 presents the communication protocol and language of RCEI. Section 4 adds some implementation details, and finally Section 5 explains what are the conclusions of this research.

2 Background

The need of communication between narrative environments and controllers have been in the field since the very first projects on IDS. In most cases communication is just performed using a proprietary format, with no special intention of establishing a general or reusable language. Three projects with communication mechanisms comparable to our proposal have been chosen for its consideration in this section.

The first one is the Interactive Drama Architecture [3], an IDS proposal that includes an automatic director of the interactive experience implemented as a rule-based system. This architecture is interesting because it has features of a mixed approach, in which both a centralized director (or drama manager) and semi-autonomous (directed) characters collaborate in order to develop an expressive, variable and interesting plot. The controller of the story basically sends messages that are basic commands for a non-player character available at the environment for the player to interact with, messages such as "explore the environment", "get this item", "go to that room", "say something to the player", etc.

The second one is Zocalo service-oriented architecture [4, 5], designed for creating interactive narratives within game-based environments in which direction by planning is performed by Web services running on different machines. It is one of the first projects that take seriously scalability, security and interoperability issues of IDS applications' software components. Its communication formats are well documented, so they can be reused when developing extensions to the architecture. Content of the messages (mainly operators) have been found relatively coupled with the semantic specification of Longbow's input, a main planner that this research group uses, and more clearly coupled with the planning paradigm.

Finally the third one is Shadow Door agent interface [6], an agent control interface for the game engine of Neverwinter Nights (NWN [7]) and the starting point of the code of our project. It allows external applications to control one single character in the game. Using this interface developers can implement external controllers, coding them in arbitrary languages (as Lisp or Java), for the game play. An extension to the game module called Neverwinter Nights Extender (NWNX [8]) is necessary, and also special scripts for receiving commands and passing them to the character, and sending facts (observations) that happen inside the world to the external controller.

3 Communication Protocol and Language

The RCEI communication protocol is blocking and synchronous, at the same time the sending of messages must be strictly alternate. First, the remote controller must begin the interchange between both extremes because, generally, the answers of the environment will be *expected facts* -that will confirm the system's *commands-* or *unexpected facts* as consequence of long-term actions produced by the execution of the commands combined with the actions performed by the interactors and other autonomous entities of the fictional world. Second, the first message of the virtual environment must be an identification message, listing every condition referred to the initial state that the environment must know. And finally, the remote-controlled environment must be who finish the communications sending an ending message to the environment, although this also could be an unexpected error message when something goes wrong at that side of the connection or if the blocking of the controller delays too much.

The communication language uses a similar syntax for both commands and facts. All of them have a subject, that it may be an agent of the environment or the environment itself, and also all of them has a process in order to notify the kind of action, which can be relative to the environment or any object or agent. The other fields in the command (or fact) are variable according depending on the parameters needed for each type of instruction.

There are three special pairs of meta-commands and meta-facts with a different structure; these are *begin, end* and *synchronize*. These commands have a subject and a predicate with a process, and two new parameters: a list of concepts and a list of relations. The functionality of these instructions -when they are commands- is starting or ending a new game performing changes (creating, deleting, moving...) the available elements of the environment. When these instructions are facts, they are useful to report the state of the environment at the beginning, at the end or at any significant moment –determined by the AI system- during the game session.

While the messages sent by the environment are interpreted as facts that have been produced recently in the environment, the messages sent by the remote controller are interpreted as "events that should happen in the environment as soon as possible", with no guarantees due to real time and non-deterministic constraints.

The basic repertory of RCEI vocabulary contains instructions relative to the simulation domain of the environment, being its expressiveness inspired on the Conceptual Dependency Theory (CDT [9]).

Firstly, there is an instruction called *speak* to perform conversations between two agents. If we want to perform more advanced conversations, we also can use the instruction *change* to modify the state of characters involved in the dialog (emotion, attitude, mood, etc.).

The instruction *move* represents values of action, gestures or grimaces of one agent with respect to a determined location. Also it represents values of expression of an agent's action with a determined meaning. For example, make gestures of anger or happiness, execute animations of social or complex activities, etc. The values of agent's movements towards a location are represented by the instruction *go;* if this instruction has no parameters it means the agent must perform a random walk.

Create and *destroy* instructions allow both creation or destruction of a location in a determined situation (linked to other locations), an agent or object, links between locations, etc.

The *change* instruction mentioned before has a great versatility for the simulation. This instruction is used for change the climate or ambient conditions of the virtual environment. It is also used to change the objects' state of things like doors, chests, weapons, lights sources, etc.

Other instructions as *attack*, *take*, *drop*, *give*, *equip* and *unequip* have been included for practical reasons and due to the game-like orientation of many stories.

4 Implementation

The RCEI language have been implemented using Java and XML technologies in an API we called jRCEI. This distribution is available on the Internet as an open source project composed by different packages such as the parser, the serializer, the API itself, a GUI for manual control and some additional testing code, including the NWN to RCEI adapter and an example scenario.

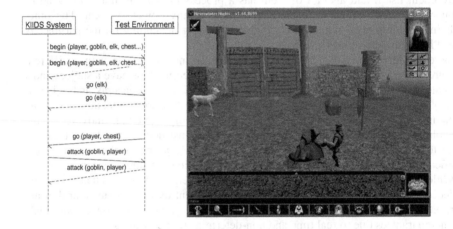

Fig. 1. Sequence diagram and screenshot of an example execution. The KIIDS system is monitoring and controlling what is happening in the RCEI test environment.

The example scenario has a set of models ready to be used in the story. After establishing the connection with the RCEI-compatible environment running in a NWN server, the KIIDS system sends the begin command. In this command, the player (dressed as a monk), a goblin, an elk and many objects (chests, flags, doors...) are described.

The environment creates everything without problems, so it returns a successful begin fact. After a short time reasoning, KIIDS sends a go command for the elk to move in random directions.

Nothing interesting happens until the player decides to go to the chest. When KIIDS incorporates that fact to its internal world model, the system reasons about it and decide that the goblin must avoid that, so it orders the goblin to attack the player.

Immediately the goblin attacks the player (note that it implies low-level decisions taken by the NWN engine, as path planning and choosing the best attack form), and the development of the story continues for KIIDS, receiving (expected or unexpected) facts and sending commands until it decides to send the end command.

5 Conclusions

Looking for a connection mechanism to make narrative environments and intelligent controllers interoperable, the KIIDS project includes a development related to a standard interface called RCEI. The objective of this interface is to provide a general engineering toolkit for building IDS applications offering flexible and efficient communication between the main system and the dramatic scenario.

The language proposed offers a basic but powerful vocabulary to communicate with the environment. While the interface is valid for both plot-oriented or character-oriented projects, now the tests have been done with the plot-oriented KIIDS director in mind. This only means that there are no special high-level commands designed for autonomous actors. Every instruction is simple, so characters, objects and the environment itself receive the same kind of information.

Extensions to the basic repertory of RCEI vocabulary are possible and simple to add. RCEI adapters at both sides of the connection must include those additions and must use them propertly. With respect to the proposal of extensions to the language, there is an important restriction: no addition of new simulation instructions can become RCEI dependent on too specific environments' or systems' specifications.

As future work we are designing new adapters for other environments based on the Neverwinter Nights 2 and Unreal Tournament 3 engines, at the same time we deals with distributed architectures and performance issues. RCEI is planned to be included in the final distribution of KIIDS, being completely open to the contributions of the research community.

Acknowledgments

This research is funded by Ministerio de Educación y Ciencia (TIN2006-14433-C02-01 project), Universidad Complutense de Madrid and Dirección General de Universidades e Investigación de la Comunidad de Madrid (UCM-CAM-910494 research group grant). Second author held a Beca-Colaboración 2006-2007 grant from Ministerio de Educación y Ciencia.

References

1. Peinado, F., Navarro, A.: RCEI, A Remote-Controlled Environments Interface (2007), http://federicopeinado.com/projects/rcei
2. Peinado, F.: Knowledge-Intensive Interactive Digital Storytelling system (2007), http://federicopeinado.com/projects/kiids/
3. Magerko, B., Laird, J.E.: Building an Interactive Drama Architecture. International Conference on Technologies for Interactive Digital Storytelling and Entertainment. Darmstadt, Germany (2003)
4. Young, M., et al.: Zocalo (2007), http://zocalo.csc.ncsu.edu/
5. Vernieri, T.M.: Web Services Approach to Generating and Using Plans in Configurable Execution Environments. M.Sc. thesis, Liquid Narrative Group. North Carolina State University. Raleigh, NC, USA (2006)

6. Zubek, R.: Shadow Door: Neverwinter Nights NPC Control Interface (2003), http://www.zubek.net/robert/software/shadow-door/
7. BioWare: Neverwinter Nights: Diamond Compilation Pack (DVD-ROM). Atari (2005)
8. Stieger, I.: Neverwinter Nights Extender (2004), http://www.nwnx.org/
9. Lytinen, S.L.: Conceptual Dependency and its Descendants. Computers and Mathematics with Applications 23(2-5), 51–73 (1992)

Bringing Interactivity into Campbell's Hero's Journey

Guylain Delmas, Ronan Champagnat, and Michel Augeraud

University of La Rochelle
Pôle Sciences et Technologies
17042 La Rochelle – France
{guylain.delmas,ronan.champagnat,michel.augeraud}@univ-lr.fr

Abstract. Joseph Campbell's "Hero's Journey" is a well-known narrative structure mainly used in cinema and literature. This paper deals with an application of this structure as a template for interactive storytelling in video games. It first presents an architecture for adaptive execution, gives the outline concerning this model and shows how to adapt it to an interactive context. A new interactive pattern is being introduced, as a model for dynamic computation of narrative.

Keywords: Interactive Storytelling, Adaptive execution.

1 Introduction

Video games are a more and more important support for training and education: they immerse the user into a simulated setting, used to reproduce real experiment while reducing the costs and the risks of real practice. [Wong, 2007] stated that video games are a more effective tool for education than traditional ways of teaching.

Within this context, the improvement of the framework of game is of first importance, because it encourages the student to further experiment. One of the important improvements is the construction of rich and detailed "stories", synchronized on cycles of training. Immersing the "player" in a story will ensure that he will play it until the end, and thus will provide an additional effort in the training process.

However, interaction for learner is needed for a better efficiency. The linear aspect of stories unrolled into games is an obstacle with the interactivity and freedom necessary to the training. The duality between stories and interactivity generally carries out to a clash between story and interaction [Juul, 1999]. This divergence leads two different ways of solving the problem: in a first category we have works about scenario design and validation of player's actions, as presented in [Young, 2004] or [Magerko, 2005], and next we find other works based on the concept of emergent narrative, introduced by [Aylett, 1999] and completed by [Szilas, 2003].

To deal with this opposition, we suggested in [Delmas 2007] a system of plot monitoring for interactive games. It generates a story during the course of execution, according to game's setting, player's actions, and plot patterns written by game designer. This first system includes for now only one basic scenario pattern, which requires evolutions.

M. Cavazza and S. Donikian (Eds.): ICVS 2007, LNCS 4871, pp. 187 – 195, 2007.

Literature has provided many works on stories' structures, such as [Propp, 1968] with Russian traditional folktales. These models can provide interesting bases to the development of scenario patterns, and most of them were already reviewed as possible tools for interactive storytelling systems [Cavazza, 2006]. Our attention focused on the "Hero's Journey" from Joseph Campbell [Campbell, 1972]. This model is based on the study of the initiatory tales in mythology. It is already used in video games design, and is considered as a standard tool for scenario writing [Dunniway, 2000]. However, this structure was designed using linear structure of stories. It is thus not well suited for more complex structures based on interaction. Our objective is to provide an adaptation of the model more convenient to support interaction, and to generate interactive stories. So we propose to integrate it in a monitoring system for interactive games, using a pattern based on Hero's Journey.

We will first present our monitoring system, and the place the Hero's Journey can take in our work. Then we will discuss about the Hero's Journey, its interests and its limits in an interactive environment. We will then present some clues to adapt this model in order to support interaction, and finally we discuss perspectives opened by this work.

2   Plot Monitoring for Interactive Narrative Games

Our works about the Hero's Journey and its adaptation to interactive games has for goal to integrate it as a scenario pattern in a plot monitoring system for games. This system, previously described in [Delmas, 2007], is designed to generate a narrative at game's execution time, relying on player's choices rather than on a pre-designed plot.

2.1   Plot Monitoring Architecture

Our system relies on the idea of generating the narrative of a game during its execution, rather than basing it on a prewritten plot. This idea enables us to provide games with freer narratives, more in accordance with player's expectations, while ensuring consistency and interest of the story.

Our work relies on the use of emergent narrative theory [Aylett, 1999], added with a plot monitoring architecture [Champagnat, 2007]. This architecture observes the course of the game, analyses player's actions and gives directives to the game in order to produce narrative. This part is similar to [Szilas, 2003], it differs on the way we consider the narrative. We make decisions relying on a global vision of narrative, instead of a local one.

This architecture requires 3 main data components:

- Game model: This model (a logical description of the game) provides us information about the different elements present in the game, their mutual relations, the ways they can interact between themselves and the ways the player can interact with them. With this model, the monitoring system can have an up-to-date vision of current game state, and make estimations about possible evolutions of the game during the play. For technical reasons, we chose to use a Petri net to implement this model. Petri net logic, enabling to consume resources to produce new ones, is well suited to a model where we consume states and interactions to produce new states.

- Narrative model: This model is used as a pattern for narrative generation. This set of rules of narrative construction is used as a guideline for development of narrative during the execution.

- Player's profile: This set of information about player allows us to make estimations about player's current and future actions, and to anticipate the choices he will make. We can use this information to generate a narrative more suited to player's behaviour.

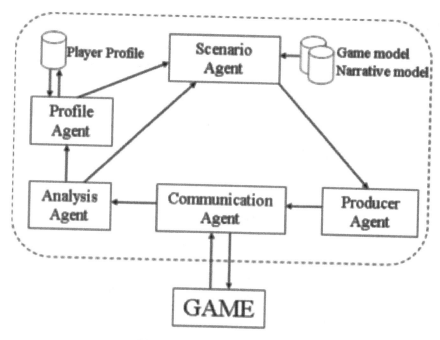

Fig. 1. Plot monitoring architecture

At the beginning of the play, no scenario is still selected. The system waits for the first actions of the player in order to select the scenario which will be the most appropriate. With each event occurring in the play (here a player-character interaction), the game sends information to the system, this one treats it then agent by agent:

The analysis agent identifies the resources related to the event and the influence of the event on the statistics of the player profile. It supplies the statistics to the profile agent and informs the scenario agent about the impact of the player upon the game model.

When the scenario agent receives new resources, it first computes the new state of the game (Petri net player). If a significant narrative step is crossed (evolution of a critical resource), the agent has to computes an adequate reaction. It first determines the conclusion with the best probability of occurring (according to proximity to current state and player's profile). It then lists all system-directed resources needed to reach this conclusion (focusing only on critical resources), and select an appropriate number of them (by referring to narrative's length and appropriate narrative constraints). The list of selected resources is then transmitted to the realization agent.

The production agent then converts this list of resources into computable instructions and sends them to the game. The game can then alter character's behavior according to the instructions (without instruction, each character follows a default behavior).

Once the narrative reaches a conclusive state, the system can put a term to the game. We keep from this execution a game log (events which occurred, caused by the player or the system), a trace of execution (various successive states) and the player profile (number and nature of interactions, statistics related to each character). This information can then be analyzed to have a retrospective vision of the play (favorites themes, player's preferences, reactions to various situations).

The main limitation to the quantity and quality of the narratives generated relies mainly on the complexity of the game model. A limited game model provides very few means of interactions to the player, and restricts the game to a small amount of predefined stories. On the opposite a really rich game model provides a great liberty of action, and allows the plot monitoring system to design various stories. However, the narrative construction model is also important, as it will be used as a pattern for narrative generation. This model has to provide consistent enough narrative, while giving flexibility to the monitoring architecture.

2.2 The Hero's Journey as a Model of Narrative Construction

We stated in previous section the importance of the model of narrative construction. Definition of such model can be a problem if we don't use a suitable reference model. However, literature provided us with a fair amount of examples of narrative construction, such as [Propp, 1970] and [Campbell, 1972]. So, these models seem to be a logical source of inspiration for our logical models.

The Hero's Journey is one of the most famous models in story construction. It has already largely been used in writing, cinema and videogames. In this context, it makes a perfect choice of basis for interactive story construction. An interactive version of the Hero's Journey will provide us with ability of generating stories with a well-tried structure, already known and approved by players.

3 The Model as We Know It

This section presents Campbell's Hero's Journey and its interest for serious games, and makes a point on the limits of the structure for interactive games. Actually, Campbell's structure is designed for linear narratives and not for interactive games.

3.1 What's This "Hero's Journey"?

The identification of this structure comes from a study of the recurring diagrams found in mythology. Joseph Campbell proposes a common pattern, including strong reference symbols: a journey from the "common" world towards another most supernatural, and the way back. This journey is also a symbolic representation of the passage from childhood to adulthood, passing by a series of trials and by facing paternal and maternal figures. The structure describes the story in 3 parts:

The Departure stands for exposure and introduction. The hero is at first immersed in his common environment, and then faced to an unexpected problem. Lacking the skills needed to resolve his problem at first, he will have to start a journey (the Quest) to an unknown environment. Only by succeeding the quest will the Hero obtain the knowledge and skill he needs.

The Initiation stands for the major part of the story. It's the core of the quest, where the Hero will have to gain knowledge and face trials in order to progress. This part ends on a major trial, during which the hero must prove both his virtue and his mastery of the elements of the quest.

The Return completes the journey by a way back t the Hero's initial environment. Back from his Quest, he still has to put the knowledge obtained in application to solve his initial problem. He proves by this way that he mastered both two worlds of the Quest.

3.2 Relevance for Serious Games

The Hero's Journey, as a description of an initiatory process, brings a convenient basis for transmission of knowledge. In a typical Hero's Journey's narrative, our hero is at first faced with an insoluble problem (start of the quest) He then has to assimilate various knowledge relative to the quest and pass trials in order to progress, ends by a ordeal trial resuming the whole knowledge acquired. Then he can come back to his world, and use his knowledge to solve his initial problem, proving his ability to put his new knowledge in practice.

In a serious game framework, we can so use this diagram as a decomposition of knowledge transmission. First the student is faced with a difficult problem, illustrating the theme of the lesson. He notices that he misses the knowledge and skills to solve it. Then the subject is divided into several elements, presented one after another, and the student must show his assimilation of the various elements in order to go on. A final test sums up the whole elements, and gives confirmation of their assimilation by the student. Finally, he is faced with the initial problem again, and can give value to his new knowledge by solving the problem, ending with a feeling of self progression.

3.3 Limits of the Model

Although very useful for writing linear narratives, this model finds limits when used for interactive narrative. Based on a sequence of linear patterns, it is not designed for a purpose of interactivity.

In a linear story, the author does not have to worry about the choices and actions undertaken by the characters, since he controls at the same time those ones and the resolution of their actions. In the same way, he can constantly choose to put in scene characters other than the hero, in order to exploit different methods of narration (even if in the case of the "Hero's Journey", the Hero remains central). However, within the framework of interactive narrative, and more in that of games, the author looses these freedoms. The player is generally identified as the Hero, and makes the experiment of the game through his adventures. The Hero must be permanently present at the time of the play, avoiding player to loose his marks. Moreover, this one must remain in the scope of the action, and not leave the player in passive position.

In addition, in a game, the player must be free of his choices and actions. His choices can then come directly against the initial scenario (which sometimes relies on precise choices from player). Finally, the player can fail: fail some trials, be mistaken, and refuses some possibilities. These failures, if they are not taken into account during the game design, can put the narrative in danger: either while compelling game to repeat some steps, leading to boredom of the player, or by causing a brutal termination of the game, ending the experiment before term.

4   Adapting Hero's Journey to Interactive Storytelling

In order to improve Hero's Journey's adaptation to interactive games, we propose some alterations to the initial model. These modifications rely on the implication of the player, the enacting of his choices, and adaptation to player's efficiency. We add new steps (*Stubborn refusal, Interference from without*, etc.) and extend the narrative scheme.

4.1   Possible Ways Towards Adaptation

As the Hero's Journey principal lack is its linear form, we proposed three suggestions of adaptation to upgrade it in an interactive narrative model. The suggestions rely on the constant implication of the player, the implementation of player's every choice and the adaptation to player's results.

On the opposite of a traditional spectator, the player must remain in the center of the action, and not be limited to a passive role. Any important action of the scenario must occur by and with him. If it's still possible to provide some cinematic sequences related to second role characters, these sequences should only be used as an element of drama, and related to player's actions (refusal of implication, failure with a test, etc).

As a result, any scene of the story must put the player at the center of the action, and its resolution must rely on player's actions. Although consequences of these actions can give place to phases where player looses control over the narrative, those should only illustrate the result of his actions, and not direct the course of the game.

As the player is central to the narrative, the story should never rely on a specific comportment. Each time that the player is given a choice (to begin his journey, accept/refuse some help, reaction to a proposal or a meeting, etc.) each reaction must be valid and allow the progression of the narrative. This one must give a suitable answer to each choice.

Often game designers are tempted to reward some "good" choices (choices which show a will of progression, the resolution of an important dilemma, etc), but this solution is to be used with parsimony: by obviously supporting specific choices, the game denies player's right to determine his acts.

Players can't always succeed at the first time, and we rarely hear of stories ending brutally because the hero made a mistake. Heroes sometimes fail, so do players.

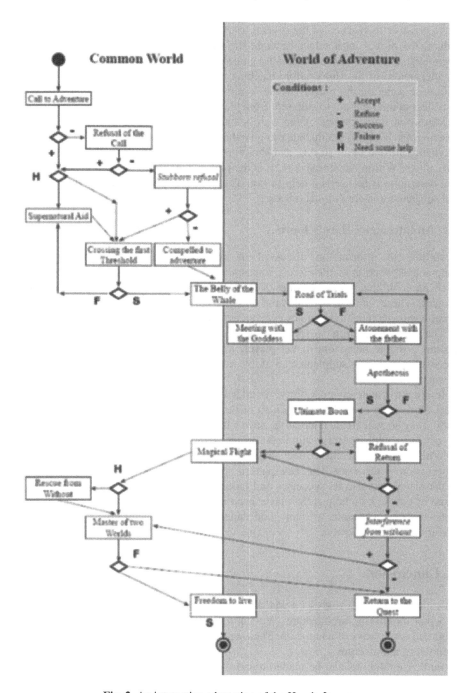

Fig. 2. An interactive adaptation of the Hero's Journey

That's why the game must take into account player's failures as much as his successes. Most of games (with notable exception of Wing Commander IV) only make possible to succeed of the several trials suggested to the player. In the event of failure, the player must either reiterate the stage, or take again the game since its beginning. These repetitions break the game's dynamics and bore the player, causing an interruption of the game before reaching its end. The game must be permissive to failure: to sanction the player (worse results, handicaps at the time of the following tests, less points) but not to stop him from playing.

Moreover, some phases of the Hero's Journey (mainly *Supernatural Aid* and the *Rescue from Without*) are intended to give the hero a support in his trials. They are not inevitably present in all stories, and should mainly rely on player's ability to pass the difficulties. Within our framework, it is the player's ability to succeed the tests which will determine if he needs a help or not. Thus, these support stages become optional and subjected to a conditional release.

4.2 An Interactive Hero's Journey

According to information discussed in previous section, we can propose an "interactive" version of the Hero's Journey (fig. 2). This new model is based on the application of the preceding rules, but also requires to carrying out some design choices. There can be several valid alternatives, according to author's needs. A version with accompanying notes is given here as an example.

The scenario pattern we propose must offer sufficient flexibility to cover the various possible behaviors of the player, and to accept his failures as much as its successes. We thus supplemented it by adding new stages and by detailing the advance.

In order to cover any possibility, we added complementary stages. Mainly optional, they allow us to open the possibilities of the narrative and to answer the unforeseen ones. They so will create alternative ways which will enable us to adapt to the choices of the player while preserve him in the story.

With the help of these new stages, it is possible to build a more detailed progression of the story. This new pattern takes into account the important decisions of the player and also its successes and failures during various trials. It is possible to assist its course by a help if the player encounters difficulties, to make him test again some trials if his results are not good enough, or to accelerate the narrative if the player voluntarily goes on.

5 Conclusion

This paper presents a study of a well-known story design model and clues to adapt it to a plot monitoring architecture. We studied interests and limits of the model, and proposed some ways of adaptation. Then we presented how to use this model in a plot monitoring architecture.

Further evolutions can be made around the use in a serious game context, with a more detailed specification of knowledge and its valorization through trials. A better evaluation of player's knowledge before the game and of player's improvements can also be a way of adapting not only the course of the narrative, but also its content.

References

[Aylett, 1999] Aylett, R.: Narrative in virtual environments – towards emergent narrative. In: Proceedings of the AAAI Fall Symposium on Narrative Intelligence (1999)

[Campbell, 1972] Campbell, J.: A hero with a thousand faces. Princeton University Press (1972)

[Cavazza, 2006] Cavazza, M., Pizzi, D.: Narratology for interactive storytelling, a critical introduction. In: Göbel, S., Malkewitz, R., Iurgel, I. (eds.) TIDSE 2006. LNCS, vol. 4326, Springer, Heidelberg (2006)

[Champagnat, 2005] Champagnat, R., Prigent, A., Estraillier, P.: Scenario building based on formal methods and adaptive execution. In: Proceeding of ISAGA, Atlanta (2005)

[Delmas, 2007] Delmas, G., Champagnat, R., Augeraud, M.: Plot Monitoring for Interactive Narrative Games. In: ACE 2007. International Conference on Advances in Computer Entertainment, Salzburg, Austria (2007)

[Dunniway, 2000] Dunniway, T.: Using the Hero's Journey in Games. Gamasutra (November 27, 2000)

[Propp, 1968] Propp, V.: Morphology of the Folktale, 2nd edn. Trans. Lawrence Scott. University of Texas Press (1968)

[Szilas, 2003] Szilas, N.: IDtension: a narrative engine for Interactive Drama. In: TIDSE 2003. 1st International Conference on Technologies for Interactive Digital Storytelling and Entertainment, Darmstadt, Germany (2003)

[Wong, 2007] Wong, W.L., Shen, C., Nocera, L., Carriazo, E., Tang, F., Buggal, S., Narayanan, H., Wang, H., Ritterfeld, U.: Serious Video Game Effectiveness. In: ACE 2007. International Conference on Advances in Computer Entertainment, Salzburg, Austria (2007)

Automatic Direction of Interactive Storytelling: Formalizing the Game Master Paradigm

Federico Peinado[1] and Pablo Gervás[2]

[1] Departamento de Ingeniería del Software e Inteligencia Artificial
Universidad Complutense de Madrid, Spain
email@federicopeinado.com
[2] Instituto de Tecnologías del Conocimiento
Universidad Complutense de Madrid, Spain
pgervas@sip.ucm.es

Abstract. During the fast evolution of automatic direction of Interactive Digital Storytelling many description of similar ideas have appeared in the academic literature. System architectures and workflows are usually presented using informal descriptions and diagrams, what makes difficult to identify what are the real contributions of each publication. In the way of establishing a safe ground for future research on this topic, this paper is a first step towards the formalization of a particular paradigm for developing automatic storytellers. The chosen paradigm is Role-Playing Game Mastering, which computational model is presented using UML.

1   Introduction

Specially during past decade, research on Interactive Digital Storytelling (IDS) has been growing relatively fast. Many papers about this topic are published each year in any of the conferences and journals that accept this kind of scientific contributions (from specific but also general fields such as Computer Entertainment and Education, Multimedia Systems, Artificial Intelligence, etc.). Some theoretical proposals have been described around the same idea: computational models for automatic control of an interactive narration.

The heart of the problem these research projects are trying to solve is a deep and well-known narratological question: the dilemma of Interactive Storytelling.

Authors of interactive narrations request some control over the plot that is unfolding in the computer of the user because they are the creators of the contents, the behaviours and the final purpose of the application; but at the same time interactors also need some control over the story they are enjoying because what motivate them is taking part in the plot as active agents and not only passive audience.

Several approaches are taken to develop an automatic direction system, and many different domains, environments and applications are used as test beds for illustrating the utility of those systems. Some of these approaches are becoming more common than others, what means they are recognized in the scientific community as valid paradigms for working in this field.

M. Cavazza and S. Donikian (Eds.): ICVS 2007, LNCS 4871, pp. 196–201, 2007.

In this paper we are presenting a preliminar formalization of a well-known theory, what we called the Game Master (GM) paradigm. This theory claims that the richer and more intuitive metaphor of an automatic director for IDS applications is a human GM controlling a role-playing game. This paradigm, sometimes too much overlooked, is a particular instance of the more general "centralized approach" to IDS management.

Because we usually found poorly detailed and informal figures in IDS research, probably because of the immaturity of the field, we propose the objective of improving and clarifying all the contributions that have appeared around te GM paradigm, describing them in a common and understandable framework.

The contents of the paper are organized as follow: Section 2 provides a short overview on IDS automatic direction related to the GM paradigm. Section 3 describes our proposal of a computational model for the system architecture and main workflow of this paradigm. Finally, Section 4 presents some preliminar conclusions of this research project.

2   Background

Widely different computational IDS approaches have been proposed in the area in which we can found those two big families of automatic direction approaches. There are proposals based on emergent behavior of non-player characters that achieve dramatic goals and approaches giving more responsibility to a central dramatic planning algorithm. Sometimes adding controllable NPCs to a centralized planner for achieving story goals or adopting a mixed approach, with a centralized director and a set of semiautonomous agents. There are also standalone dramatic planners that controls the most important narrative elements, like characters or the whole fictional world.

The idea of reusing concepts from Role Playing Games (RPGs) in the domain of IDS applications was there many years before it was published and more developed in recent research [1,2,3,4]. Empirical studies, as the theory of Louchart and Aylett, or the categorization of Flowers, Magerko and Mishra, have been specially considered for the development of our model. Peinado and Gervás's translation of GM improvising rules to the world of computational problem-solving and the introduction of characters in the continuation of that model by Swartjes, Vromen and Bloom are also considered as a main reference in our proposal.

What is more difficult to find in the papers on automatic direction for IDS application are good formalization of computational models, workflows or software architectures that give support for this complex and knowledge-driven dynamic management. In order to start using a formal modeling language, we have chosen the Unified Modeling Language (UML) [5] for drawing a visual conceptualization of a GM-based system. This OMG standard is a well-known tool for modeling software applications, well documented and with very good development tools, so we consider it useful for modeling applications as the ones were mentioned before.

3   Modeling an Artificial Game Master

In the context of this model, we make some assumptions about what an IDS system and an automatic director of an IDS system is.

First of all, we consider that an IDS system means "a computational system designed for software developers to build IDS applications" and IDS application means "a computational application designed for users (interactors) to take part in a concrete interactive experience, structured as a story represented in the computer". Sometimes behind an IDS application there is a more generic IDS system, sometimes not. In both cases it is possible to abstract the essential paradigm that researchers had in mind when designing their software, but usually for IDS application is more difficult.

Secondly, and automatic director for us means "a part of a computational system designed for the system itself to manage the experience of their potential users". This managements usually implies explicit representation of knowledge, intelligent mediation between authors and interactors and some goals or restrictions over the user experience, what it is called the multiform plot.

As we mentioned before, the Game Master paradigm is a particular case of the centralized architecture presented in many research projects. This architecture can accept some directed characters, what means they are in some way controlled by the director and therefore they have limited autonomy for developing the story. The game master can be implemented as a distributed system, even as a complex system with several components, but for control effects, only one narrative agent exists.

This section is dedicated to the computational model of the game master we formalize. There are some differences between this model and the ideas presented in other papers, but every decision is justified according to the different nature of a human GM and an "artificial" one, specially in the level of knowledge.

In figure 1 the UML component diagram of our proposal is shown. The model corresponds to a GM-based system architecture, i.e. a system with an automatic director of IDS applications following what we have called the Game Master paradigm.

In the center of the model there are two nodes: "Narrative Environment" and "Director". The first one is the virtual environment in which the narrative action is presented to the users (here called Interactors). It usually represents a 3D world with objects, locations, characters and every element needed to tell the story. Although using their imagination is also possible for the players, this environment restricts a lot that aspect of playing games. Players and environment have a good flow of information.

The second node replaces the human GM, being an artificial GM in the form of a software system. Both director and environment are communicated because they send and receive information, but in this case specific adapters are needed because interfaces for both nodes can be quite different due to the different nature of an AI program and a graphic or multimedia engine. Inside the Director there is a Knowledge Model and extensions for each domain of knowledge that the

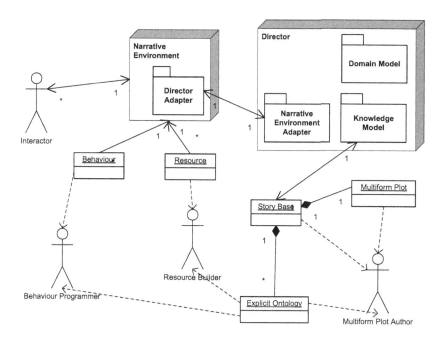

Fig. 1. A model of an automatic director inspired in a human Game Master

director needs in order to understand what is happening in the story and to intervene accordingly.

The Adventure, the plot draft that the human Game Master used to follow, it is called Multiform Plot in this model, developed also by an external Multiform Plot Author. This multiform plot is also the input for the environment, but because of the format it can be easily integrated in the Story Base and taken as part of the knowledge model of the director; so dependency with the Multiform Plot is implicit, but included in the model. The Story Base usually contains complete plots or some partial plots with elements that are useful in order to reuse old material when directing a new story.

Here clearly the Director is not the author of the multiform plot, but it can add some successful experiences to the Story Base, even in real time due to the capabilities a computer has and a human being has not.

Resource Builder and Behaviour Programmer are the two roles of the people involved in creating the material for the virtual environment. The game system must be ideally implicit in the environment, so Interactors can discover it at the same time they play. Director do not need to depende on those things because the communication with the environment is enough fluid to check that during each significant situation in the story.

An explicit representation of knowledge is needed, an Explicit Ontology, what is just a part of the knowledge the Interactors have about the fictional world, but enough for the Director to understand what happens in the story. In real life there is a strong game background and common sense assumptions shared by the GM and the players, but here all that knowledge is limited to the basic information about the game that can be coded in the ontology.

This model is being applied in the development of the centralized knowledge-intensive automatic director of the Knowledge-Intesive Interactive Digital Storytelling (KIIDS) system [6]. This director uses Case-Based Reasoning to model the kind of decisions a GM takes to create on the fly the next scene he is trying to introduce in the game.

4 Conclusions

In this paper we present a computational model of a human game master. It is designed as a centralized intelligent system, replacing the human GM, that perform some automatic control over the dynamic development of the story. Far beyond *mediation*, the system *directs* the story towards well defined goals using a multiform plot for that.

World and specially characters are not considered as truly narrative agents, just as non-completely autonomous extensions of the game master (the behaviours of the Narrative Environment represent those characters). Shared knowledge between players, GM, adventure authors and game system builders is replaced by an explicit ontology incorporated in the knowledge model of the Director. Data structures are unified in a story base, supporting multiform plots and complete stories. Communication interfaces between the Narrative Environment and the Director appears, because data flow now it is not transparent and fluid as players talking with the GM was.

The preliminar formalization presented here could be a step forward to the information interchange in our field. Although this paper has no room for other UML diagrams that describe low-level details of our model, the basic ideas have been presented.

The final goal is to make the community move towards better presentation of their ideas and results, using UML or other formal languages (maybe more appropiated for low-level description) to express, compare and evaluate different approaches, finding compatibilities and synergies, distributing the work in small parts, looking forward a better understanding of what IDS is and how it can be controlled by the computer.

Acknowledgements

This research is funded by Ministerio de Educación y Ciencia (TIN2006-14433-C02-01 project), Universidad Complutense de Madrid and Dirección General de Universidades e Investigación de la Comunidad de Madrid (UCM-CAM-910494 research group grant).

References

1. Louchart, S., Aylett, R.: Towards a narrative theory of virtual reality. Virtual Reality 7(1) (2003)
2. Peinado, F., Gervás, P.: Transferring game mastering laws to interactive digital storytelling. In: Göbel, S., Spierling, U., Hoffmann, A., Iurgel, I., Schneider, O., Dechau, J., Feix, A. (eds.) TIDSE 2004. LNCS, vol. 3105, pp. 48–54. Springer, Heidelberg (2004)
3. Swartjes, I., Vromen, J., Bloom, N.: Narrative inspiration: Using case based problem solving to support emergent story generation. In: International Joint Workshop on Computational Creativity, London, UK (2007)
4. Flowers, A., Magerko, B., Mishra, P.: Gamemasters and interactive story: A categorization of storytelling techniques in live roleplaying. In: Futureplay, London, Ontario (2006)
5. Object-Management-Group: Unified modeling language. http://www.uml.org/
6. Peinado, F.: Knowledge-intensive interactive digital storytelling system. http://federicopeinado.com/projects/kiids/

FearNot! – An Emergent Narrative Approach to Virtual Dramas for Anti-bullying Education

Ruth Aylett[1], Marco Vala[2], Pedro Sequeira[2], and Ana Paiva[2]

[1] MACS, Heriot-Watt University, Riccarton, Edinburgh. EH14 4AS, UK
ruth@macs.hw.ac.uk
[2] INESC-ID and IST, Tagus Park, Portugal
Ana.Paiva@inesc-id.pt

Abstract. Overview of the FearNot! system for demonstration.

Extended Abstract

FearNot! is a story-telling application originally created in the EU FP5 project VICTEC and now extended in the FP6 project eCIRCUS [eCIRCUS 07]. It has applied ideas from Forum Theatre [Boal 79] to the domain of education against bullying. In Forum Theatre, sections of an audience take responsibility for a specific character in the unfolding drama, played by an actor who always stays in role. Episodes in which the actors improvise within an overall narrative framework are broken by interaction sections in which the audience sections talk over with 'their' character what they should do in the next dramatic segment. The actor is free to reject advice that seems incompatible with their role, and may also suspend a dramatic episode if it seems necessary to get further advice.

In FearNot!, dramatic episodes are generated by the bullying behaviour of one of the characters, who victimizes another of the characters (Fig 1.). These are

Fig. 1. One character victimizes another in FearNot!

M. Cavazza and S. Donikian (Eds.): ICVS 2007, LNCS 4871, pp. 202–205, 2007.

John:What should I do?
Mark:hit him in the face
John:So you think I should hit him back?

Fig. 2. The user advises the victim using free text input

graphically-embodied in 3D cartoon-like form within school and other related environments, with overall scenarios that have been collected from school students themselves in the UK and Germany. Between episodes, the victimized character seeks advice from the child user, of age 9-11, who is able to enter free-text input (Fig 2.). This advice changes the internal state of the character, who may then behave differently in the next episode. The educational aim is to allow children to explore the space of responses to bullying given that there is no strategy guaranteed to work, though some strategies are more often successful than others.

Creating believable characters that give the illusion of life allowing the user's suspension of disbelief is essential for FearNot! because not only is believability a precondition for an empathic relationship between characters and users – required to meet the educational outcomes - but also, because in a dramatic environment, user engagement depends on gripping stories being told and for this characters must be believable.

Characters select actions autonomously within episodes through an emotion-driven architecture, FAtiMA [Dias & Paiva 05] that uses OCC-based cognitive appraisal [Ortony et al 88, Elliot 92] along with coping behaviour [Lazarus 91] at both reactive and predictive levels, as shown in Fig. 3. The story within a specific episode thus emerges from interaction between the characters, producing an emergent narrative [Aylett et al 06]. Episodes are set up by a narrative facilitator agent, that chooses which characters will be present and in which location.

Characters have also been equipped with an autobiographic memory [Ho et al 07] so that they can refer to incidents from past episodes in interacting with the child user. The overall system also integrates a language processor and has been implemented

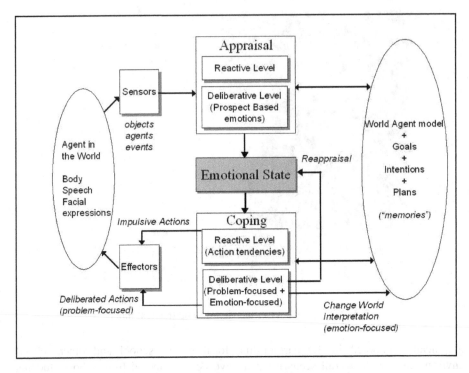

Fig. 3. The FAtiMA agent architecture

within a generic environment, ION, which supports a variety of visualisation in the current case the open source graphics engine Ogre 3D has been used for 3D visualisation.

A scripted version of the system has been extensively evaluated [Hall et al 05] in order to test whether the characters seem believable to children and whether they are able to empathise with what happens to the characters in the stories. The results were positive, and a longitudinal study of the impact of the current version will be carried out in schools in the UK and Germany in September 2007.

We propose a demo of FearNot! in which users will be able to interact with the system, playing the role of the child user.

Acknowledgements

This work was partially supported by European Community (EC) and is currently funded by the eCIRCUS project IST-4-027656-STP. The authors are solely responsible for the content of this publication. It does not represent the opinion of the EC, and the EC is not responsible for any use that might be made of data appearing therein.

References

Aylett, R.S., Louchart, S., Dias, J., Paiva, A., Vala, M., Woods, S., Hall, L.: Unscripted Narrative for affectively driven characters. IEEE Journal of Graphics and Applications 26(3), 42–52 (2006)

Boal, A.: Theatre of the Oppressed. Theatre Communications Group, New York (1979)

Dias, J., Paiva, A.: Feeling and Reasoning: a Computational Model. In: Bento, C., Cardoso, A., Dias, G. (eds.) EPIA 2005. LNCS (LNAI), vol. 3808, pp. 127–140. Springer, Heidelberg (2005)

Elliot, C.: The Affective Reasoner: A process model of emotions in a multi-agent system. PhD Thesis, Illinois (1992)

Gratch, J., Marsella, S.: Tears and fears: Modeling emotions and emotional behaviors in synthetic agents. In: The Fifth International Conference on Autonomous Agents (2001)

Hall, L., Woods, S., Aylett, R., Newall, L., Paiva, A.: Achieving empathic engagement through affective interaction with synthetic characters. In: Tao, J., Tan, T., Picard, R.W. (eds.) ACII 2005. LNCS, vol. 3784, pp. 731–731. Springer, Heidelberg (2005)

Ho, W.C., Dias, J., Figueiredo, R., Paiva, A.: Agents that remember can tell stories: integrating autobiographic memory into emotional agents. In: AAMAS. Proceedings of Autonomous Agents and Multiagent Systems, ACM Press, New York (2007)

Lazarus, R.: Emotion and adaptation. Oxford University Press, NY (1991)

Ortony, A., Clore, G., Collins, A.: The cognitive structure of emotions. Cambridge University Press, Cambridge (1988)

From ActAffAct to BehBehBeh:
Increasing Affective Detail in a Story-World

Stefan Rank and Paolo Petta

Austrian Research Institute for Artificial Intelligence
Freyung 6/6, A-1010 Vienna, Austria
{stefan.rank,paolo.petta}@ofai.at

1   Introduction

Story-worlds are virtual worlds inhabited by synthetic characters that provide
an environment in which users participate actively in the creation of a narrative. Implementation approaches range from plot-driven to character-based
[4,7]. Character-based approaches require synthetic agents with autonomy and
personality. Affective agent architectures [13,2] are used to construct such autonomous personality agents, and computational models of emotion are seen as
a prerequisite for the required emotional and social competences. The present
paper reports on ongoing work based on the experiences gained in earlier work,
in particular TABASCO [6] and ActAffAct (Acting Affectively affecting Acting
[8,10]). The following section reviews details of the earlier approach towards creating a story-world to generate cliché stories, while the later sections present the
changes in scope and approach adopted in our current work.

2   ActAffAct: Goals, Approach and Results

The ActAffAct project researched a bottom-up approach to imitating emotional
characters interacting in a story-world. The goal was to achieve the unfolding
of a plot-like structure while limiting the use of external macro-level control—as
traditionally exerted by, e.g., a director. The ideal level of external control would
be none at all, resulting in the emergence of plot from the characters' interaction,
effectively turning the agents into reusable roleplayers. A basic assumption of the
project was that emotions—as described in appraisal theories [5,12,1]—can provide the links between actions that render a plot plausible. More specifically, the
interplay of motivational constructs and the subjective evaluative interpretation
of changes in an agent's environment provide for the causal and emotional connections that can lead to the unfolding of a story, given an environment set up to
be prone to conflict. We implemented a simple 2D world (see Fig. 1) populated
by four agents parameterised to roughly correspond to archetypical dramatic
character types: hero, mentor, villain, and victim. Further, the world contained
some objects to be used to instigate conflicts by helping, hindering, challenging, and rewarding agents. An appraisal-based architecture was implemented to

M. Cavazza and S. Donikian (Eds.): ICVS 2007, LNCS 4871, pp. 206–209, 2007.

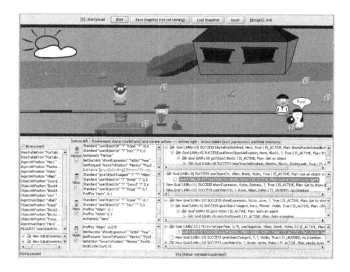

Fig. 1. The ActAffAct viewer application

control the characters. It used a pragmatic approach to integrate an appraisal theory [5] into a belief-desire-intention type plan-based agent framework [3].

ActAffAct was a first step towards the goal of dramatically and emotionally believable software agents, and it succeeded in creating dramatic structures, if for a rather limited notion of drama. Even so, the direction held promise for further work. A significant aspect of *interactive* drama to remain excluded was interaction itself, i.e., the interaction between one or more human users and the system. For real-time interaction to be possible in an emotionally meaningful way, we concluded that the disambiguation, structuring, and valuation of information acquired in sensorimotor interaction provided as a part of appraisal would need to be integrated at a lower granularity. The simulation of sensing and acting in a virtual world by exchanging pre-structured symbolic information does not match the intricate relation between perception and appraisal in real life. Further, research efforts in the European Network of Excellence Humaine[1] corroborated a focus on the pervasive role of emotion in humans and its operationalisation in a virtual agent.

3 BehBehBeh: Goals and Approach

BehBehBeh (Behaviour Behooving Behaviour [9,11]) is based on reconsidering the building blocks of affective agent architectures in order to provide for a rich and reasonably complete integrated agent architecture while delineating clearly all modelling shortcuts due to technical reasons or related to the scenario targeted. For BehBehBeh, the environment was changed to a simulated 3D world

---

[1] Human-machine interaction network on emotions, http://emotion-research.net

Fig. 2. Disgust, the first episode modelled in BehBehBeh

including a physics simulation. From the start, the objectives of this new version prioritise interaction with a user. All interaction with the environment is modelled as a dynamic process, and several concurrent modalities are to be included (simplified vision, hearing, smell, movement, and basic object manipulation). In order to achieve such a richer model of the internals of an affective agent, we propose to use concurrent communicating *processes* as model building blocks; these acquire and use *resources* that model the embodied limits of the agent itself. Basic types of resources are the processing time available to the agent and the communication channels for inter-process communication. The agent's abilities to interact with its environment are also abstracted as resources, to be used and controlled in a timely manner by its internal processes. Shortcuts required to achieve practical results are also reflected and marked as resources. While this approach towards a richer model of internal processes initially leads further away from the goal of interactive drama, we consider it a necessary step towards affectively satisfying interaction with virtual beings. In order to reduce the complexity of creating a complete affective model based on these building blocks, we focus on a series of specific emotional phenomena, modelled incrementally; as very first phenomenon we chose an episode of disgust (see Fig. 2).

4   Conclusion and Future Work

BehBehBeh is work in progress, aimed at overcoming limitations identified in earlier work by incrementally modelling emotional episodes using bounded resources and concurrent processes. These building blocks are motivated by the needs of modelling a physical system, by the characterisation of emotion in psychological theories, and by practical implementation concerns. Future work includes the steady addition of models covering further emotional episodes, building architectural abstractions as the need arises. To verify consistency of the models, they will all be integrated in a single game-like scenario.

Acknowledgements. The Austrian Research Institute for Artificial Intelligence is supported by the Austrian Federal Ministries for Science and Research and for Transport, Innovation and Technology. This research is supported by EU's FP6 NoE HUMAINE (Contract No.507422) and the Austrian Funds for Research and Technology Promotion for Industry (FFF 808818/2970 KA/SA). This publication reflects only the authors' views. The EU is not liable for any use that may be made of the information contained herein.

References

1. Frijda, N.H.: The Laws of Emotion. Lawrence Erlbaum Associates, Mahwah, NJ, USA, London, UK (2007)
2. Gratch, J., Marsella, S.: The Architectural Role of Emotion in Cognitive Systems. In: Gray, W.D. (ed.) Integrated Models of Cognitive Systems, pp. 230–242. Oxford University Press, New York (2007)
3. Huber, M.J.: JAM: a BDI-theoretic mobile agent architecture. In: Proc. of the 3rd Annual Conf. on Autonomous Agents, pp. 236–243. ACM Press, New York (1999)
4. Mateas, M., Stern, A.: Façade: Architecture and Authorial Idioms for Believable Agents in Interactive Drama. In: Gratch, J., Young, M., Aylett, R., Ballin, D., Olivier, P. (eds.) IVA 2006. LNCS (LNAI), vol. 4133, pp. 446–448. Springer, Heidelberg (2006)
5. Ortony, A.: On Making Believable Emotional Agents Believable. In: Trappl, R., Petta, P., Payr, S. (eds.) Emotions in Humans and Artifacts, pp. 189–212. MIT Press, Cambridge, MA, USA, London, UK (2003)
6. Petta, P.: The Role of Emotions in a Tractable Architecture for Situated Cognizers. In: Trappl, R., Petta, P., Payr, S. (eds.) Emotions in Humans and Artifacts, pp. 251–288. MIT Press, Cambridge, MA, USA, London, UK (2003)
7. Pizzi, D., Charles, F., Lugrin, J.-L., Cavazza, M.: Interactive Storytelling with Literary Feelings. In: Paiva, A., et al. (eds.) ACII 2007. LNCS, vol. 4738, pp. 630–641. Springer, Heidelberg (2007)
8. Rank, S.: Affective Acting: An Appraisal-based Architecture for Agents as Actors. Institute for Medical Cybernetics and Artificial Intelligence, Medical University Vienna, Master Thesis (2004)
9. Rank, S.: Building a computational model of emotion based on parallel processes and resource management. In: Cowie, R., de Rosis, F. (eds.) Proc. of the Doctoral Consortium at ACII2007, Lisbon, Portugal, September 12-14, 2007, pp. 102–109 (2007)
10. Rank, S., Petta, P.: Motivating Dramatic Interactions. In: Agents that Want and Like: Motivational and Emotional Roots of Cognition and Action, AISB, University of Sussex, Falmer, Brighton, UK, pp. 102–107 (2005)
11. Rank, S., Petta, P.: Basing artificial emotion on process and resource management. In: Paiva, A., et al. (eds.) ACII 2007. LNCS, vol. 4738, pp. 350–361. Springer, Heidelberg (2007)
12. Scherer, K.R.: What are emotions? And how can they be measured? Social Science Information 44(4), 695–729 (2005)
13. Trappl, R., Petta, P. (eds.): Creating Personalities for Synthetic Actors. LNCS, vol. 1195. Springer, Heidelberg (1997)
14. Trappl, R., Petta, P., Payr, S. (eds.): Emotions in Humans and Artifacts. MIT Press, Cambridge, MA, USA, London, UK (2003)

Affective Interactive Narrative in the CALLAS Project

Fred Charles[1], Samuel Lemercier[1], Thurid Vogt[2], Nikolaus Bee[2],
Maurizio Mancini[3], Jérôme Urbain[4], Marc Price[5], Elisabeth André[2],
Catherine Pélachaud[3], and Marc Cavazza[1]

[1] School of Computing, University of Teesside, United Kingdom
{f.charles,s.lemercier,m.o.cavazza}@tees.ac.uk
[2] Multimedia Concepts and Applications Group, Augsburg University, Germany
{vogt,bee,andre}@informatik.uni-augsburg.de
[3] IUT of Montreuil, University Paris VIII, France
{m.mancini,c.pelachaud}@iut-univ.paris8.fr
[4] Faculté Polytechnique de Mons, Department of Electrical Engineering,
TCTS Lab, Belgium
jerome.urbain@fpms.ac.be
[5] BBC Research, Tadworth, Surrey, United Kingdom
marc.price@rd.bbc.co.uk

1 Introduction

Interactive Narrative relies on the ability for the user (and spectator) to intervene in the course of events so as to influence the unfolding of the story. This influence is obviously different depending on the Interactive Narrative paradigm being implemented, i.e. the user being a spectator or taking part in the action herself as a character. If we consider the case of an active spectator influencing the narrative, most systems implemented to date [1] have been based on the direct intervention of the user either on physical objects staged in the virtual narrative environment or on the characters themselves via natural language input [1] [3]. While this is certainly empowering the spectator, there may be limitations as to the realism of that mode of interaction if we were to transpose Interactive Narrative for a vast audience.

Spontaneous audience reactions are not always as structured and well-defined as previous Interactive Narrative systems have assumed. If we consider that the narrative experience can be essentially interpreted as generating various emotional states (e.g. tension) which derive from its aesthetic qualities (e.g. suspense [6]), a logical consequence would be to analyse spectator's emotional reactions and use these as an input to an Interactive Narrative system. Such an approach would actually constitute a "feedback loop" between an Interactive Narrative inducing emotions and the analysis of the quality and intensity of such emotions expressed by the user. It is notoriously difficult to accurately detect and categorise spontaneous affective states occurring when users are engaged with various media. This is why we have revised the affective loop described above and, in an attempt to improve the elicitation of user emotional reactions we have inserted a virtual agent, acting as a co-spectator into that loop (see an illustration of the installation in Fig. 1).

The system can now be described as comprising i) an interactive narrative using traditional plan-based generative techniques, which is able to create situations exhibiting different levels of tension or suspense (by featuring the main character in

M. Cavazza and S. Donikian (Eds.): ICVS 2007, LNCS 4871, pp. 210–213, 2007.

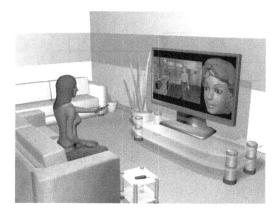

Fig. 1. Affective Interactive Narrative installation

dangerous situations) ii) an expressive virtual character (implemented using the Greta system [4]) whose role is, by accessing the internal data of the narrative planner, to exaggerate the emotional value of a given scene so as to make it more visible to the user and iii) affective input devices, which at the current stage of development of the system are limited to an affective speech detection system (EmoVoice [5]) and a multi-keyword spotting system detecting emotionally charged words and expressions.

Overall, the system operates by generating narrative situations of various levels of intensity and tension, which are conveyed to the user via the additional channel of the expressive character. The system then detects in real-time the emotional state of the user, in this first version mostly through its vocal reactions[1]. Finally, the emotion detected is used as a feedback on the story generation system to reinforce (positive feedback) or slow down (negative feedback) the narrative tension of the generated story.

2 System Overview and Results

We present a brief overview of the integrated system for the Affective Interactive Narrative installation (see Fig. 2) as well as some early results. The visualisation component is drawn from the character-based interactive storytelling system developed by Cavazza et al. [1] on top of the UT 2003™ computer game engine (Epic Games).

The narrative engine is essentially a HTN planner determining for the main virtual actor what action it should take next. The actions selected are passed to the game engine, in which they are associated to corresponding scripts describing the physical realisation of the action (including specific animations). Our first experimental prototype is based on a similar plot to Lugrin's *Death Kitchen* interactive narrative [2].

---

[1] Because vocal reactions correspond to a strong level of arousal, the expressive character plays an active role in increasing the user's reactivity. Future versions of the system will include the analysis of paralinguistic input (including silence) and video analysis of user's posture.

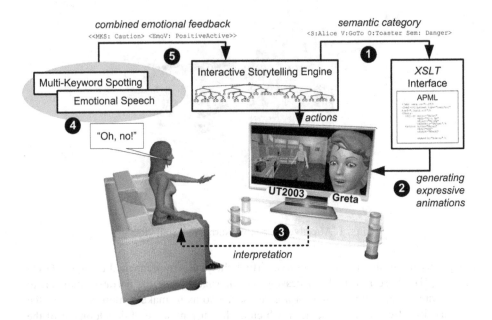

combined emotional feedback
<<MKS: Caution> <EmoV: PositiveActive>>

semantic category
<S:Alice V:GoTo O:Toaster Sem: Danger>

Fig. 2. System overview illustrating the sequence of processes

The overall plot consists in having the virtual character carry out everyday tasks in the kitchen where there is a great potential for dangerous tasks to take place. Unlike Lugrin's system which is based on emergent narrative paradigm, our prototype supports the specification of the narrative via the description of the virtual character's behaviour using a plan-based representation of everyday activities. The influence on the interactive storytelling engine comes from the emotional feedback portrayed by the user visualising the plot unfolding on the screen.

For instance, the virtual character is about to carry out a dangerous task in the kitchen, such as walking over a spillage on the floor. This dangerous situation is highlighted by the expressive virtual agent by playing the animations of the appropriate facial expression generated in real-time using our Java-based software interface which translates the information provided by the interactive storytelling engine into the appropriate APML commands using XSLT. The reaction from the user can be to warn the virtual character by shouting utterances such as *"Oh no!"*, *"Ah no!"*, *"Oh my god!"*, which are interpreted by the multi-keyword spotting component as a cautionary utterance. The EmoVoice component analyses the acoustic features of the utterance to recognise the emotional aspects of speech. This component incorporates so far three emotional classifications: *Neutral*, *PositiveActive*, and *NegativePassive*. The level of arousal (*PositiveActive*) defined from the user's utterance generates a high value of influence on the narrative engine by means of a dynamic change in the heuristic value. The remaining planning process is then influenced by the modified heuristic steering the subsequent selection of tasks towards a less dangerous set of situations.

3 Conclusion

We have described a first proof-of-concept implementation of our system, whose purpose was mostly to validate the concept of feedback loop and experiment with the various constraints on the system's response times. Such a prototype would not be able to support user reactions to narrative "instantaneous" events (fall of an object, impact of a missile) unless these are somehow announced or the action is artificially slowed down. We are however devising mechanisms for progressive tension generation that would be able to announce events of intense narrative significance before these are actually generated by the system. This would in turn make possible to process the user's emotional reaction to actually have an influence of the story unfolding, rather than just record emotions and reactions *a posteriori.*

Acknowledgements

This work has been funded in part by the EU via the CALLAS Integrated Project (ref. 034800, http://www.callas-newmedia.eu/).

References

1. Cavazza, M., Charles, F., Mead, S.J.: Character-based Interactive Storytelling. IEEE Intelligent Systems, special issue on AI in Interactive Entertainment, 17–24 (2002)
2. Lugrin, J.-L., Cavazza, M.: AI-based world behaviour for emergent narratives. In: Proceedings of the ACM Advances in Computer Entertainment Technology, Los Angeles, USA (2006)
3. Mateas, M., Stern, A.: Natural Language Understanding in Façade: Surface-text Processing. In: Göbel, S., Spierling, U., Hoffmann, A., Iurgel, I., Schneider, O., Dechau, J., Feix, A. (eds.) TIDSE 2004. LNCS, vol. 3105, Springer, Heidelberg (2004)
4. Poggi, I., Pelachaud, C., de Rosis, F., Carofiglio, V., De Carolis, B.: GRETA. A Believable Embodied Conversational Agent. In: Stock, O., Zancarano, M. (eds.) Multimodal Intelligent Information Presentation, Kluwer, Dordrecht (2005)
5. Wagner, J., Vogt, T., André, E.: A Systematic Comparison of Different HMM Designs for Emotion Recognition from Acted and Spontaneous Speech. In: ACII 2007. LNCS, vol. 4738, pp. 114–125. Springer, Heidelberg (2007)
6. Cheong, Y.G., Young, R.M.: A Computational Model of Narrative Generation for Suspense. In: AAAI 2006 Computational Aesthetic Workshop, Boston, MA, USA (2006)

Creating Interactive Poly-Artistic Works: The ConceptMove Project

Olivier Delerue[1], Stéphane Donikian[2], and Gildas Clénet[2]

[1] IRCAM, 1 place Igor Stravinsky, 75004 Paris
Olivier.Delerue@ircam.fr
[2] IRISA/INRIA, Campus de Beaulieu, 35042 Rennes
{donikian,gclenet}@irisa.fr

Abstract. Poly-artistic works often come up against two kinds of problems: heterogeneity of technologies on the one hand, and lack of abstraction to write the global structure of a piece on the other hand. To avoid the endless start from scratch approach, we present our project ConceptMove that addresses these issues. ConceptMove is a unified paradigm for describing interactive art pieces. This paradigm led us to code generation in order to automatically solve common issues. Last but not least, we propose an intuitive and user-friendly authoring tool that makes it possible for authors to easily write down their ideas.

Keywords: Interactivity, poly-artistic works, unified paradigms, code generation, temporal constraints.

1 Introduction

Interactive poly-artistic works is a type of expression becoming increasingly common nowadays. Consequently, users, specta(c)tors, expect more and more to play an active part in these works. Such works include for instance the *Virtual Museum of Contemporary photography* by Ahad Yari Rad, *Topologies de l'instant* or *Seule avec loup* by N+N Corsino, *Schlag!* by Roland Auzet, or *Waves* by Andrea Cera and Herve Robbe... Such creations always require the use of a wide range of technologies (3D video and audio display, video and audio synthesis, body tracking...): a large number of computer environments, software and frameworks have been created to fulfill these needs. These include for instance Max/MSP for audio processing, OpenMask [1] for 3D graphics, Life Forms [2] for the animation of human movements... Standards as well have been studied such as VRPN [3] or VRML for virtual realities as well as communication protocols between applications (OSC for instance).

However, despite this important profusion in terms of technical tools, several issues remain unsolved when realizing such artistic works. First, in the context of collaborative arts, existing frameworks do not provide means for conceptualizing art pieces for contributors coming from different artistic areas (composition, choreography, video, 3D graphics...). Second, establishing communications between software or hardware components is often complicated. Finally, the communication process and its language have to be redefined from scratch for each new realization.

M. Cavazza and S. Donikian (Eds.): ICVS 2007, LNCS 4871, pp. 214–218, 2007.

2 The Concept Move Project

We address these issues in ConceptMove, a project funded by the French ANR research program RIAM. Our objective is to facilitate the realization of interactive poly-artistic art pieces in several ways. First, the communication process should be as transparent as possible to the users. Second, the artists should be in a position to use their favorite environments or software components in order to fulfill their ideas. And last, we wish to provide a symbolic shared area to specify the relationships between the different artistic worlds so that artists coming from various domains have a common language to start working on. Thus, the key idea is to describe poly-artistic interactive art pieces in a most generic way, regardless of the various software, hardware and environments that will be used to implement concretely the functionalities. Such description is represented in Fig.1 where the art piece has been formalized with temporal entities organized in time using the Allen's relations.

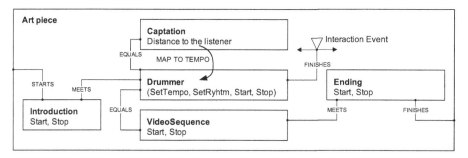

Fig. 1. Simple sketch of an interactive art piece using Allen's relations

In this simple sketch, the art piece is composed of six temporal objects (including the art piece overall container) and a number of temporal relations established between the temporal objects: when the piece starts, the Introduction is immediately started and followed right away by the central section composed of the tracking activity, the drummer and the video sequence linked together by « equals » relations. During this section the tracking module transmits listener position events to be mapped to the drummer module tempo parameter. The central section finishes exactly when the expected « interaction event » occurs. This leads to the Ending section witch finishes the piece.

In the following section we show how this description is used in order to generate automatically computer code for implementation in the selected environments.

3 Transformations and Code Generation

Once the overall description of the piece is achieved with the meta-language, including interactive specifications and temporal constraints, it is time to choose what environment or programming language the different people involved wish to use. As this XML description will be the source of different plug-ins (currently implemented are Max/MSP, Pure Data, Listenspace, OpenMASK, Java), there is technically no limitation in the range of software one can use. Next development may for instance consider addressing OpenMusic, Flash, and Eyesweb [4]. This architecture can also communicate with existing material, assuming they already had an OSC communication: the generated code will automatically match the particular protocol.

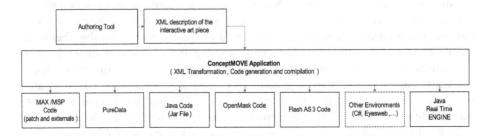

Fig. 2. Overall transformation process

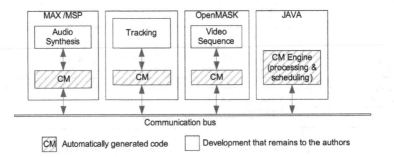

Fig. 3. Illustration of the generated code in several environments

The code generator (Fig. 2), with given IP address and port information, will then generate a low level interface for each requested environment. This interface will then be easily used at a high level in this environment (Fig. 3). For instance, a MAX/MSP developer will be able to establish a communication with a Java application, simply by using its send / receive common objects. This part, handling the communication, relies on an existing standard, WSDL, which allows describing the way an application communicates with the rest of the world. But there are also complementary temporal constraints that enable hierarchical and complex relations between temporal objects. This makes it possible for the code generator to create the "engine" of the art piece, e.g. a simple application that will schedule events in real time. This application will send start and stop events on time, but will also receive requests to start or stop temporal objects from the outside, enabling this way dynamic modification of temporal structures, through interaction for instance. Such constraint requests will of course be ignored if they turn to be inconsistent with written script of the piece. The written script is and stays the main reference and score for generated material and structural events.

4 Authoring

Authoring remains an important issue since the whole description of the art piece has to be specified in an XML format, which is not usable directly by the artists. A prototype of authoring tool has been created and can be seen on Fig.4.

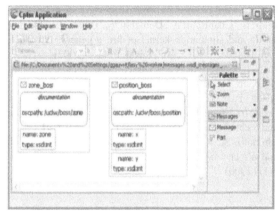

```
<wsdl:message name="zone_boss">
 <wsdl:documentation>
   <wsdl:oscpath value="/uclw/boss/zone"/>
 </wsdl:documentation>
 <wsdl:part name="zone" type="xsd:int"/>
</wsdl:message>

<wsdl:message name="position_boss">
 <wsdl:documentation>
   <oscpath value="/uclw/boss/position" />
 </wsdl:documentation>
 <wsdl:part name="x" type="xsd:int" />
 <wsdl:part name="y" type="xsd:int" />
</wsdl:message>
```

Fig. 4. View of the XML authoring tool (left) and equivalent XML code (right)

This tool is implemented as an eclipse plug-in and allows specifying the art piece from the most abstract level down to the implementation details. Once the piece is fully described, the authoring tool generates and equivalent XML description that will then be used for the transformation and code generation described previously.

5 Conclusion

After analyzing the brake that slow down artistic creation in poly-artistic works, we developed, within the ConceptMove project, a meta-language with the aim of solving some of these problems. This language, a XML dialect, describes communications and time constraints of a piece, in a unified paradigm. Even if this approach may not be suitable for some situations needing fine grained interactivity (score following to name one), it proposes a convenient formalism for lots of other situations like virtual and augmented realities, as well as interactive narration. Finally, after addressing the main issues through code generation, we proposed an intuitive graphical authoring tool that places the XML meta-language at a comprehensive level.

References

1. Margery, D., Arnaldi, B., Chauffaut, A., Donikian, S., Duval, T.: Openmask: Multi-threaded or modular animation and simulation kernel or kit: a general introduction. In: Richir, S., Richard, P., Taravel, B. (eds.) VRIC 2002, Laval, France (2002)
2. Landis, J., Chapman, J., Calvert, T.: New Directions in Dance. In: Notation of Dance with Computer Assistance, pp. 169–178. Pergamon Press, Oxford (1979)
3. Taylor, R.M., Hudson, T.C., Seeger, A., Weber, H., Juliano, J., Helser, A.T.: Vrpn: a device independent, network-transparent VR peripheral system. In: ACM Symposium on Virtual reality software and technology, pp. 55–61. ACM Press, New York (2001)
4. Camurri, A., Hashimoto, S., Ricchetti, M., Trocca, R., Suzuki, K., Volpe, G.: Eyesweb - toward gesture and affect recognition in interactive dance and music systems. Computer Music Journal 24(1) (2000)

Author Index

Lecture Notes in Computer Science

Sublibrary 3: Information Systems and Application, incl. Internet/Web and HCI

For information about Vols. 1– 4443
please contact your bookseller or Springer

Vol. 4662: C. Baranauskas, P. Palanque, J. Abascal, S.D.J. Barbosa (Eds.), Human-Computer Interaction – INTERACT 2007, Part I. XXXIII, 637 pages. 2007.

Vol. 4658: T. Enokido, L. Barolli, M. Takizawa (Eds.), Network-Based Information Systems. XIII, 544 pages. 2007.

Vol. 4656: M.A. Wimmer, J. Scholl, Å. Grönlund (Eds.), Electronic Government. XIV, 450 pages. 2007.

Vol. 4655: G. Psaila, R. Wagner (Eds.), E-Commerce and Web Technologies. VII, 229 pages. 2007.

Vol. 4654: I.-Y. Song, J. Eder, T.M. Nguyen (Eds.), Data Warehousing and Knowledge Discovery. XVI, 482 pages. 2007.

Vol. 4653: R. Wagner, N. Revell, G. Pernul (Eds.), Database and Expert Systems Applications. XXII, 907 pages. 2007.

Vol. 4636: G. Antoniou, U. Aßmann, C. Baroglio, S. Decker, N. Henze, P.-L. Patranjan, R. Tolksdorf (Eds.), Reasoning Web. IX, 345 pages. 2007.

Vol. 4611: J. Indulska, J. Ma, L.T. Yang, T. Ungerer, J. Cao (Eds.), Ubiquitous Intelligence and Computing. XXIII, 1257 pages. 2007.

Vol. 4607: L. Baresi, P. Fraternali, G.-J. Houben (Eds.), Web Engineering. XVI, 576 pages. 2007.

Vol. 4606: A. Pras, M. van Sinderen (Eds.), Dependable and Adaptable Networks and Services. XIV, 149 pages. 2007.

Vol. 4605: D. Papadias, D. Zhang, G. Kollios (Eds.), Advances in Spatial and Temporal Databases. X, 479 pages. 2007.

Vol. 4602: S. Barker, G.-J. Ahn (Eds.), Data and Applications Security XXI. X, 291 pages. 2007.

Vol. 4601: S. Spaccapietra, P. Atzeni, F. Fages, M.-S. Hacid, M. Kifer, J. Mylopoulos, B. Pernici, P. Shvaiko, J. Trujillo, I. Zaihrayeu (Eds.), Journal on Data Semantics IX. XV, 197 pages. 2007.

Vol. 4592: Z. Kedad, N. Lammari, E. Métais, F. Meziane, Y. Rezgui (Eds.), Natural Language Processing and Information Systems. XIV, 442 pages. 2007.

Vol. 4587: R. Cooper, J. Kennedy (Eds.), Data Management. XIII, 259 pages. 2007.

Vol. 4577: N. Sebe, Y. Liu, Y.-t. Zhuang, T.S. Huang (Eds.), Multimedia Content Analysis and Mining. XIII, 513 pages. 2007.

Vol. 4568: T. Ishida, S. R. Fussell, P. T. J. M. Vossen (Eds.), Intercultural Collaboration. XIII, 395 pages. 2007.

Vol. 4566: M.J. Dainoff (Ed.), Ergonomics and Health Aspects of Work with Computers. XVIII, 390 pages. 2007.

Vol. 4564: D. Schuler (Ed.), Online Communities and Social Computing. XVII, 520 pages. 2007.

Vol. 4563: R. Shumaker (Ed.), Virtual Reality. XXII, 762 pages. 2007.

Vol. 4561: V.G. Duffy (Ed.), Digital Human Modeling. XXIII, 1068 pages. 2007.

Vol. 4560: N. Aykin (Ed.), Usability and Internationalization, Part II. XVIII, 576 pages. 2007.

Vol. 4559: N. Aykin (Ed.), Usability and Internationalization, Part I. XVIII, 661 pages. 2007.

Vol. 4558: M.J. Smith, G. Salvendy (Eds.), Human Interface and the Management of Information, Part II. XXIII, 1162 pages. 2007.

Vol. 4557: M.J. Smith, G. Salvendy (Eds.), Human Interface and the Management of Information, Part I. XXII, 1030 pages. 2007.

Vol. 4541: T. Okadome, T. Yamazaki, M. Makhtari (Eds.), Pervasive Computing for Quality of Life Enhancement. IX, 248 pages. 2007.

Vol. 4537: K.C.-C. Chang, W. Wang, L. Chen, C.A. Ellis, C.-H. Hsu, A.C. Tsoi, H. Wang (Eds.), Advances in Web and Network Technologies, and Information Management. XXIII, 707 pages. 2007.

Vol. 4531: J. Indulska, K. Raymond (Eds.), Distributed Applications and Interoperable Systems. XI, 337 pages. 2007.

Vol. 4526: M. Malek, M. Reitenspieß, A. van Moorsel (Eds.), Service Availability. X, 155 pages. 2007.

Vol. 4524: M. Marchiori, J.Z. Pan, C.d.S. Marie (Eds.), Web Reasoning and Rule Systems. XI, 382 pages. 2007.

Vol. 4519: E. Franconi, M. Kifer, W. May (Eds.), The Semantic Web: Research and Applications. XVIII, 830 pages. 2007.

Vol. 4518: N. Fuhr, M. Lalmas, A. Trotman (Eds.), Comparative Evaluation of XML Information Retrieval Systems. XII, 554 pages. 2007.

Vol. 4508: M.-Y. Kao, X.-Y. Li (Eds.), Algorithmic Aspects in Information and Management. VIII, 428 pages. 2007.

Vol. 4506: D. Zeng, I. Gotham, K. Komatsu, C. Lynch, M. Thurmond, D. Madigan, B. Lober, J. Kvach, H. Chen (Eds.), Intelligence and Security Informatics: Biosurveillance. XI, 234 pages. 2007.

Vol. 4505: G. Dong, X. Lin, W. Wang, Y. Yang, J.X. Yu (Eds.), Advances in Data and Web Management. XXII, 896 pages. 2007.

Vol. 4504: J. Huang, R. Kowalczyk, Z. Maamar, D. Martin, I. Müller, S. Stoutenburg, K.P. Sycara (Eds.), Service-Oriented Computing: Agents, Semantics, and Engineering. X, 175 pages. 2007.

Vol. 4500: N.A. Streitz, A.D. Kameas, I. Mavrommati (Eds.), The Disappearing Computer. XVIII, 304 pages. 2007.

Vol. 4495: J. Krogstie, A. Opdahl, G. Sindre (Eds.), Advanced Information Systems Engineering. XVI, 606 pages. 2007.

Vol. 4480: A. LaMarca, M. Langheinrich, K.N. Truong (Eds.), Pervasive Computing. XIII, 369 pages. 2007.

Vol. 4473: D. Draheim, G. Weber (Eds.), Trends in Enterprise Application Architecture. X, 355 pages. 2007.

Vol. 4471: P. Cesar, K. Chorianopoulos, J.F. Jensen (Eds.), Interactive TV: A Shared Experience. XIII, 236 pages. 2007.

Vol. 4469: K.-c. Hui, Z. Pan, R.C.-k. Chung, C.C.L. Wang, X. Jin, S. Göbel, E.C.-L. Li (Eds.), Technologies for E-Learning and Digital Entertainment. XVIII, 974 pages. 2007.